Henry Kingsley

Tales of old Travel

Henry Kingsley

Tales of old Travel

ISBN/EAN: 9783743314139

Manufactured in Europe, USA, Canada, Australia, Japa

Cover: Foto ©ninafisch / pixelio.de

Manufactured and distributed by brebook publishing software (www.brebook.com)

Henry Kingsley

Tales of old Travel

TALES OF OLD TRAVEL.

RE-NARRATED

BY

HENRY KINGSLEY, F.R.G.S.

Third Edition.

WITH ILLUSTRATIONS.

*The bodies and the **bones** of those*
  *That strove in **other days** to pass,*
*Are withered in the **thorny close**,*
*Or scattered blanching **on the grass**.*
He gazes on the silent dead:
  "They perished in their daring deeds."
This proverb flashes through his head,
  "The many fail: the one succeeds."

London:
MACMILLAN & CO.
1870.

LONDON:
R. CLAY, SONS, AND TAYLOR, PRINTERS,
BREAD STREET HILL.

CONTENTS.

	PAGE
MARCO POLO	1
THE SHIPWRECK OF PELSART	40
THE WONDERFUL ADVENTURES OF ANDREW BATTEL	56
THE WANDERINGS OF A CAPUCHIN	78
PETER CARDER	113
THE PRESERVATION OF THE "TERRA NOVA"	122
SPITZBERGEN	142
D'ERMENONVILLE'S ACCLIMATIZATION ADVENTURE	161
THE OLD SLAVE TRADE	186
MILES PHILIPS	210
THE SUFFERINGS OF ROBERT EVERARD	237
JOHN FOX	264
ALVARO NUNEZ	273
THE FOUNDATION OF AN EMPIRE	308

LIST OF ILLUSTRATIONS

	To face page
PELSART PREVENTED FROM REACHING THE ISLAND	44
FATHER DENIS AND HIS NEGRO GUIDE	89
D'ERMENONVILLE SEES THE RIO GRANDE	175
THE OLD SLAVE TRADE	203
THE MEETING OF MILES PHILIPS AND THE GREY FRIAR	233
THE DESERTION OF ROBERT EVERARD	243
EFFECTS OF A CYCLONE	274

TALES OF OLD TRAVEL.

MARCO POLO.

IN the thirteenth century the wonderfully rapid aggregation of innumerable small Tartar tribes into one vast swarm, guided in its ceaseless work of destruction by a succession of absolute and pitiless hands, those of Ghengis Khan and his generals, and grandsons, the sons of Tuli; filled all Europe with alarm. That alarm grew into terror after the fall of Cracow in 1240, when Baatu Khàn, with half a million of flat-faced and short-legged warriors, routed the chivalry of Europe under the Count Palatine of Saxony, and desolated Eastern Europe in all directions.

The wildest notions prevailed about the savageness of these conquering Tartars. Yui of Narbonne, in his letter to the Bishop of Bordeaux, quoted by Matthew Paris, narrates as having occurred under his own eye at the siege of Neustadt, in Carniola, horrors far too hideous for repetition here. This same siege of Neustadt having being relieved by the Duke of

Austria, eight Tartar prisoners were taken, one of whom was discovered by the Duke of Dalmatia to be an English renegade; a man who had desperately diced away his fortune and his self-respect in that awfully abominable city Acre; wandering from land to land, making uncouth noises as though he were dumb, clothed in a sack, and looking such a sorry dog that the meanest thief passed him with contempt, and the charity of the good was excited towards one whom it had pleased God to thrust down so low. He rambled on, thus prolonging life for a season. "Albeit every day by rashness of speeche and inconstancie of heart he endangered himself to the deuil" (poor fellow, *that* seems likely enough), until falling sick in Chaldea he bethought himself of learning one of the Tartar tongues, and subsequently many others. He was entertained by the Tartars, and afterwards employed as interpreter-envoy to threaten the King of Hungary, and try to make him yield to the Tartar chief that kingdom which they afterwards overran.

This man first gave the Europeans some distinct though slight notion of the Tartars, or Mongols, as they were among themselves. His account was possibly not worth *very* much, seeing that his care was to please his captors by representing the Tartars as the fiends which they believed them to be; and, moreover, only had his life spared having "made such oathes and protestations as (I think) the deuil himselfe would haue been trusted for." The most remarkable part of his testimony was as to the wonderful absence of quarrelling and brawling among the Tartars. For the rest he seems truthful but adverse, as he was bound to be. His testimony is of little value to us, as he was followed by others abler and certainly more respectable than himself; but to omit mention of him in a book of adventure would be a great fault, seeing that a well-written account of his adventures, could one get such a thing, would form probably a stranger story than any told in this book.

About 1245 matters became still more complicated with these Tartars. The Carizmians (shepherds of the Caspian) rolled headlong on Syria, and the union of the Franks with the Sultans of Aleppo, Hems, and Damascus was insufficient to stem the violence of the torrent. They pillaged the Holy City, almost destroyed the military orders, and profaned the Sepulchre, and generally undid the work of Frederic II., the fervour of the fifth Crusade now burning very low. The worst of it was that the Tartars themselves, under Baatu Khan, were in hot pursuit. Immediate action on the part of his Holiness became necessary. The fiends of Tartars must instantly be converted to the Roman Catholic faith, lest a worse thing befall us. His Holiness (Innocent IV.) "took action" immediately, pitched the Saracen alliance overboard, and sent four very foolish Franciscan monks, Ascelin and others, by no means Xaviers, to convert these sons of Tartarus.

It would be humiliating to dwell on the hopeless folly of the whole expedition. They found the Tartar "horda," or tent, the quarters of the expelled Carizmians, and came barefooted in their miserable garments before the mighty general, who could then have overrun Europe, demanding the submission of his master the great Khan to the Pope, of whom these barbarians had never heard. Baatu, on the other hand, had never heard of the Pope. These worthy friars seemed to him impudent madmen: they told him that the Pope was lord of heaven and earth, and that the Khan must send his submission to him, or, &c. &c. The Tartar asked about the Pope's armies, victories, and so forth, to which they had nothing to answer in any degree satisfactory; and, to bring a somewhat painful matter to an end, he treated them badly, and dismissed them with a bit of Parthian contempt. The Pope having sent for *him* to give in allegiance, he thought he could not do better than send for the Pope. The Pope (so the mighty savage expressed himself) was a dog; and moreover, if that pope did not come to *him* and do homage, there was an, &c. &c. behind that pope which he would do well to think about. There is little doubt that the Tartar general would have carried his threat into execution had he thought the Pope of sufficient importance, which luckily he did not. The whole adventure of these four good men, whose courage we must not for a moment forget was simply magnificent, and who would have been proud of martyrdom, was in the end ridiculous and humiliating. Conceive the exasperation which a well-trained Jesuit would have felt towards these four simple cloister babies.

John de Plano Carpini, the Minorite friar, though he was profoundly ignorant (like the rest of the world) of the geography of those parts, and although he was credulous* to the extent of believing in a

* As a good instance of this, "Ad 'Parossitas' venerunt, qui paruos

nation of men without joints to their legs, who, if they fell down, could not get up again without help, yet has left behind him a very interesting and very sensible account of the Tartars. He went this same year, 1246, out from Europe, and by a more northerly route; actually getting within half a day's journey of the capital city of Karakorum, a distance of 3,500 miles from Kiew, his place of departure. Carpini behaved much more wisely than the poor Prædicants, and was treated much better. He merely told Baatu, and Ajuk, his cousin, that the Pope had seen with surprise and grief the unfortunate habit the Tartars had of murdering his subjects, and recommended them to become Christians. He had no very great reason to complain of his treatment, except that it was contemptuous, and that the whole thing was an utter failure. He had the singular good fortune to see the installation of Ajuk Khan, son of the Ogadai, grandson of Ghengis, the first cousin of Baatu, conqueror of Russia and Hungary. It was a magnificent spectacle, held a few miles out of Karakorum. The wealth exhibited was gigantic, and the good friars themselves seemed to have attracted some sort of contemptuous wonder by the mere meanness and poverty of their appearance. The first day the Tartars were all clad in white, the second in scarlet, the third in blue, the fourth in baldakin: which circumstance will explain to us the

---

habentes stomachos et os paruum, non manducant, sed carnes decoquunt, quibus decoctis, se super ollam ponunt; et fumum recipiunt, et de hoc solo reficiuntur." The Tartars were so far advanced in civilization, as to make fun by cramming a traveller.

curious theatrical behaviour of the Poli in Venice, at their celebrated return supper, years later. Carpini after this ceremony was forgotten, and nearly starved, but at last dismissed with a letter to the Pope. The Khan offered him an ambassador, but he declined; and the reasons he gives for his refusal show him to have been a very shrewd man, and, what is more, a gentleman. "These ambassadors," he argued, "would be mere spies, and seeing the disturbed state of Europe, would be the more encouraged to make war on us, seeing how we are divided against ourselves. The hatred of the Europeans to the Tartars is so great, that they would be assuredly slain: 'Gentes enim nostræ arrogantes sunt et superbæ;' and the Tartars never rest till they have avenged the death of an ambassador;" and altogether thought they would do their 3,500 miles back again, in the dead of winter, without the ambassador, and so started. The Empress-mother, widow of Ogadai, had the woman's pity for those in distress, and possibly also the woman's reverence for the priest, let him be of what denomination he chose: for she gave "each of us a gown of fox-skins, with the fur on the outside, and a piece of purple." But "our Tartars stole a yard out of every one of them, and out of that which was given to our servant, they stole the better half." The thieves! of course they did; was it not their profession? The good and brave Carpini returned to Kiew after incredible hardships, with apparently slight results. But I think that no one who has ever read his quaint, simple, honest story, can avoid admiring him. He was not a mere fanatical ignorant baby, like Ascelin; but he was a mere monk, and a mere monk was not the thing wanted: a Jesuit was required. And Jesuits were not at that time invented.

Rubruquis, the last friar who attempted the conversion of the Tartars in this century, was the cleverest, and we must be brief with him. He was sent by Louis the Saint in 1253, in reality to attempt to bring about an alliance between the Crusaders and the Tartars against the Saracens, but ostensibly to inquire into the truth of reports, most likely spread by the Nestorians, that the Tartar princes were Christians. The first prince he came to was Sartuck, whom he met on the Volga. Sartuck's people looked on the report as to their Christianity as an offensive imputation, which was not to be repeated. Being evidently puzzled, however, and believing their mission to be too important for him to decide, he sent Rubruquis, Friar Bartholomew of Cremona, Goset, "the man of God," Turgemannus, "and Nicolas, my servant, whom I bought at Constantinople, with some part of the alms bestowed on me, (!)" to Baatu, of whom we have heard before. Baatu sent them on to Mangu, and Mangu sent them home again. The whole expedition was without results. He tells us of Prester John, in whom he has small faith. He says, what is perfectly true as far as it goes, that Prester John was Ung Khan, a Mongolian prince of the Nestorian persuasion, who was killed in the wars with Turgis Khan in 1203. Though Rubruquis travelled through his so-called dominions, half a century after his death only a few Nestorians had ever heard of him: he was scarcely worth their notice. The other few circumstances which seem to float to the surface after reading Rubruquis, are that the Nestorian priests beat a board instead of ringing a bell, which reminds us of one of Mr. Curzon's admirable sketches, made six hundred years later, in a book* which is a strange contrast to Rubruquis. Another thing one remembers, is that the gipsy queen Cotata was a Christian, though her husband Mangu was not. Rubruquis's book is, like Carpini's, most excellent and interesting reading.†

This was the third and last attempt in this century, of the cloister upon the faith of the barbarians. The monks, from the silly Ascelin, to the shrewd Rubruquis, had done their best most nobly, but the time was not ripe. The great opportunity was to come. When it came, a merchant, and not a priest, was the man who had the chance of seizing it. But the cowardly priests deserted the merchant, and the thing was never done, and perhaps never will be.

With an apology for this tedious, but I hope correct introduction, I will at once begin on my main theme.

It was in the year 1250, that two noble Venetian gentlemen, Nicolo and Maffeo Paolo, or, as we will say in future, Polo, left Venice, on an adventurous trading journey among these very Tartars, of whom we have been saying so much.

---

* Monasteries of the Levant.

† Rabbi Benjamin, of Tudela, was before them all (1160), but he is only the Arthur Young of the Tartar revolution, and is beside as credulous as his equally noble brother Jew, Joseph Wolff.

It is certain that they had heard of the adventures of the Minorites and Prædicants with Carpini, among these people, though Rubruquis was not yet started. The communication between Venice and the East in those times must have been very frequent. The enormous wealth, spoken of by Carpini, must have excited their curiosity and their trading instincts to a great degree. They started accordingly, taking with them a great store of jewels.

They travelled slowly, and arrived in due time at Constantinople, where Baldwin II. was at that time emperor, and here they stayed for some time. They then crossed the Black Sea to the port of Soldavia (Sinope? Sukum Kali? or was it Trebizond?) from whence they proceeded to the court of Barkah, one of the Baatu branch of the descendants of Ghengis, to whom they presented all their jewels, receiving still more beautiful presents in return, a kind of gentlemanly traffic at once courteous and remunerative.

Signor Nicolo, the elder of the two brothers (who at this time, if it is true that he married and had a son after his ultimate return to Venice, must have been under thirty years old), had, when he quitted home, left his good lady big with a child whose name is a household word throughout Europe and civilized America to this day. He now, after some two years, felt a natural longing to see his signora and the unknown baby, and to find out if all had gone right with them, and so they essayed to turn homewards. Alas! the good signora had slept for some years peacefully in her grave among the lagunes, and the unseen baby had grown into a gallant and beautiful young man before the wearied eyes of the brothers Polo were permitted to rest upon the "stones of Venice."

Their host Barkah fell out and went to war with his dear uncle, the mighty general Hulagu Khan, and of course was signally defeated, and the Poli had to fly. The way to the sea was closed to them, and so they made south to the city of "Guthacam," on the Tigris, a town which I am not able to identify. They now struck to the eastward, across the great salt desert of Persia, a distance of nearly 1,300 miles in a straight line, though they probably made much more of it, for they seem to have kept to the desert on purpose, making no mention of having halted anywhere, not even at Teheran, which was directly in their way, until they arrived at Bokhara, beyond the limits of Persia. There is nothing very surprising in this, for it is perfectly evident that these Tartar prince cousins were allowed, so long as they obeyed the head Khan at Karakorum, to make war on one another *ad libitum*, and indeed upon the death of Kublai they scorned submission to the central authority altogether. This is the more remarkable because private quarrelling among the people was strictly forbidden.

Barach, Khan of Bokhara in those days, seems to have been a far superior person to Joseph Wolff's friend of our own times: he gave them a good reception, and they stayed with him for three years.

Meanwhile Mangu Khan had died very soon after the visit of Rubruquis, and Kublai Khan, his brother, younger son of Tuli, the mighty general, son of Ghengis Khan, had succeeded him. He belonged to the military branch of the family: his brothers Baatu and Hulagu are well known to the readers of history, Baatu as conqueror of Eastern Europe, the victor of Lignitz; Hulagu as the conqueror of Persia, the destroyer of the *Assassins*, and the Old Man of the Mountain. Kublai was more of a politician than a warrior. The change of habits which had begun with his uncle Octai had been further developed by his brother Mangu. The Tartars no longer lived in tents, but in houses; and Karakorum, at first a mere depôt for plunder, had developed into the handsome town compared by Rubruquis to the town of St. Denys, and was still developing into the still grander town seen by the Poli. Already had a Paris goldsmith found his way to the very centre of the Great Steppe, and was beating the holy vessels of the Hungarian and Polish churches, plundered by the great Baatu, into epergnes and centre pieces exceeding in magnificence and equalling in taste those of the most admired European civilization.

At the end of three years, an ambassador going from Prince Hulagu to Kublai Khan found these two charming Venetian gentlemen at the court of Bokhara, speaking the Tartar language fluently. The ambassador urged them strongly to go with him and see the mightiest prince on the earth, and after a little hesitation and consultation they consented, and turning their backs upon Venice once more, and their faces to the East, thus added nearly three thousand more miles to the already hopeless distance which lay between them and home.

After a year's weary and dangerous travelling, they

arrived at Tai Guen, on the Houng-ho, and stood in the presence of the great Khan himself, who seems to have been a right royal person. He received them with great courtesy, and questioned them about many things, but the conversation from the first seemed to turn on the Pope and Western development of the Christian religion. They had many audiences of him, and he grew more and more delighted with them, and at length he determined to send them as ambassadors to the Pope.

The request to the Pope was that he should send him a hundred men learned in the Christian religion, who should instruct him and his people in the truths of Christianity. He declared that he had a profound devotion for our Lord, believing Him to be the only true God; and he charged Nicolo and Maffeo to bring him back some of the oil which burns before the Holy Sepulchre at Jerusalem. He then dismissed them on their most important errand.

Ascelin, Carpini, Rubruquis, had all been treated with contempt by these Tartar khans. But Kublai, the first prince of his race who had been brought up in all the refinements of a Chinese education, was also the first to desire a close and earnest acquaintance with such Christianity as he could get. Why was this? Probably for many reasons. The court lady party was certainly Nestorian. He was in want of a religion, and at last, says careful Gibbon, left the pure and simple religion of his great ancestor (seventy boiling cauldrons, and seventy enemies thrown into them, good Mr. Gibbon, out of your own mouth) to sacrifice to the idol Fo. The correct

Mosheim also says, "We learn from the best accounts and the most respectable authorities that—" (the Nestorians flourished through these times) — "that several kings and grandees of these nations had either been instructed in the Gospel by their ancestors, or were converted to Christianity by the exhortations of the Nestorians." Which of the grandees besides a man with an unspellable name, by all authority, one of the Khans of the Kercutes, whose skull was set in silver *pour encourager les autres chrétiens* we know not. It was evident that Nestorianism, with its miserable *unmeaning* superstitions, would not satisfy the soul of the Chinese-bred gentlemen, who afterwards sacrificed to Fo under fail of anything better. But he had heard of (I think not seen) men of gentle demeanour, of simple and pure life, and of very humble aspect and appearance, who had come thousands of miles, patient through every form of discomfort and danger, to his brother and his uncle : not carrying and bringing presents, but bringing defiant messages, such as it was death to bring: calm, dignified, and self-possessed, amidst all the brutal contempt which had been heaped upon them. Men who expected death for the faith's sake, if with fear, yet with unutterable longing for the crown of martyrdom it would bring—men who, with all their silly superstition, represented very fairly the first and purest age of Christianity. Who dares laugh at these noble monks ? And now there came to this perfectly-finished Chinese gentleman, two gentlemen, Nicolo and Maffeo Polo, who were the most perfect and charming gentlemen ever seen ; who professed the same faith as these ragged monks, and would kneel to them to receive their blessing; kneel to those monks who had refused to kneel to his terrible headlong brother, not from pride, but—lest the others who knelt should be invoking the devil.

There is no chapter in the history of human stupidity so sad as the story of these noble monks. Had there been a Xavier to the fore at this time, the Roman Catholic form of religion would have counted one hundred million more adherents than it has now, "*sans compter le petit Mortara.*"

This Kublai Khan was grandson of Ghengis Khan, of whom one can read in chapter lxiv. of Gibbon's "Decline and Fall," and elsewhere. I seem to make out from very various sources, that he was born either in 1215, or 1218; that he succeeded to the throne, after the very short reign of his elder brother Mangu; that he was a little under forty years of age when Nicolo and Maffeo Polo came to him; and that, after a reign of some thirty-eight years, he died at about the age of seventy years. The Tartars put his death in 1292; the Chinese in 1295. The former are evidently right, for they are confirmed by the Poli. Evidently a gentleman, although the stupidity of the church of those times would not allow him to become a Christian.

Kublai Khan dismissed his beloved Venetians. He sent with them one of his great men called Chogatul, who was not only to see them safe through his kingdom, but also to go on to the Pope himself. But he also gave them something more important than the safe-conduct of a nobleman; namely, an engraven plate of **gold, signed** with his name; by **the presentation of which,** throughout **their journey, they were** furnished with every travelling necessity, and **had the** country entirely at their service.' Poor Chogatul fell sick after three weeks travelling, and they were forced to leave him behind and go **on their** way alone. Yet this wonderful talisman of **a gold plate** acted like magic. The arm **of** Kublai Khan **was a long one, for he** played Frederick the Great over **more thousands of** miles **than** did **the** Prussian **king** over **hundreds.** They **were** everywhere courteously **assisted** through their long journey by the subjects of the Khan; **most** discourteously received by **nature, who spread such** stumbling blocks in their path **in** the way **of weather** and floods, that they were three years in reaching the Armenian **port** on **the Black** Sea, which Ramusio calls Giagga.

From hence they sailed to Constantinople, passed the Archipelago, **and then held across the Mediter-**ranean sea **to Acre.** The **reason of** this retrograde movement eastward **is** probably **this**: that at the **Armenian port they could** only find a ship bound **to that** port, **and from that** port they were perfectly sure of a passage westward. For **we must** remember that in the year **1268 the seventh** Crusade was getting on hand. **St. Louis** was preparing for his **fatal** expedition **to** Carthage; Antioch was lost, and **our Henry III.** had obtained **a grant of one tenth of the Church** revenues for **three years. In April 1269, when they** arrived, Prince Edward (Edward I.) with **his** glorious thousand **of** Nazareth, and his more glorious Queen **Eleanor the** Wound Sucker, were nearly due. Commercial intelligence might not have travelled fast in those days, yet it is not wildly impossible that some shrewd Armenian merchant may have got an inkling that there would be a plethora of half a million (about the sum raised by Henry III.) of British gold at Acre that year; or at all events a vast congregation of dandy and extravagant Crusaders; and may have chartered a ship with the necessaries of life to that starving, immoral hell upon earth, Acre; for a description of which town in this very year, you must consult indispensable Gibbon again. However, the two Paolos reached here in A.D. 1269. And the compiler's brother assisted, on board the *Pique* frigate, in blowing it up, for the last time at present, in A.D. 1840.

The Churchmen were pretty busy in Acre this year. The brothers Paolo, with their mission to the Pope, a mission which seemed so very promising with regard to the spread of Christianity in the East, found here a very eminent Churchman indeed; a legate of the Apostolic See, "Tibaldo Visconti di Piacenza," by one account: "Theobald, a native of Placentia, Archbishop of Liege," in Teutonic protestant eyes; no less a person than Pope Gregory X. afterwards: about whose efforts for the junction of the Greek and Latin Church one may read in one's Mosheim and elsewhere. This good man, who was doing his duty in that horrible Acre, told them of the death of Clement IV. and advised them to wait till a new Pope was elected before they went back to the Khan.

So the two gentlemen started for Venice, 1269. Nicolo's wife was dead, but the boy baby whom he had never seen, had grown into a. glorious young creature of nineteen, handsome, clever, witty, and accomplished. Men remember this youth even now, and they call him MARCO POLO.

Was it that Venice was dull, now that one dear face was gone, and one dear voice only heard in dreams for twenty years now silent? Was it that many friends were dead, and those who were left could scarcely have known them, or even, they say, their speech? Was not the Khan, too, waiting their return, and all kinds of unknown honours and wild adventures attending them at the court of the mightiest monarch of the time? Beyond all, were they not in the prime of life, and the travel fever strong on them?

> "I cannot rest from travel; I will drink
> Life to the lees: all times I have enjoyed
> Greatly, and suffered greatly, both with those
> That loved me, and alone; on shore, and when
> Through scudding drifts the rainy Hyades
> Vext the dim sea: I am become a name,
> For always roaming with a hungry heart."

It is difficult indeed to guess the motives of men who have been dead for five hundred years, and have left no sign behind them; but there seems to have been no shadow of a purpose with them of staying at home: and so there departed with them, this time persuaded, easily enough I do not doubt, their splendid young son and nephew: to accompany them in an expedition, the progress of which seems almost like the dream of a madman. These three started together to walk and ride, principally over land, from

Venice to Pekin. And what is more, they did it, and went further afield still before all was over.

No pope was elected for above two years, and getting anxious lest the Khan should think they had broken faith with him, they left Venice and returned to Acre, where Theobald of Placentia still was. Having been to Jerusalem and procured the holy oil for the Khan, they unwillingly set out from Giazza, unwillingly because they had missed getting a commission from the Pope. The legate however gave them a letter, and they went. Hardly were they gone, when the decision of the cardinals arrived at Acre. Theobald of Placentia was elected Pope, and took the title of Gregory X. He at once sent swift messengers after our three travellers with fresh letters in his new name, and also added to their company two preaching friars of great learning and piety, brothers Nicolo and Gulielmo. To these friars he gave letters and privileges, authority to ordain priests and bishops, and power of absolution in all cases; they also carried presents and the papal benediction to the Khan. The Master of the Temple accompanied them as far as Giazza.

However great was the piety and learning of these two monks, we cannot rank their courage high. On arriving in Armenia, they found the country at war with the Sultan of Babylon, and were instantly terrified into giving their letters to the three Polo's, and returning with the Master of the Temple. The three Poli went on, one fancies, laughing at the cowardice of the foolish monks.

They went, I think, to Trebizond, or another seaport in **Armenia, for I cannot verify** "Giazza." Thence to Erzeroum, Ishera Meshid, Balkh, this time leaving Bokhara to the north. Then by Badakshan **in the** Hindoo Koosh, where young Marco **fell** sick, but as usual lost no time in acquiring knowledge (the indefatigable young man—what a senior **wrangler or** double first he would have **been : one hopes he was** not **a** prig, though one knows he was a dandy). This illness detained them at Badakshan **for a year,** after which they went on to Khotan, and passed over **the** southern end of the **Great** Steppe of Cobi, **near the bases** of the **Kuen Lung** mountains, which bound Thibet on the **north ; the** rivers all flowing northward, and losing themselves in small swampy lakes, which disposed of their waters by evaporation. **They** came then to Kunchow, the most north-westerly **town** in the present Chinese dominions, where they **stayed** some time, having made **a** journey **of nearly 4,000** miles eastward from the Black **Sea.**

At this point **Kublai** Khan, **now** at his residence of Tai Guen, some 200 miles south-west of Pekin, heard of their coming, and sent **to meet** them. He soon had **his** old friends brought **before** him, and for the first time saw young Marco. " **And** who may that be ? " he asked the **Russian autocrat who had** received the Chinese education, **with** slightly sardonic politeness. " My son and **your** majesty's servant," answered the Venetian neatly enough; after **which one** may imagine a general Kootoo, ending in **a thorough** good understanding.

The Pope's letters and presents, and the holy oil, which they had fetched from Jerusalem during their detention at Acre, were duly presented. Young Marco was a success, and was taught to write among the other young noblemen, during which instruction he contrived to learn four languages—Mongol, Turkish, Manchu, and Chinese. He was a great success. So began their twenty years' residence at the court of Kublai Khan.

This is the place to mention my belief with regard to Marco Polo's geography, and to say this: that the more it is examined, the better it will stand examination. His geography was, of course, to some extent hearsay geography, as was that of Speke, for instance. But Speke's hearsay-geography has been most wonderfully verified by Baker, and Marco Polo's geography is shown to be more true in proportion as human knowledge increases. Mr. Cooley, in his "Maritime and Inland Discovery," gives a most excellent resumé of Marco Polo's travels, which is admirable for the verification of proper names. His object however was merely scientific, mine is romantic; but I can assure my reader that I will stick to the texts as closely and as inexorably as he. The simple story in this case is so much more wonderful than anything one could invent, that there is no temptation to decorate it.

The dreadful "Old Man of the Mountain, chief of the tribe of Arsacides," now corrupted into "Assassins," had been with all his beautiful and terrible surroundings destroyed by Prince Hulagu in 1262, before the arrival of Marco. But Marco heard a great deal about him. The sect of which he was the last Imam, or head-priest, had existed in the mountains south of the Caspian, near Teheran, for above 160 years, and had a colony, the terror of Crusaders, established at Mount Lebanon. Moadin had imitated as well as he could the Mahomedan heaven. Between two mountains, in a valley similar to that in "Rasselas," accessible only by one fortified wicket, he had made a paradise or park of surprising beauty, in which were means for the perfect gratification of every sense and every passion. He found youths of fierce and dauntless aspect, between the ages of twelve and twenty, and to them discoursed of the joys of Paradise, and of his power to take those there who would implicitly obey his behests. The youths were shortly afterwards drugged, and carried, in a state of insensibility, to the garden among the mountains, and on awaking found themselves in the enjoyment of every sensual pleasure known to man. After a few days of this, they were again secretly drugged and carried back to the outer world, firmly believing in the supernatural power of their chief, and ready to commit any number of fearful crimes in his service, in the hopes of once more realizing that delicious dream from which they seemed to have awakened. The daggers of these fanatics were felt alike by Crusader and Mahomedan, and the original organization must have expanded into a vast secret society; for in 1280 we find that no less than 40,000 of them were attacked and destroyed in Syria by the Mamelukes. The original nest of them in the north of Persia was attacked by the irresistible Prince Hulagu. After three years' siege the entrance was forced, and thousands of short-legged, broad-shouldered Tartars rushed yelling into the beautiful garden. It is difficult to imagine the peculiar horrors of the scene which must have followed; the instantaneous ruin of what was probably one of the most beautiful places in the world; the wailing of the miserable women, and amidst all, the Assassins fighting desperately like hunted cats among their trampled flowers.

The experiences of the Poli, during their twenty years' residence in China, are of course very interesting, and prove the truthfulness of their narrator by the critical examination. For one instance:—They told him that an incombustible cloth was made from the salamander, a serpent which could exist in fire. He examines the matter for himself, and denies the existence of the salamander, proving that the cloths in question were made from a fibrous mineral, so well known to us now as asbestos; and, what is more, gives the details of its manufacture, even describing the way in which the gritty particles are separated from the asbestos by comminution. He was no *gobe-mouche* traveller. We, however, have to do with incident.

Mangu and Kublai, the two most intelligent princes of the race of Ghengis, were as eager to subsidize foreign talent as was Frederick the Great, or as are the Russian Government of the present day. Rubruquis had already seen a Parisian goldsmith at Karakorum, under Mangu, forging the chalices from Hungarian churches into epergnes to decorate the riotous dinner-table of the Mongolian conqueror. Such talent as that of the Poli was not to be held cheap. Marco, apparently the most brilliant of the three, was entrusted almost at once with the most delicate missions, **but his father and** his **uncle** had the luck **and** dexterity **to render at the first** such important service as must almost, for a time, have eclipsed the popularity of the younger Polo.

Previous to 1269, the year of the Poli's **return to** Venice, the Tartars had conquered that small part of China which lies north of the Hoang-ho, known to them and to our poets as **Cathay:** not only holding possession of that part of **the city** of Pekin which is **to** this day called **the Chinese** Quarter, but having erected on the other side of the Hoang-ho a **new city,** even now known as the Tartar Quarter, outside which stands, as I understand it, the very Summer **Palace** which was sacked the other day by the French and English. South of the Hoang-ho, however, they had not penetrated, and all China proper was governed by an amiable and philanthropic prince called Fanfur, a prince devoted entirely to the **exercise of** humanity and to the care of his people, save in one point—he neglected his defences; and Kublai Khan, having no earthly cause **of quarrel with** him, only a "manifest destiny" to act with, acted on his manifest destiny, invaded him without the slightest pretext with an overwhelming army, drove him from his dominions, and annexed China; rather a large stroke of business in our degenerate eyes, but nothing in those days.

He treated Fanfur's wife, who fell into his hands, like **a** gentleman; and no doubt the Chinese inhabitants were treated as well as they could expect to be by **a** victorious **army** of Tartars. **But** there was one hitch **in** the proceedings. The **city of** Say-gan-fu (Siang **Yang?**) remained in the rear, refusing **to be** taken on any terms; not threatening communication with the base of operations (because such feeble-minded subtleties were unknown among the Tartars, whose base of operations, like that of all the invading tribes of barbarians, of whom they were the last, was the last town they had plundered; who not only made the war support the war, but pay for the next one), but merely holding out through a kind of pig-headed loyalty — a very Basing-house of a place. They were surrounded with water on three sides, and were too difficult a nut to be cracked by bows and arrows. At this exasperating point the two elder Poli came forward, and with the help of some Nestorian artificers, constructed *catapults*, and took the city triumphantly. Does the reader see the great historical importance of this siege? It is this: it destroys in one moment the old schoolboy fiction, believed in by nine hundred and ninety-nine people out of a thousand to this day—that the Chinese knew the use of gunpowder before the Western nations. The Poli make no mention of gunpowder; and if the besieged had used it, there would have been small chance of the Poli taking the city with catapults. Gibbon's shrewd eye detected this fact at once, and it has been on record some eighty years; yet open any common book of information and you find the old fiction repeated, that the Chinese had known the use of gunpowder 3,000 (30,000, if you like) years before the western nations.

It may be, to a certain extent, interesting to mention that Marco found not a Prester John, but a Prester George, grandson probably of the man whose name, heaven only knows why, is in our mouths to this day. Prester George was a mere nobody; smaller even than his grandfather Ung, who probably has gained a more lasting reputation on smaller grounds than any man who ever lived. Ung was posthumous father-in-law to Ghengis Khan, and a Nestorian. Ghengis asked his daughter in marriage, and he returned an insulting answer, Ghengis' affairs being at that time low. Ghengis invaded him, cut off his head, married his daughter, and had his skull set in silver. How his wife liked this treatment of her father I cannot learn. One never would have heard of the man, had it not been that the Catholics determined that there *should* be an orthodox Church in Northern Asia, and not finding one, in a sort of way, canonized this man. Honest Rubruquis pricked the bubble, but it has not burst even yet.*

In person Kublai Khan was of the middle stature, a comely handsome man, of very fresh complexion, bright black eyes, well-fashioned nose, and a finely-formed body. He was a man of great physical courage, and before his accession to the throne had shown himself a successful general on more than one occasion, though apparently not such a soldier as his brothers Baatu and Hulagu; but since his accession

---

* Another Prester John, or "Pretre Janni," was afterwards made, on much the same grounds, out of the Negus of Abyssinia. Francesco Alvarez went as ambassador to him. Another result of that strange view of Catholicity, which has been more rudely shaken than ever by the reply of the Greek bishops to Rome last month. From Carpini one sees that the idea of "one God, one faith, one baptism," was not enough for Rome. She must have one ceremonialism, or all was naught. And she has got her answer.

he had only been once into the field, in 1280, to suppress the rebellion of Naram, his uncle, and Caydu, his nephew. On this occasion Kublai handled a force of 460,000 men, and by swift and careful marches fell upon Naram, at the head of 400,000 men, before Caydu could effect a junction with him, routed his army, and captured him. It is noticeable that of Kublai's army 360,000 were cavalry, and only 100,000 foot; these last being principally composed of his own falconers and huntsmen. After this victory he once more retired to his favourite pursuits of statesmanship and sporting.

His favourite sports were falconry and cheetah hunting. He had also wolves trained like the cheetahs. He flew his hawks and "eagles" at large four-footed game as well as fowls. Some of his larger hawks could actually disable a wolf. After the gout came on him, he took to hunting from a castle carried by two elephants. There were regular officers to signal the game, and when the signal reached the imperial elephant, the roof of the castle was taken off, and Kublai sat up. His ordinary retinue of falconers was 10,000. When encamped with his courtiers for hunting purposes, their tents had the appearance of a noble city. As a good instance of barbaric ostentation, the Khan's great hunting-tent was lined with sable and ermine. The size of the tent is not given, but although the estimate of it is greatly exaggerated, yet it was evidently a very large pavilion; so much larger than any other, that our good Marco's imagination seems to have run riot a little. I make a rough calculation that it would cost about 1,200*l.* to line a tent seven feet square and high with second quality sable; if lined with imperial sable the cost would be one-third more, say 1,600*l.* Ermine is a somewhat dearer skin, taking into account that it is smaller; so even on these insufficient and understated data the Khan's pavilion must have cost an inconceivable sum. Skins, particularly sable, seem to have been dearer then than now: 16*l.* is, I believe, the full price for imperial sable, even in Russia (the fur is never seen here); for black fox about 50*l.* the skin. Here we read that 2,000 sultanines of gold were often given for so much sable as would make a pair of "tests." The Tartars called sable the "queen of furs," as, indeed, it is to this day, excepting only the black fox, with which, of course, they could not be acquainted, as it comes from Arctic America.

The ostentation of this wonderful Khan was only equalled by his wealth. Although there must have been an accumulation of the precious metals, almost rivalling, one may guess, any which the world has seen before or since—or certainly enormous—no bullion whatever was circulated in the form of coinage: it was all kept for purposes of luxury and display. The only medium of commerce throughout the empire were imperial assignats, of mulberry paper: of course valueless any distance beyond the limits of a revolutionary empire like that of the Tartars. Within the limits of that empire, however, or at all events about the principal seats of government, they seem to have retained their full value. Merchants from foreign parts, who brought precious stones and other articles *de luxe* to the imperial court and to the palaces of the satraps, were paid in this paper. They converted it before their departure into solid articles of merchandise, and apparently went away perfectly satisfied, for they came again. Whether this was a perfectly healthy financial system, it is not for me to decide. It had, however, the merit of "working well."

The value at which human life was held at this time in this empire was decidedly low, but not lower than one could expect. With one exception, there seem to have been no fierce and sanguinary customs; and human life seems only to have been recklessly, yet, as things still go, fairly enough sacrificed in maintaining order and in prosecuting war. The exception to which I allude was the "custom," at the burial of any of the divine royal race of Ghengis Khan. It was customary, while taking the royal corpse to be buried in the Altai, for the escort to kill every one they met on the line of march, and send them to Hades to be slaves of the dead Khan. Of course it may be said that the remedy lay with the people themselves, who had only to keep out of the way; but whether through ignorance of the custom, or through recklessness, the people sometimes met with a terrible disaster through this silly custom. At the funeral of Mangu, elder brother of Kublai, no less than 10,000 peasants were killed in this way, very possibly by coming to stare at the cavalcade.

Again, human life was not always respected in such a trivial matter as that of observing curfew. After curfew had rung from the great bell of Pekin, no man was allowed to stir abroad from his house, except in cases of extreme necessity—such as that of a woman in labour, and then he could move only with a light, as lately at Warsaw. For any infringement of this rule he was arrested and taken to the police-court, where he was beaten with cudgels, and very often died under the beating. In such rough police as this, the military government of the rude and powerful Kublai shows poorly beside the benign and gentle rule of the humane Fanfur whom he conquered.

Such briefly was the court at which the three Venetian gentlemen lived for some twenty years, and at which they obtained the highest honours and distinctions; and during which residence the southern part of China was conquered, and Japan attacked; the brave Japanese being too strong for the Tartars. Marco, the youngest of the three, and evidently the favourite, was actually governor of the conquered town of Yang-cheu-feu for the usual space of three years. They were getting also enormously rich, and they had quite taken to the Tartar language and manners. They were princes in China. They had, as one says, nothing to wish for in this life. Only they got home-sick, and nothing would do for them but they must see Venice before they died.

Who was the first to suggest the homeward journey we do not know. It may have been Marco, now forty years old, sick of vulgar barbaric ostentation, and pining for civilization and art, of which he had only had a glimpse as a lad, and which he remembered only in day-dreams. It may have been Nicolo, longing to lie beside the wife of his early manhood in the graveyard in the Lagune. It may have been the good bachelor uncle Maffeo, longing to tell his wondrous story on the Place of St. Mark, to such gossips as remained after forty years, or to their sons or grandsons. It may be that all three desired the offices of that religion which they still professed. Who can tell? But the idea once started by some one of the three, was adopted by the others. What worth was life, what worth was wealth without Venice?

The Khan would not hear of it. Did they want riches? They should have three times as much as they had. Why would they leave him? Out of pure affection he would not allow them to depart.

A very short time afterwards, Argon, or Arghun, a Mongolian prince of Persia, lost his wife Bolgana, who, on her deathbed, prayed him that he would marry no other wife than one of her own family, which was of Cathay. Upon this, Arghun sent three ambassadors, Ullatai, Apusea, and Coza, to Kublai Khan, to beg a princess of the required family. Kublai granted their request, and a very beautiful young lady of seventeen, by name Cogalin, was selected for the noble destiny of Queen of Persia; and the three ambassadors started westward with their precious charge. The poor young lady was destined to be most unfortunate in this journey. The dismemberment of the empire of Ghengis Khan, which was in reality consummated a year or two afterwards, at the death of Kublai Khan, had already begun. The wars among the different Tartar princes were already so bloodthirsty, that the very **authority of the** old **Khan** was insufficient to frank even an Imperial **party** through what were still nominally his **dominions.** After **eight** months' ineffectual attempts to proceed, they returned baffled.

It was at this time that Marco had returned from one **of** his innumerable adventures, having been sailing some ships of the Khan in the Indian seas. He described these seas **as** being so very pleasant, that the three ambassadors at once went to Kublai and begged that they might proceed round India **by** sea to the Persian Gulf, and that the three **Poli, as** men skilled in navigation, should accompany them. After **a** little anger at the ambassadors **for** making such **a** disagreeable request, he granted it, and dismissed his beloved Poli with every show of affection, **a** splendid present of rubies, and their expenses for two years, making them promise to return.

They started with fourteen ships of four masts each, some of which contained nearly three hundred **sailors.** They made Java in three months, preferring the straits of Sunda **to the** straits of Malacca. **After** this they made a long **voyage** of it, and sickness visited them, carrying off **six** hundred of the sailors, and two of the ambassadors, leaving only Coza alive.

It could not, however, have been altogether an unhappy voyage. There were the two elder Poli, sedate, polite, well informed. **There** was the gallant, elegantly-dressed Marco, now close on forty, a dangerous man to **have the** fetching home of a bride who had never seen her lover, though she were to be Queen of Persia. There **was** Coza, a man whom **I** (I cannot tell why) have set down for a man like Polonius; and lastly, there was the **beautiful** princess herself; **that was the group.** Depend upon it, there were pleasant evenings **on the quarter-deck; some** evenings under the tropic stars, when the sea was calm, and the subdued hum of some great Indian city was borne upon the warm night wind, to mingle with the lazy flapping of the sails, and the lap of the water around the ship's side: Princess Cogalin, in after-days, in the whirl of a great revolution, must have remembered this voyage, **one** would think, as the happiest time in (I **guess)** her not very happy existence. Forgive **my** trying, by the help of **strong** probabilities, to rescue **one** piece of real life out of the great dark past.

They were eighteen months reaching the Persian Gulf; and when they got to Ormuz, Arghun **was** dead, and there had been something like a revolution. One Chiciato governed the kingdom for Arghun's son Chagan, **a youth under age, who** was at Arbor Secco, on the **confines of Persia, with** sixty thousand **persons, for** the guard of certain passages against the enemy; a matter which there **is** neither **time nor** inclination **to edit.** Chiciato ordered the ambassadors **to take the princess to** Chagan, and marry her to him, which was duly done by the three Poli. Let us hope **that our friend the pretty princess** found herself more **suitably matched with the** youthful Chagan than she could have been with the more elderly Arghun; and in leaving her, thank her for her company **so far.**

Chiciato gave them fresh passports of travel, in the name, be it remembered, of the still mighty Kublai Khan, which **passports decreed that any** who opposed them, or who refused to assist them, should be put to death. With these powers they started for Trebizond, but on their way thither, they heard news which shut out their old Chinese haunts from them, and relieved them from the promise they had given to return. They must seek their kind old friend and patron elsewhere than at the Summer Palace at Pekin, if they would see him again. Kublai Khan was dead.

He was about seventy-seven, and had reigned thirty-eight years, having made but one failure during his reign—the unsuccessful attack on Japan. Among the four more eminent brothers, sons of " Tuli the General," Mangu, Baatu, Hulagu, and Kublai— Kublai was certainly the greatest, as well as the gentlest and most civilized. His civilization and his gentleness he, in part, no doubt derived from his Cathayan education. He could be extravagantly generous—so can most people who have the plunder of half the world in their coffers; but he could be chivalrous to women, witness his treatment of the Queen of Fanfur, who defended Southern China against him with considerable success, after her craven and effeminate husband, the philanthropist, had fled. He could love those who were worth loving, and be just to them, witness his behaviour on the departure of the Poli. He was a very great statesman, a man of great personal courage, and a general who could handle his three hundred thousand men in a stricken field with eminent rapidity and success. He would have been a Christian (and made his subjects so also, which is more to the purpose), if they had given him a fair chance. But he was dead, and the Poli, in spite of their regrets for him, must have been glad to find themselves free to remain in their still-loved Venice.

It must have taken a considerable time, in the disturbed state of the Tartar empire, for the news of the death of the Khan to reach them, and they travelled slowly, for they touched at Constantinople and at Negropont, arriving in Venice in the year 1295. This confirms the *Tartar* date given for the death of Kublai Khan, against the Chinese: the former make him to die in 1292, which is plainly correct; the latter in 1295, which is impossible if the Poli received the news of his death between Ormuz and Trebizond. The two brothers and the uncle, however, beyond all dispute, arrived at their house in St. John Chrysostom Street, in Venice, in the year 1295.

Now that they had touched Western civilization once more after an absence of twenty-six years; now that they had a chance of comparing themselves to other people, they found that they had turned into Tartars, in dress, in manner, and in speech. No one knew them, and but few believed in them. It was actually necessary for them to prove their own identity; and, while proving this, they determined to take the popularity of Venetian dandyism by storm at the same time. For this purpose they resolved on a supper party, the like of which has seldom been seen, and which must be considered one of the great supper parties of history.

They assembled what the gentlemen who write the evening and dinner-party business in our newspapers would call the "rank and fashion" of Venice; who no doubt came willingly enough, were it only for the sake of talking over these three finely-dressed people afterwards. They found themselves received by the three Poli, bowing in gorgeous dresses of crimson, rich even for those days, when a dandy put half his estate on his back and legs. Never were seen such clothes; but they were not good enough for the Poli to sit down to supper in. Begging to be excused, they changed them for suits of crimson damask, still more exasperating to the Venetian dandies, and gave the priceless crimson satin suits to the servants. These, however, were not good enough to wear while drinking with their guests; so before dessert they threw these also to the servants, and came forth flaming in crimson velvet. This trick, as I before noticed, they had got from the Tartars.

But they reserved their great surprise until the servants were sent away, and they were over their wine. Then they produced their Tartar coats, their belts, and other travelling gear, and ripped them open before the astounded guests. One after another the great jewels fell clashing on the table, and lay blazing in little heaps in the light of the lamps. One would like to have been at that supper party had it only been to see the collection of rubies which the Khan gave them as a parting gift. Taking every sort of probability into account, it is extremely doubtful if such a collection of jewels has been seen together. When we consider that they had been trading advantageously for twenty-six years among the ravagers of the East and West, and had converted everything they could into jewels, it must have been a great collection. Among them, they say, were some old family jewels well known to some of the guests, which led to the acknowledgment of their identity. This seems to me the most improbable part of the story. However, the popularity of the Poli was assured.

Life was now over for the two uncles. Uncle Maffeo became a worthy magistrate, and lived apparently until his nephew returned from captivity; for he not only confirmed his nephew's account of their adventures everywhere in society, but on his deathbed to his confessor affirmed every word of them to be true. It is said also that Marco's father, Nicolo, in despair of his son's return from Genoa, married and had three children. This is not the sort of thing which would be idly invented, one would say, unless one considers that we are told by the closest and most unimpeachable critics that about one-third the things known as historical facts must have been invented in simple idleness. Pettigrew's pamphlet on Amy Robsart is a good illustration of the way these inventions may be exposed. Were it in any way worth speaking of, I should doubt this second marriage of Signor Nicolo's. He had been forty years travelling, and even if he were only twenty-five when he began he would now be seventy. The probability is that he was, considering that he was the elder brother, at least seventy-five. If one puts on to this the time of Marco's captivity, long enough to make him despair of ever seeing him again, one at least gets him up to eighty. This exceeds by six years, unless I am mistaken, the dates of a case well known to lawyers. As if it was of the least importance.

It was God's will, however, that Marco Polo should not rest from his labours as yet. A very short time after their return, Lampa Doria, the Genoese admiral, came to the island of Curzola (the long island E.S.E. from *Lissa*, off the coast of Dalmatia, in this last year become so famous, and distant some twenty-five miles) threatening Venice. The Venetians sent out, under command of Andrea Dandolo (I think he was grandson of Enrico Dandolo, conqueror of Zara, and grandfather of Andrea the historian, friend of Petrarch. I am not sure, doubtless there are many who are), a large number of ships to oppose them. Marco Polo commanded a galley in this great fleet, which was superior in numbers to the Genoese. In the very same water, close to the very same island, where we saw the other day Tegethoff and Persano ramming and pounding at one another, did Doria and Dandolo pound and ram at one another in the year of grace 1296. The bones of the Venetians and Genoese of the thirteenth century lie lowest; upon them are the bones of the Austrians and Italians of the nineteenth. A little off, the men of Hoste and his English lie quietly in the ouze of the Adriatic. Not a very remarkable instance; for if you examine Europe from end to end it is only one great grave of bones, thicker in strategical points than elsewhere—useless bones buried just too deep for the plough to turn them up and utilize them. The world is better for the expenditure; but has it not been done with some mismanagement and extravagance? The Venetians were totally defeated, and Marco Polo, fighting in front, was wounded, taken prisoner, and carried to

Genoa. It was in his captivity here that he wrote his travels.

He found that he had to repeat them so often, that it would be better to write them down, and so, sending to Venice for his notes, he, with the assistance of one Rustigielo of Pisa, wrote down his travels in *Latin*, somewhere about 1298. From this a translation was made into Italian, and the Latin MS. became rare—so rare, indeed, that the Italian was taken to be the original, and was translated back into Latin by one Francis Pepin, or Pepuri, a monk, who abridged it by the order of his superiors. It is a copy of this MS. which is in the library of the King of Prussia, and was printed at Basle by Reinecius. About 1550, however, Giovanni Bamusio, the collector of travels, Secretary to the Ten at Venice, had lent him by Signor Chisi the rare original Latin MS. of 1298; from this, and with an enthusiastic admiration for his fellow-townsman, he composed his account of Marco Polo's travels, which must be taken as the most authentic form of them. Hakluyt has, it appears, copied from the monk Pepin's abridgement, which makes Purchas very angry: perhaps the good Secretary to Archbishop Abbot was not sorry to prick a hole in the coat of his great contemporary.

Marco continued four years in captivity at Genoa before he was released. On his return home, at the age of fifty, he married and had two daughters, Moretta and Fantina, but no sons. These two young ladies must have therefore had between them all the enormous wealth of the family (for I do not believe in Nicolo's marriage), and most probably married some very eminent men. It would be interesting, were it possible, to know which of the noble Venetian families had, or have, Polo blood in their veins.

He died as he had lived, admired, beloved, and respected as much among the Venetians as among the Mongols, having served the State of Venice as faithfully as he had served the Khan. It is on record of him that he was a very *humble* man. Where he is buried is, for some reason, uncertain. Sansorino, however, the Venetian printer, distinctly says, "under the passage to the Church of S. Lorenso on the islet Gemelle." *Requiescat.* I like what I know of him so much that I am sorry to bring the pleasant labour of writing a short account of him and his friend the Khan to a close.*

* PEDIGREE OF KUBLAI KHAN.

The following is a little scheme of the Tartar dynasty which I made out from various sources for my use three years ago. As it does not differ from the narrative of Gibbon, it may be presumed to be nearly correct, although the spelling is different. For instance, one of the monks calls Ajuk "Gayuk;" another, "Cuyne" (Khan).

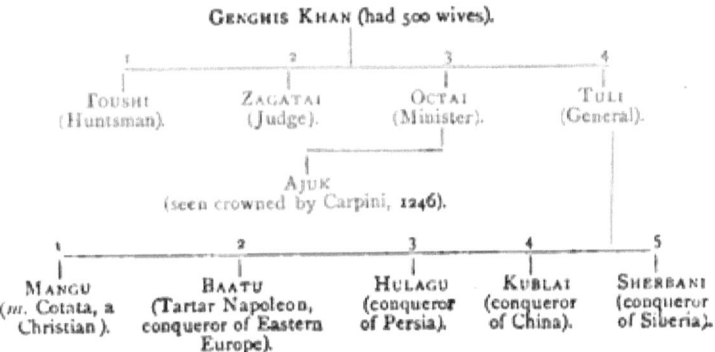

As far as my knowledge goes, the most powerful and most able family which has ever been known on our globe, the ablest of them all, Kublai, asking for Christianity, which the Papacy supplied; as we see.

THE SHIPWRECK OF PELSART.

IN these days, when the *Columbian* runs 14,000 miles in 55 days, and the *Argo* actually goes round the world in 125 (four months), we can hardly understand how the sailors of older times endured their wonderfully arduous voyages without going melancholy mad. That they were more often on shore is true, but nevertheless, the long periods of confinement at sea, combined with the—in those days—ever-present scurvy, must in many cases have made the worst of them very reckless and very desperate.

The cause of these few sentences was my remarking, that the ship *Batavia*, commanded by Francis Pelsart, which sailed from the Texel in October, 1628, had been nine weary months at sea, when the accident happened about which we are going to hear. It may in some way account for the conduct of some on board.

In those days of imperfect chronometers, or no chronometers at all, longitude was a very great difficulty, even as it is now among small and ill-found craft like the fruit brigs when they venture into the ocean; they being almost entirely dependent for their longitude on the bigger ships, which are better found with instruments; as any one who has sailed in the Bay of Biscay will testify. It is no wonder then, that the captain of the *Batavia*, having been separated from the rest of the Dutch fleet, for a time not specified, by a storm, found himself utterly at a loss as to his whereabouts as to longitude, though perfectly correct as to latitude.

Any schoolboy going in for a competitive examination in geography could give him his longitude in these days, with, most likely, a feeling of contempt towards the hard-headed Dutch sailor, and a feeling of complacency at his own superior wisdom, as if he had found it all out himself. His longitude was about 115°, and his latitude was about 30°. He had got himself driven into one of the queerest and most out-of-the-way corners on the face of the globe; a place which is nearly as queer and nearly as little frequented now as it was then: near the place called Houtman's Abrolhos; but at that time it had not even such an outlandish name as that. Houtman's Abrolhos is on the east coast of Australia.

You must trust a second hand to edit Pelsart truthfully. It is not difficult, for his narrative is very clear, and many are more familiar now with those latitudes than he was. It was a night in June, in the depth of winter, you will remember, and there was a fair cold wind from the pole, for the ship's course was N.E. and by N. The moon was full and high, and, although Pelsart does not mention it, the sky was of a deep splendid purple, and the Southern Cross was hanging in the air like a boy's kite ready to topple and fall. Pelsart was ill and in his cabin, and the officer who was in charge only saw, as he thought, the moonbeams reflected on the glorious purple sea. But he was mistaken. That brighter light on the wandering waves which were following the wind towards that meeting which never takes place and never will, was not the effect of moonlight. If he had kept a sharper look out he would have seen it. That frosted silver meant "breakers," and before he had done thinking about his sweetheart among the tulips at Rotterdam, the ship had struck, with that dull, ripping, riving noise which no man out of Bedlam wishes to hear twice.

Pelsart was on deck in a minute. Of course, the first thing he did was to turn out the master and blame him severely for what had happened, and to ask in what part of the world he was. The master excused himself by stating that they were in a part of the world where no man had ever been before, which was true.

Finding that there was more water before than behind them, they threw the cannon overboard, in hopes that she would, when lightened, drift free. Such was not the case, however: she continued striking heavily; and while they were still employed a furious storm of wind and rain came travelling up on the wind and burst over them. They now cut away their mainmast; but it was of little good, for it would not go overboard, but lay hampering the deck. They could make out two small islands close to them, and a larger one eight or nine miles off. On these islands Pelsart, having thought it over, determined to land the women, children, and sick people, who were out of their wits with fear.

Day dawned at last upon this horrid night. The master returned from examining the islands about nine o'clock, and an hour after they began to take off the women and children, using the more diligence as the ship apparently began to break. About 160 people were moved during the day,—120 to the large island, and 40 to the smaller one. They also worked at getting up their bread, but unluckily gave less thought to the water. And some of the crew getting brutally drunk, they only landed twenty barrels of bread and very little water. The captain stuck by his ship, doing all he could amongst the drunkenness and destruction, until the master came off to him from one of the islands to say that it was no use sending any more provisions on shore, for that the people were wasting those they had. Pelsart immediately went on shore to see after these matters, and found them almost without water. He made an effort to get back to the ship and to get them some more water, but the weather was too heavy. The carpenter swam from the ship to the boat to tell Captain Pelsart what sad condition they were in on board the ship. Pelsart got him to swim back and tell them to make rafts and float ashore on them; but the weather getting worse, he had, to his great grief, to return and leave his lieutenant and seventy men on the point of perishing.

The people on the islands were in a sad plight also. There was on the small island, where there were but forty people, only forty gallons of water. On the larger island, where there were 120, there was still less. Under these circumstances, the people of the small island urged the captain, with murmurs, to go and seek water on the neighbouring islands. His answer was perfectly manly and fair. He would go if those on the big island would consent; but that sooner than leave his ship's company without the consent of the whole party, he would return to the ship and perish with his lieutenant. He therefore turned his boat's head towards the large island, to get the consent of the people there. He now found that his crew were in a state of respectful mutiny, of which his coxswain was ringleader. They positively refused to allow him to land on the island, and, on his endeavouring to leap overboard, used force to restrain him, only permitting him to write a few lines in his table-book, saying that he was gone for water, and to throw it ashore. Whether they were determined, at all hazards, to retain possession of the captain's person, as being the only one who could navigate them home, or whether they were affectionately anxious for his safety, and for that reason would not let him land among the large islanders, it is hard to determine now. They had their will, however, and in the end the matter was settled thus:—The captain got a paper from all his men, saying that it was their wish that he should depart in search of water; and so, having spent a day or so in reconnoitring, he put a deck to his long-boat, and on the 9th, five days after the wreck, he was off the coast of Australia, with a smaller boat either in tow, or in company.

At that time the nearest point of human civilization was at Batavia, in the island of Java, a good fifteen hundred miles away. The whole of the great

Pelsart prevented from reaching the Island.

THE SHIPWRECK OF PELSART.   45

land east and south of him was then, of course, a lonely desert, whose silence was only now and then broken by the yells of the sparse and miserable savages, when they fell out about their filthy, stupid women, or their horrible food. But I met a gentleman at a great dinner-party the other day who lives not forty miles from this place. This gentleman had taken a house in Belgravia during his sojourn in England on business, but was going back to his great copper works there directly. To readers not conversant with Australian geography, it may be interesting to mention that this place where Pelsart was looking for water, and where the Geraldine Copper Mines are now, is no part of Australia of which he has probably ever heard, but lies some two thousand miles west of Melbourne. I only mention this to make Captain Pelsart's account of the coast more interesting. People will begin to believe in Australia some day.

Although the most interesting part of this story will be found in the mishaps which befel the shipwrecked people left on the two islands, yet, as we must follow Captain Pelsart, it will be better to do so at once; and to come back to the others, and to the *dénouement*, later.

"Pelsart's Group" of islands are nearly the most southerly of that little archipelago now called Houtman's Abrolhos, and which stretches some fifty miles north and south. He seems very much to have miscalculated the distance between the islands and the continent, which he makes sixteen miles, but which Stanford makes far more. It is no great matter. There is little doubt that he, in his boat, with his mutinous, but respectful crew, was the first discoverer of this wonderful new copper-bearing country, which is now helping to enrich the already rich Swansea; that he approached it on the 9th of June, 1629; and that it remained undiscovered, or, to be more correct, utterly unsettled and unutilized for two hundred years or more. *We* have got it now, of course, as we have got most of the good things, though we are said to want ideas. The country is not good, but better than Westmoreland or Perthshire, leaving alone its copper or gold.

Pelsart made the coast, as far as we can tell, about Geraldstown or Port Grey. Geraldstown is, I believe, to Port Grey what Melbourne is to Williamstown. They saw a cove, and tried to make it, but the surf on the bar was too much for them, and they went northward, having missed, one supposes, the mouth of the "Irving" river. Had they made this, there would have been a very different story to tell. He describes the coast as similar to that about Dover; but it is familiar enough to many people now.

They made no land now, until they were in 24°, where some of the men swam ashore through the ocean rollers. This must have been Cape Cuvier. The men found naked savages, who ran away from them, but no water. They then sailed for ten days, when they landed again in 22°, and got some rain-water. This was probably on the great cape which defends Exmouth Gulf from the seaward; nay, one may say almost certainly so.

Here there comes a singular proof of the perfect

correctness of Pelsart's narrative—" strong enough to *hang* a man "—even if there was the slightest doubt of his story, of which there can be none. His distances and his dates (one fears through able editors) are sadly at fault, to a cursory reader. They are so obviously at fault, that they are without doubt mere clerical errors; you get from the *twenty-fifth* back to the *sixteenth* in a way which surprises you, till you see that the printer has printed "16" instead of "26." Again, when at the north-west cape, where we have just left him, he is looking for the river of Jacob Remescens (what river was that? what old story of Dutch discovery, lost for ever, does *that* suggest to us?) he gives us his latitude, and proves not only the truth of his story, but his own excellent navigation. The most westerly point of Australia was passed days before, at Dirk Hartog's Island in 26°; since then the coast had been bending slightly eastward, slightly out of his course, but he had held to it in hopes of finding water. At this point, the exact latitude of which he gives, it bends suddenly, almost at a right angle, to the eastward, and it became necessary for him to make across the ocean for Batavia. The editor makes this only *one* hundred miles from the scene of his shipwreck, whereas it was as he had come, at least four. Reading that he had only come one hundred miles, and that at this point he determined to push for Batavia instead of going back, one would accuse him of cowardice; but when one comes to see that he had come four hundred miles before a strong south wind, at an average rate of sixty nautical miles a day, one must hand him back his certificate, and declare that he did for the best in pushing for Java.

Of course he saw no more of Australia after this; his course was N.E. across the ocean. He reached Batavia on July the second, twenty-four days out, distance, as he made it (it is impossible, as any sailor will tell you, to be particular), fifteen or sixteen hundred miles. The only great ocean boat voyages which compare to this, are Bligh's, after the mutiny of the *Bounty*, twelve hundred miles; the voyage of the *Mystery* to Melbourne in 1854 (the distance, as she made it, say some ten thousand miles); Bass's whale-boat voyage; and the voyage of a Portuguese from Goa to Lisbon, round the Cape, in a canoe. One finds it difficult to give the palm; but it certainly remains between Pelsart and Bligh; as usual, in nautical adventures, between the Englishman and the Dutchman. I suspect that Pelsart's boat was bigger than Bligh's, because he put a deck to it before he started. The *Mystery* was a twelve-ton boat, with a cabin. About the Portuguese canoe I am in want of information, and of belief.

It is evident, however, that Pelsart's expedition is worth recalling. But what went on in the two little islands, opposite my friend S——'s house, in the year 1629, is stranger and more interesting than the mere fact of a man getting himself blown from Geraldstown to Batavia. We return to the shipwrecked folks on the sandy islands, "among whom," says our able editor, in his old style, "there happened such transactions, as in their condition, the reader would little expect, and perhaps will hardly credit. In order to their being thoroughly understood, it is necessary to observe that they had for supercargo one Jerom Cornelis, who had been formerly an apothecary at Harlem."

Jerom Cornelis was about the last man who succeeded in getting from the wreck; in fact, he spent ten days on her before he got to land on one of the yards. In the absence of Captain Pelsart he had to take the command.

He now suddenly came out in his true colours, as one of the most treacherous and bloodthirsty ruffians one reads of in the history of piracy. He determined to surprise the captain when he returned, and with a few faithful followers to turn pirate. For this purpose it became necessary to butcher all the honest men of the party, which were, we may suppose, a very large majority.

His first action was to separate the honest men, and take them in detail. For this purpose he despatched Mr. Weybhays and the chaplain with forty men to another island to look for water. Weybhays found water and made the signal agreed on, he lit three fires; but they were unnoticed, for the massacre on the larger island had begun.

Between thirty and forty were killed on the occasion, and his fiendish plan had so far prospered; only a few poor fellows had cast themselves into the sea, and gained Weybhays, with their horrid tale of treachery and murder. But two other great obstacles remained,—Weybhays and his party of forty-five on the island where they had newly landed, and the party of forty which had originally landed on a

E

smaller island, as will be remembered; either of these parties might, from these islands, give the captain warning, and must be removed.

Weybhays's was the strongest party. So Cornelis begun with the others first. They made but little resistance, and were all mercilessly butchered, with the exception of five women and seven children. Of the five women, two, one has reason to fear, were the chaplain's daughters: one of these Cornelis took to himself, and the other he gave to his favourite. We can go no further with this part of the story.

He now broke out into the most frantic profligacy and folly. The merchants' chests were broken open, and from the rare and rich stuffs which were being carried to the Indies, he and his followers had made fantastic uniforms, covered with gold and silver lace, and so swaggered about the desolate sandy islands among the laughing sea-gulls. He drew up his code, this wretched assassin, and had his troop of guards clothed in his livery of scarlet. The temptation of the piratical mind, of the rapid, treacherous, infinitely cruel and wicked tiger-like mind, seems to be towards a tiger-like gaudiness, and babyish display. I think the reader will find that this passion for absurd dandyism is general among pirates. Any how, the image of this man, elbow deep in blood, strutting up and down in what was then the most desolate and lonely island in the world, bedizend in silks and satins, is a very strange one, and one not easily forgotten.

But the new "Captain-General," as he called himself, had to make war, and began to make it. The sturdy, honest Weybhays, with his five-and-forty equally honest comrades, and the chaplain, had to be exterminated. After a few days of miserable folly and profligacy, he embarked twenty-two men in two shallops, to exterminate them. They were well armed, but there was evidently no gunpowder on either side, as that would have finished the question quickly. These twenty-two pirates returned to the large island, well beaten. Another expedition of thirty-seven men was then sent out, but they came back more severely worsted than the others. The noble Weybhays and his men were only armed with staves having nails driven into their heads; with such poor arms, they boldly dashed into the water, and beat the murderers back.

It became necessary for the pirate to negotiate. Pelsart, ἀναξ ἀνδρῶν, might return any hour, and then ? what chance was there for the red-handed rebel against the sturdy Weybhays, plus the terrible Pelsart? *He* knew well enough how the cowardly rascals in his train would sneak away from him and submit, before the inexorable clear eye of the master, who had the awful and mysterious science of navigation at his fingers' ends; who could sail for a month at sea without seeing land, and could say, to-morrow, at noon, we shall see land, and there will be palm-trees on the shore. The master, who could do this miracle, and who in storm or battle had been the foremost and the most cool, appointing each man to his place in the midst of the most terrible confusion, might arrive to-morrow, and, with Weybhays and his fifty men at his back, quietly and calmly ask for an explanation of what had been going on in his absence. The idea was terrible. Nothing for it but negotiation and treachery.

Negotiations were opened. **Peace** was agreed on on the following grounds : Weybhays and his party were to remain undisturbed, but were to give back a little boat in which a honest sailor had escaped to Weybhays and his party (this was evidently to prevent Weybhays from communicating with the dreadful Pelsart). Weybhays, on the other hand, was to have some of the stuffs they had plundered from the merchants' chests to make clothes withall, for the honest men were sadly in want of them. Such were Cornelis' negotiations, and the truce was agreed on. His safety, however, lay, not in negotiation, but in treachery.

Among the party of Weybhays were certain French soldiers, and, through these men, Cornelis, with his fox-like intellect, saw, or thought he saw, that he could get the better of Weybhays. There had been a great deal of going and coming between the two islands during the negotiations, which were principally carried on by the good chaplain ; and the night before the ratification of the treaty (or apparently the night before) he managed to get some letters conveyed to these French soldiers, offering them six thousand livres (£240) a-piece if they would betray Weybhays.

I suppose French soldiers have always been the same. I suppose that on the receipt of these letters, they compared them one with another, put their legs very wide apart, and began walking up and down in front of one another, looking savage, and twitching their heads; and that at last one of them said sharply "*Non*," at the back of his nose; and that all the others said "*Non*," also, each looking at the other, as if the insult had come from his comrade, and he was prepared to fight him, or his own brother, and on the slighest notice.

However this is imaginary, the fact is, that these noble Frenchmen carried their letters to Weybhays, and laid them before him.

When Jerom Cornelis came the next morning, Weybhays was perfectly ready for him. Cornelis came across with the clothes he had promised Weybhays, followed by only three or four men. Weybhays attacked them, killed three or four, but, better than this, captured Cornelis in his tom-fool's dress, and bound him tight.

One Wonterloss made his escape and got back to the other island, to rouse his fellow-conspirators. Things were so desperate now with them, that they made an immediate effort to rescue their head-centre, by attacking Weybhays. They were badly beaten, and almost before the strife had calmed down, and they had got back to their island, Pelsart was among them.

Not a beaten, thirsty fugitive in the ship's pinnace: far otherwise. One of the solemn and terrible Dutch frigates of those times, the *Sardam* (she could not have been at Chatham) was seen slowly sailing towards the wreck; and Pelsart was on board of her.

There flashes instantly before one's mind's eye, a picture which, although the subject is 200 years old, must be faithful. Three bright yellow islands, crowned with myrtle-like shrubs, which rise out of the fuming sand; around them a brilliant blue sea under a deep blue sky. On the beaches of these islands, groups of men are moving about towards one point. Beyond the islands, in the ocean, is a wreck holding up its gaunt ribs above the little braid of silver surf which surrounds it. And, slowly sailing towards this wreck, comes one of Vandervelde's own, solemn, majestic frigates: but not as one would see her in one of his pictures, cloudy and dim, in a driving Dutch mist, but made so bright and brilliant by the crystalline Australian atmosphere, that each rope stood out like a wire, each block like a bead, each reef-point on her snowy sails like a silken thread upon white satin. Such must have been the picture which Jerom Cornelis, bound without hope of rescue, must have seen and cursed that spring morning.

Pelsart, to his great joy, saw a great cloud of smoke rising from one of the islands, and knew that his people were not all dead. He had put some wine and provisions in a boat, and was advancing towards the island when he was met by the faithful Weybhays in his boat, who begged him to hurry back to his ship, as the mutineers intended to surprise her; and at the same time told the horrid story of the murder. While he was doing so, two boats appeared, and the captain rowed back for his life, just gaining the deck of the *Sardam* in time.

To his great astonishment, for Weybhays could hardly have had time to tell him more than the mere fact of the murder, Pelsart saw two boats come alongside, filled with men in scarlet uniforms laced with gold and silver, and armed. He demanded what they meant by coming alongside armed. They replied they would let him know when they got on board. He ordered them to throw their arms overboard, or he would sink them alongside. Resistance was utterly useless, and they surrendered, and were put in irons. John Bremen, the first of them who was examined, owned to having murdered twenty-seven. That night Jerom Cornelis was brought on board heavily ironed.

It now remained to seize the rest of the conspirators, and they prepared to attack them the following morning. But, when they had landed, the rebels made no resistance; they were utterly cowed, threw down their arms, and submitted.

The *Sardam* stayed about the wreck until she had weighed some chests of silver. The jewels distributed by Cornelis among his followers were all recovered; and then a council of war was called as to whether they should try the prisoners there, or take them to Batavia. Considering the great quantity of silver on board the ship, they determined to judge them on the scene of their crimes, in preference to incurring the danger of carrying them to Java. They were accordingly tried and executed; and Pelsart sailed away, leaving the lonely islands to their original solitude and desolation.

THE WONDERFUL ADVENTURES OF ANDREW BATTEL.

THE captivity of Andrew Battel among the Portuguese, and his hair-breadth escapes in Equatorial Africa, where he lived for eighteen years, are well worth relating as an example of the style of life often led by the happy-go-lucky English sailor in Elizabeth's time; perfectly ready to go anywhere, or do anything which came to his hand. To find a thorough Andrew Battel now-a-days, you must, I think, go to Portugal; they wander more and are found in stranger seas than the sailors of most other nations.

He was an Englishman, a sailor, of Leigh on the South Essex coast (last station before Southend), and in the year 1589 joined the expedition of one Abraham Cooke of Limehouse, who had fitted out two little craft for an adventure to the river Plate, an enormous distance for such exceedingly small vessels, whose names were the *May Morning* and the *Dolphin*. In what capacity, or in which ship Andrew went, he does not say, and indeed he has a somewhat involved way of telling his story, all along; although it is evidently *meant* to be perfectly true, and undoubtedly is so, with very few exceptions which will be perfectly obvious to the reader.

They started in May, and getting, after a few rebuffs, a fair wind, sailed down Spain and Portugal, and soon found themselves becalmed under the Grain Coast, just below Sierra Leone, with the men sickening so fast with the scurvy, that by the time they had slipped along about 300 miles to Cape Palmas, scarcely one was sound. Here, however, they got some "refreshing," and recovered. How very strange it was that these men, who, like all sailors, knew that with plenty of lemon-juice you could avoid that hideous disease, the scurvy, did not think of carrying some of this precious juice along with them. It was 250 years longer before any one thought of carrying lime-juice to sea.

Feeling better, they bore down on the little Portuguese island of St. Thomas, which lies just on the equator. On another island near the south end they found a village full of sick negro slaves, sent there to recruit. Having refreshed themselves with the fruit of the island, the piratical rascals returned thanks to Heaven by burning the hospital village, and running up the side of the island, came to the town of St. Thomas, "but durst not come near, for the castle shot at us." One can hardly help wishing that it had hit them.

They then took a short cruise out of sight of the island, in this part of the Gulf of Guinea, apparently with a view of deceiving the lynx-eyed Portuguese governor as to their whereabouts, but without success, for on returning to the other side of the island for water, they found that he had "ambosked" a hundred men in the wood by the watering-place, who thrashed them handsomely, killing one man and wounding several. It became evident that there were more kicks than halfpence going on this side of the Atlantic, and so Abraham Cooke, commander of these two little tubs, determined to set sail to the other side of it, which he did, making the coast of Brazil in thirty days, at "Ilha Grande" (mouth of the Rio Grande, below Cape St. Roque?) probably a point between Natal and Pernambuco. This was a distance of 2,000 miles or more in thirty days, that is to say, some 70 miles a day on the average, not bad sailing for two little craft of fifty tons! This fact seems to one worth remembering.

At this island, which I cannot find, they stopped twelve days and refitted; what else they did there I cannot quite make out; we must remember that, in all probability, Andrew's reminiscences were dictated to the clerk of Southend over rum and water; either the clerk at this point began to get disguised in liquor, or Andrew, finding himself in a Christian country, got cautious and respectable; or else they were both tipsy together. I cannot say how it was, but the narrative here is hazy. They sent the *Dolphin* home for one thing. They did something else here which I cannot understand. An unlucky little Portuguese pinnace "happened in" there, "and they presently went aboard" and took the merchant out of her. Whether the merchant was a consenting party or no, Andrew does not say, he only tells us more hazily than before, that the merchant took them to a part of the island where there was a banished man who grew plantains; and then this merchant, finding himself in the hands of the Philistines, laid them on to a good thing about some "caravels," from the town of Buenos Ayres. He told them that with this fruit (the plantains of the banished man), they would get easily to the river Plate; in short, evidently wanted them to go there, or further, as long as they left him alone. That is all I can make out about this part of the adventure. Either through caution or through drink, Andrew Battel is as indefinite in his explanations as a good Secretary of the Admiralty.

His very vagueness is, to me, a proof of his truth.

You *must* not ask a sailor too many questions. Only the other day, a retired collector of her Majesty's Revenue (who had been in his time a privateer's man), a very old friend, was describing to me the masterly way in which he had dodged a French corvette, in the last war, on to shallow water off one of the banks on the coast of Holland. The French corvette could not follow his schooner across the bank; he was running over it, with the shot dropping further and further astern each moment, as the Frenchman found her water shoaling: he had escaped, when the night lifted a little, and showed him the dreadful spectacle of a BRITISH frigate right on his course. He jammed down his helm and held northward over the bank, trusting in his desperation that there might be water enough. "But why didn't you run on for the British frigate?" I asked; "and get under guns." I was silenced with a lofty look of contempt. I asked no more questions. You must not ask a sailor too many.

It is perfectly legitimate to tell this very little story here. This is a book of adventures.

Abraham Cooke, of Limehouse hole, commander of this queer little expedition, egged on by the Portuguese merchant, evidently anxious to get rid of him, still thought well of the expedition to the river Plate, and having victualled his ship with the "banished man's" plantains, sailed south, and came to the island of *Lobos Marinos*,* at the mouth of the river Plata, which was covered with seals and sea-morses in immense quantities, upon which they lived thirty days. They made one attempt to run up to Buenos Ayres, and cut out a small vessel, but failed, and getting into terrible straits for want of provisions, gave up the voyage and came northward to the island of San Sebastian, a short distance to the south of Rio Janeiro. There they went ashore to fish, and some of them being famished, went up into the woods to gather fruit. A canoe full of Indians had arrived at the other side of the island, and, creeping up, surprised five of them, of whom was Andrew, and carried them off to Rio Janeiro as prisoners. Upon this loss of five of his men, Abraham Cooke of Limehouse sailed away in the *May Morning*, and never was heard of again.

Andrew was not detained long at Rio. He and one Torner were sent to Angola, in Africa, to the town of St. Paul, and put in prison; but not for long: the Portuguese seeming to have made great use of their prisoners of war, and he was sent "up the river

* Isla de Lobos, some sixty miles from Monte Video, on the same side of the river.

Quanza to a garrison town 120 miles up." Now I wish to call attention to this slight proof of his accuracy. The river which comes on at St. Paul is called Coanza to this day, and just 120 miles up it stands the town of Aco. He had forgotten the name of the town, but not the distance to it; and it is further worthy of notice that his latitude and longitude are wonderfully correct.

He was now appointed pilot to the governor, Hurtado de Mendoza; but immediately afterwards fell ill, and lay eight months so at St. Paul. Here, he says, he was much hated as an Englishman, and remembering the burning of the negro village at St. Thomas's not so long before, one can scarcely wonder at it. His first voyage for the Governor was to Tarza, at the mouth of the Congo, for elephants' teeth, wheat, and palm-oil, in which he was successful. Then he went up as high as Loango, making such excellent bargains as 120 lbs. of ivory for a yard of cloth, and dealing in "Irish rugs," whatever they are; he gave Mendoza great satisfaction, and had his liberty for two years and a half.

He now made an attempt to escape. A Dutch ship coming in to the port, offered to take him off. He was already secreted on board, when he, the hated Englishman, was betrayed by some Portuguese, and taken out of the ship by the sergeants of the city. He expected that the Governor would put him to death, but he did not, merely banishing him for life to the fort of Massagano, to help in the conquest of those parts.

After remaining here for six years, he made another

effort to escape. Massagano stands on the river Coanza, which falls into the Atlantic at St. Paul, and his plan was to seize a canoe, and drop down the river for a certain distance, then striking northward, to enter the territory of Congo. He opened his plan to four Egyptians and seven Portuguese, who consented to join him, and the whole twelve, having secured a canoe, and taking with them twelve muskets with ammunition, dropped down the river Coanza as far as a place called Mani Cabech, and there, carefully sinking their canoe, they struck northward into the bush.

They were scarcely eight degrees from the line, and their sufferings were very great from heat and drought. They struggled on, however, most courageously in a north-western direction, fording one river infested with crocodiles. They had to pass within twelve miles of the town of St. Paul, and the negroes were evidently anxious for their capture. They refused them water, and Andrew and his companions were obliged to extort it by threats of using their fire-arms. At last there was a collision with the negroes, and four of the latter were killed. By this time, of course, the news of their escape had spread. On the morning of the seventh day they found themselves pursued by the Captain of St. Paul's and a host of negroes.

The Portuguese at once hid themselves, but Andrew and his four Egyptian comrades still kept their courage, and made efforts to escape. They were useless. The fugitives were brought to bay in a little wood, and dispersed by a volley of musketry. Andrew, now finding himself alone, came out with his musket loaded, and coolly announced that, unless he got a promise of life, he would "die there among them"—a grim sort of threat, with so much meaning in it that the Captain immediately gave his word of honour as a soldier, and Andrew submitted.

He was now cast into prison, with an iron collar round his neck and heavy bolts on his legs, and only released when condemned to banishment for life. He now was forced to join in the half war half slave-hunt which the Portuguese were carrying on in the south. They went on plundering, burning, and carrying away captive for two years, annexing the dominions of one petty prince after another, and apparently enlisting his army; for at the end of this time the Portuguese army amounted to fifteen thousand men. At this time Andrew Battel was wounded, and, I suppose in consequence of his services, was allowed to go to the city to be cured. This gave a new turn to his mode of life.

A frigate was sent south to the Bahia de Vaccas below Novo Redondo, and among the sixty soldiers on board of her went Andrew. Their principal object was to supply the city of St. Paul with meat, and so, having made up a cargo of cattle, with some copper, a sweet wood called cacongo, wheat, and beans, the captain took the frigate north, and left the fifty soldiers to collect cows. They built a fort, and got together some five hundred head against the return of the frigate; but on her second voyage back their attention was diverted from the cattle-trade in another and more profitable branch—the slave-trade. This produced a remarkable new series of ramblings for Andrew

Sailing along the coast of Benguela, close to the highlands of San Felipe, they saw upon a promontory, a large concourse of men; and knowing that in the then state of society in Africa, no great crowd of men could get together unless for purposes of war, and would, therefore, have slaves for sale, they anticipated some fine trade, and found their anticipations realized beyond their hopes.

These newly-seen people seem to have been a most remarkable nation. They were a nomadic cannibal tribe, who, says Andrew Battel, came first, some fifty years before, from Sierra Leone, and had fought their way in that time down here to Benguela (a distance of say 3,000 miles). Considering the distance Andrew travelled with them in his long sojourn amongst them, I do not see any reason whatever to doubt this. However, here they were, intensely eager for trade, and intensely easy to deal with. They sold the Portuguese slaves for the value of one real a-piece, which a day's sail off, at St. Paul, were worth twelve mille reys.*

Such wonderful customers deserved encouragement. The chief of the Gagas was in a little difficulty. He wanted to cross the river Corea, and cut the throats of the people on the other side, a perfectly inoffensive tribe: would the Portuguese lend them boats? The villains did so, with the greatest of pleasure, putting them over eighty at a time, and firing on those who opposed them with their muskets. Surely one of the very foulest deeds ever done. At twelve o'clock, the cannibal fiends had, with the assistance of their Christian brethren, formed line of battle, and rushed

* Pigafetta tells us much about them.

howling on the unfortunate Benguelans, who were quickly overcome. A horrible slaughter ensued, one hundred chiefs having fallen, whose bodies were eaten by the Gagas. The rest of the nation, men, women and children, were either eaten or sold to the Portuguese, who, after committing this abominable piece of wickedness, began a smart trade with the Gagas, making three voyages to and from St. Paul in five months, evidently doing such a piece of slave-trading as has seldom been equalled.

At the end of five months, however, the Gagas had moved, one of their necessities, palm-wine, not being procurable in Benguela. Such customers were not to be lost sight of, fifty men were told off to go after them up the country, and the ship waited at San Felipe.

These horrible friends were as easily traced as a swarm of locusts, or a column of the migratory ants spoken of by M. du Chaillu. After two days' march, they came upon a town which had been burnt and plundered by them. To the unhappy chieftain of this town, Mofarigosat, according to Andrew Battel, they sent a negro they had bought of the Gagas, with the lie that he had been sent to bring them (the Portuguese) to the Gagas' camp. This made him welcome them through terror of the Gagas; but he soon began to see what wonderful allies they would be for him in his wars. They were the first white men he had ever seen with their muskets, and he used every means to induce them to stay with him, persuasion first, no doubt; but he afterwards seems to have threatened force, for they became alarmed. They

F

promised him that if he would let them go, they would return in two months, and to this Mofarigosat reluctantly consented, only on condition that a white man should remain as hostage. They agreed to the terms; some were for casting lots as to who should remain, some were opposed to it. What need? was there not an Englishman? Let the heretical English dog stay. And so they marched off: I suppose back to the ship, having had enough of following their cannibal friends; and the hostage left was, of course, Andrew Battel.

At the end of two months, no Portuguese appearing, Mofarigosat began to treat him with great rigour. Most of the chieftains were for putting him to death; but the chief would not have it, still hoping for the Portuguese. After a time he was set at liberty, still retaining his musket and powder. He lived an uneasy, vagabond life among them for a short time, and at last determined to run away to his cannibal friends the Gagas.

Walking all night, he came to a beautiful town in a wood, the streets of which were so shaded with Alicondo cedar and palm, that they were darkened by them. He calls the town Cashil, and funnily enough calls the chief of it Lord Cashil. Here, by good luck, he found some of the Gagas, and went away with them.

Of his wanderings for the next sixteen months with these people, it will be as well to say that, geographically speaking, they seem to have been confined to the sierras behind the Portuguese settlements, from the latitude of the present St. Felipe to that of St.

Paul, or a little higher. We should also say something of this wonderful tribe of nomadic cannibals with whom he consorted, in preference to the Portuguese.

Their numbers of fighting men appeared to be about sixteen thousand. Their great necessities seemed to be human flesh and palm-wine, and they seldom seem to move forward as long as a supply of the latter lasts, which was not very long, as they cut down the trees to obtain it. On the march they never passed a single night without making a stockade and placing a guard. They spent considerable time in some regions: always invading on this plan. They went in and erected a fort; the inhabitants were sooner or later sure to attack them behind their works, giving them a vast advantage. Letting the inhabitants exhaust themselves by these efforts, they watched their opportunity, and finished them. On this plan they claimed to have worked their way through the country from Sierra Leone in fifty years.

But what was most astonishing about these people was their system of policy, which I should think, as far as I have read, was without parallel in the history of the world. In its fiendish wisdom and its intense wickedness it may seem almost incredible; but it would be a vastly more incredible thing to believe that it was all invented by the sailor brain of Andrew Battel. The man who had imagination enough to dream of such an ineffable horror might have written "Frankenstein" or the "Arabian Nights."

These Gagas, these conquering cannibals, had wives who bore them plenty of children, *but these children were all buried alive as soon as born.* The tribe was recruited in this way. When they sacked a negro town, the conquered men and women were eaten or sold, but the girls and boys were kept, the women for wives, the boys for warriors. The boys were trained to the use of arms, but wore a collar round their necks until they brought an enemy's head to the chieftain. Then, and then only, they got their privileges as men. Cowards of any age were put to death and eaten.

Just look what the results of this policy must have been; how the means were so wonderfully adapted to the end. To what end? To the training of a race of cannibal savages, practised to valour from their youth, without any ties of country or family. What wonder that they walked through Africa, desolating like locusts, from their home (not such a great distance from Dahomey, of which we have heard lately), and in fifty years had gone three thousand miles. And look at another nightmare view of the case. These Gagas were not a nation or a race; they were a *sect*. When Battel met them swarming on the cape near the modern town of Novo Redondo, not a single individual of the original propagandists, or a single one of their progeny, remained alive. They were a mixed body of all the tribes on the African coast, between 12° S. and 10° N. Yet their devilish faith held them together in a body so compact that no more innocent tribe dared face them. What constitutes a nation—tradition or race?

As to the credibility of Andrew Battel's account of them, it would be a less effort for me to believe in table-rapping and all that sort of thing, than to believe that a Southend sailor would have had genius enough to invent such an extraordinary system of policy. Besides, Father Merolla, the Capuchin Jesuit, eighty years later confirms him about these people, supposing that his Giaghi were these Gagas, of which there is no doubt to a very great extent. He mentions their cannibalism, their overrunning the kingdom of Congo before his time, and their witchcraft, which was his life-long trouble, and in which he believed far more devoutly than did the English sailor. We have no room here for Father Merolla and his quaint superstitions, but they are *very* quaint. His entire belief in an omnipresent Devil who was not to be trifled with; his belief that these poor wretches of negro charlatans were in personal communication with that Devil; the way he had them put to death, or worse, carried slaves to Brazil; his story of the negro Lord down South, who pretended he could bring rain, and of his partner cursing the air in that part of the country, so that there was no rain for seventeen years; his credulity and shrewdness in matters of natural history; his great kind-heartedness; and his amazing fanatical cruelty in matters of religion: all these things are very wonderful to those who have never examined the self-history of such a mind before. One ends by loving the man, but his book is very wearisome. St. Dunstan and tongs is very funny, but it palls on one at last. The man was well educated, and knew his Latin poets to some extent. There is not a wilful lie in the book, but a great number of mis-statements. It is idle work reading such books as Van Helmont and Merolla.

All this leads us into a long train of thought, which

every man must follow for himself. Who invents these ghostly superstitions of savages? "The Devil," says good and shrewd Father Merolla the Franciscan, "*Bouche va toujours*," says the political economist. They are both right. One believes in the Devil and in political economy also, not to mention certain other things; but if the Devil and natural necessity *formed* the policy and religion of savage tribes, who was the person or cause which *shaped* it? Who invented their ceremonies for them? Who taught Eyre's Australian natives to do one astounding thing, and Captain Baker's African natives to do another equally idiotic? Were these ceremonies sent down from the Tuileries, or did the Speaker leave the chair, and were they invented by the collective wisdom of a Committee of the whole House? Are they the remnants of a superior state of civilization, or are they the first blind efforts of a people trying to rise to higher things? Probably as much one as the other. No Australian native could, after endless cycles of civil engineering, invent the boomerang, any more than a European can make a good one. Probably nowhere on the face of the globe is there either a race or a man with sufficient initial vitality to invent a creed so inexorably devilish and so well suited to the end aimed at as that of these Gagas. And again: ceremonies, as we learn from the most ceremonial of Churches—that of Rome—are no more than human speech, arbitrary. Brompton will explain to benighted folks the meaning of ceremonies which to them appear astounding. Has not a man lately in Protestant Prussia been fined for speaking flippantly of the holy coat of Treves?

Of course it served him right. But all ceremonies had some meaning in them before they got themselves developed, these African ceremonies among the number. We know who developed them, but we do not know who had the wit to originate them. They meant something originally; but there is no African Stonyhurst, and so the key to them is lost.

Andrew Battel's stay among these strange savages must have been more than two years. Getting tired of them and their fighting, he rejoined the Portuguese at Massagano, 100 miles up the Coanza from St. Paul de Loanda. There he found a new governor, Senor Juan Continho, who had orders from the King to get possession of the mountains of Cambambe higher up, where there were mines. He was allowed seven years' rent of all the goods and slaves carried thence, and had to build three castles—one at Demba, one at Cambambe, and one at Bahia de Vaccas. This Senor Continho evidently had his fortune before him, and was so wonderfully liberal that mulattoes and negroes came in numbers to serve him. One of his first expeditions was one which it is very difficult, if worth while, to understand; for Andrew Battel is most confused, or all the maps I can find are wrong. However he sent back to Massagano for some of the best soldiers, and Andrew Battel was despatched among them. There was a great battle at the end of the campaign, in which he calculates the opposing forces at sixty thousand, which is of course like every account of every battle ever written—an enormous over-statement with regard to numbers. They made great slaughter among the men, and took all the women and children captive. In the midst of his glorious triumph, however, the just and generous Senor Juan de Continho died, and went to render an account of his deeds.

The new captain was a cruel man, and the volunteers began rapidly to desert. At this time important news arrived for Andrew. Some Jesuits came up and brought the news that Queen Elizabeth was dead, and that James had made peace with Spain (1604); he must now have been from home fourteen years. He now petitioned the Government for his release, and his petition was granted certainly, but immediately recalled by the cruel Governor, as he wished him to go on an expedition. Now this Governor had served his three years, and another was expected immediately, on whose arrival there would be proclaimed, as was usual in such cases, a general amnesty to all deserters. Andrew accordingly determined to take to the woods till he should come.

That night he left the city secretly with two negro boys; carrying five pounds of powder and a hundred bullets. From Massagano, which is on the Coanza, he crossed to the river Bengo (which falls into the sea close to the north of St. Paul of Loanda in Bengo Bay), and after some days went on to the river Dande, the next one northward. Here he determined to stay while his negroes went to gather information. They came back with very serious news indeed. The new Governor would not arrive for another year. He was now in a sad strait. He must either keep the woods for that time, or return to the city to be hung, for having run away twice: it had come to that now. He decided naturally enough on the former course, and moved up to the Lake of Caganza, a lake about eight miles across, some six and thirty miles up the river Bengo from the mouth.

Here he seems to have had somewhat good quarters for six months; at all events, snug ones. The Bengo, not being like the Coanza, navigable for 120 miles, has no towns on it, while the latter has many; therefore, although near enough to the city, he was in a country where few whites were at all likely to come. His food was venison of different kinds, and fish out of the lake, with sometimes a little Guinea corn which his two negroes exchanged for dried fish. He, however, got tired of this, and determined to try the Atlantic!

There grew on the lake, he says, trees, "membre," as light and as soft as cork; with these he fashioned a half raft, half boat, formed a sail from a blanket, and made three oars. He railed his boat round to prevent the sea washing him out, and with his two negroes, ventured boldly across the lake and into the river Bengo. In six and thirty miles they were in the dangerous bar at the mouth, which they managed to get over in safety, finding themselves now in the open ocean. They hoisted their sail before a fair wind, and pointed their boat's head northward for Loango.

That night he passed at sea in his curious raft, and the next day he saw a pinnace coming after them, full sail, over those pleasant seas. He does not say what his thoughts were when he saw her, but he must have been rather anxious, for the rope was, so to speak, round his neck, and to avoid her was of course impossible. His joy, however, must have been very great, when he found that she was commanded by an old friend and messmate of his, who was bound for St. Thomas (where we burnt that negro hospital sixteen years ago), and that he gladly gave him a passage to Loango. What became of his wonderful boat or his two faithful negroes he does not say. The boat, we will suppose, was cast adrift. Let us hope that he did not sell his two friends: but it is sadly likely.

He now spent three years with the King of Loango. His geography and distances again seem perfectly good according to such maps as are at my command. I will, therefore, say no more about it, but go on with what is more our business, his personal experiences. For during his residence here he either penetrated into the gorilla country himself, or at all events heard a great deal about it, apparently from very good authority. He gives us a sketch of the geography, pretty correct, up to the River Mayamba, in the third parallel, and he speaks as from personal experience of Cape Lopez, which is not a hundred miles from the Gaboon; altogether his description of the gorilla country is perfectly rational, and it agrees with Du Chaillu's account of the same region in a most wonderful manner. Perhaps it will not be very interesting to give his account, since every one is interested in and knows those regions just now.

The province of Mayamba is so overgrown with wood that you can travel thirty days in the shade. The woods, Andrew tells us, are so infested with baboons, monkeys, apes, and parrots, that it is dangerous to venture among them. Of these, the pongo is more dangerous than the engeco. The pongo is in all his proportions like a man, except the legs (which have no calves), but is of a gigantic size. When it walks on the ground, it is upright.' It sleeps in trees and makes a covering over its head to shelter it from the rain.

One sees that in the main he corresponds with M. du Chaillu, though it is very likely he never saw a gorilla. I think, on the whole, that M. du Chaillu scarcely is fair to him, when he says that his accounts of the gorilla are mere travellers' tales. Andrew Battel, as a common sailor naturally would, confused the habits of the gorilla with those of the nshiego mbouvè (pongo and engeco, as he calls them), making the former the builder of the shelter-shed in the trees, instead of the latter, though I doubt if he confuses either with the chimpanzee. He also says that they walk upright, and that they go in bodies (which are very harmless errors, for they attacked M. du Chaillu on foot), and that they beat away the elephants. With the exception of these errors, Andrew's account of the gorillas agrees exactly with M. du Chaillu's : as, for instance, " The young pongo hang upon their mother's belly with their arms clasped around them." This and other circumstances about them, though written two centuries before he was born, confirm his statements in the most remarkable manner, and should, we think have met with a little more acknowledgment.

There are two other circumstances in which Andrew Battel confirms M. du Chaillu most remarkably,

Battel tells his story about the trial by the poison *imbunde*, and its effects—effects which we cannot give in a book of this kind. At p. 288 M. du Chaillu gives an account of the action of the *mboundu* poison, which would read like a copy of Andrew Battel, were it not that M. du Chaillu brought a leaf of it home, and that it was identified by an American botanist as a new species of *strychnos*: evidence in favour of M. du Chaillu, which it would be more than ungenerous to question. Merolla, eighty years later, mentions a similar trial by poison, but a little more south than Battel's northernmost, and Du Chaillu's southernmost: he calls it *bolango*, but it is all told in a miserably, superstitious manner, after which the straightforward, common-sense of the English sailor is infinitely refreshing.

Again, the following passage reads rather startling after M. du Chaillu's discovery of the little gipsies, which he announced last autumn.

"To the north of Mani Kesock (King Kesock) are a kind of little people called Matambas, who are no bigger than boys twelve years old, but very thick; they live only upon flesh which they kill in the woods with their bows and darts—they bring in elephants' teeth and tails. If any strangers pass their dwelling they immediately remove. They kill the pongos with poisoned arrows.

Here we have Du Chaillu's dwarf gipsies much about where they should be, dealing in elephants' teeth and tails. The tails of Andrew Battel puzzled me till I turned to Du Chaillu, and found that elephants' tails were a great fetish. And so, being on dangerous grounds, I leave the reader to decide for or against them both.

After following Andrew so long, one would have been glad to know how he got home again, and how soon he dictated his travels; but of this one finds nothing. They were, I should guess almost certainly, dictated to Purchas himself, or to one of his agents, to form part of his second great book, "The Pilgrims." The distance between St. Martin's Ludgate, and the sailors' haunts about the Pool being very small.

THE WANDERINGS OF A CAPUCHIN.

The good Capuchin Friar, Merolla, who followed our present hero to the same parts of Congo fifteen years afterwards, gives a far more elaborate account of the strange missionary life in Congo than does Denis de Carli of Piacenza. But as Merolla is undoubtedly dull to read unless he gets into some frantic fight with the native sorcerers (where he is more than amusing, sometimes absolutely absurd), we have thought it better, in this attempt to bring old Catholic missionary life in Africa before the reader, to use Father Denis in preference to Father Merolla; always, however, illustrating the former by the latter. Father Denis seems to have been a very noble person, and we hope that his most curious wanderings will interest the reader as much in this necessarily abridged account of them, as they did the compiler when read by him at large.

In 1666, the "Annus Mirabilis," in the popedom of Alexander the Seventh, fifteen Capuchin missionaries were despatched "by the Cardinals de propaganda fide," with patents of the following privileges, which are surely worth the idlest reader's attention for a minute :—" To dispense with any irregularity except incurred by bigamy or wilful murder. To dispense and commute simple vows, even to that of chastity, but not that of religion. To dispense with marriages within the second and third degrees, and for pagans converted to keep one of their wives. To absolve in cases reserved to the Pope. To bless church, church stuffs, and chalices. To give leave to eat flesh and white meats, and to say two masses a day in case of necessity. To grant plenary indulgences. To deliver a soul out of purgatory, according to the intention of the priest, in a mass for the dead said on Monday and Tuesday. To wear secular clothes in case of necessity. To say the Rosary for want of a breviary or any other impediment. To read forbidden books, *except Machiavel*."

The above italics are ours. The particular prohibition against Machiavelli, then dead 140 years, seems to an ignorant man like forbidding a "Pass" country curate to yield to the lively and seductive style of Hallam's "Middle Ages," and not to debauch his ideas of right and wrong by getting up the definition of an "appanage." However, people and popes are generally found to understand their own interests; and with this curious commission Denis de Carli set out on his wild and curious journey. One Michael Angelo, of Reggio, was to be his companion in this great journey. Father Denis went to his native town of Piacenza to meet him, and having met, set out for Genoa together, where the other missionaries were to embark. And so they were carried to Lisbon, to take ship for the Brazils; their ultimate destination being Congo.

The old round of the Portuguese merchantmen in those days seems to have been this: it was certainly "composite" sailing, to use Maury's term; but it was no composition between the shape of the earth and prevailing winds, but a composition between prevailing winds and the filthy lucre of gain. A man who wished to reach the west coast of Africa set his head steadily for the north-west coast of South America; the rounding of Cape Verde was not to be done against the N.E. trades without steam. The N.E. trades would carry him nearly to the line, and in some cases over it. He could then proceed away on his S.E. trades till he got to Bahia or Pernambuco (Fernambuco they call it.) Getting to Pernambuco, or Bahia, he would discharge his cargo, and, loading with dye-woods and cotton, cross to the coast of Africa on the S.E. trade-wind, and then, filling up with ivory and gold, go home almost free on the S.E. trades for his first 600 miles, unless, indeed, he had crossed light and empty, and had got a cargo of slaves, in which case he would go nearly close-hauled back to the Brazils again.

These high-minded young men (for they could not number sixty years between three of them), sailed accordingly from Lisbon, and were three months in reaching Pernambuco; glad to arrive in safety, for there had just occurred a great sea disaster which had made every one a little nervous, and as a strange old piece of sea-experience may be worth mentioning. The ship *Catarinetta*, with 400 souls on board, coming round very richly laden from Goa, passed the Brazils in safety, but under the line got some sickness on board, which carried off the master and all the best hands. The captain (a military man, like Monk of Albemarle, for instance, who was afloat himself this very year, and not making a very first-rate business of it either) was, of course, quite unable to navigate his ship, and she drifted about the line for seven months, until, after consuming all their provisions, including cats, dogs, rats, and shoes, they were reduced from 400 souls to five, among whom was the captain. They determining to cast lots as to which of them was to be eaten, the four sailors insisted on exempting the captain from the horrid lot, while he insisted on undergoing it, only anxious to keep some one of the party alive to clear his own honour, as it would be undoubtedly said of him in Portugal that he had carried off the inestimable cargo, which was even then beneath his feet, for his own ends. The lot fell on the captain, but they would not kill him, preferring to die, like good Catholics, and were rewarded by sighting land almost immediately. Only the captain and one sailor were ultimately saved. This story is evidently true, though the good Father has played Russian scandal with it a little. For instance, they could scarcely have had on board seven months' water.

The good man gives us another story of the foundation of the church of our Lady of Nazareth near Pernambuco, and a very pretty one too; but our business is not to print foolish popish legends, however well invented or well told. He, however, tells his stories simply and well.

Though not so intelligent or so much of a man of

the world as Merolla, he tells us one or two things about the Brazils which are noticeable, and omitted by the other. According to him, the slave-trade between the west coast of Africa and Pernambuco amounted, in 1666, to 10,000 head annually. Of the losses in the middle passage he will tell us presently. They were employed on sugar, tobacco, cotton, cutting dye-woods, and working cocoa and ivory.

Here, if one may be allowed to notice such a trivial circumstance, both Fathers Denis and Angelo, and, after twelve years' interval, Father Merolla, first made the acquaintance of chegoes, or "jiggers;" and both, strangely enough, are more than half inclined to believe that they were one of the ten plagues of Egypt;* an effort to fight back for the Mosaic cosmogony which is very ecclesiastic. The late Mr. Waterton, one remembers, kept a tame one on his toe, and tried to bring it over to England, with a view to acclimatization, but failed. Captain Thomas Cringle, R.N., also liked them at first; but Father Denis, and afterwards Father Merolla, did not, as Cringle's nigger puts it, "like tickle." They are very loud in their denunciation of these parasites. Father Denis is somewhat inclined to go to the length of denouncing them as "Pharaoh's lice," but, as he says again, "they are smaller than lice." Now no gentleman, unless he has been in the Crimea, is supposed to know what a louse is like. But one cannot help thinking that Father Denis

* Merolla alludes here to one of our present heroes. "Father Michael Angelo de Gualtini hints as much in a letter to his father from Fernambuco."

was something of a gentleman. The reader must judge for himself.

The Ceremonialists of the present day, even at Rome itself, would hardly get up such a spectacle as was seen by Father Denis at Pernambuco, in 1666, on the Feast of the Rosary in the church of Corpo Santo: 10,000 ells of fine coloured silk (draped, we suppose, from the clerestory gallery); a lofty tabernacle, covered with silk embroidered with flames of gold; a silver galloon over it; ravishing music, and—10,000 slaves landed per annum. Some may say, "Their life here among Christians must have been an improvement on their old African heathenism." We say nothing, but only quote good Father Merolla twelve years later, and so leave the reader to palter with slavery and popery as he chooses.

"To uphold the sugar-works a vast number of slaves are required: some there are who have no less than 500 slaves for this purpose, and whose labour is so hard and sustenance small, *that they are reckoned to live long if they hold out seven years.*"

So much for the civilization of the negroes in those times. Fathers Denis and Michael Angelo had to go on across the Atlantic, and see the negroes before they were civilized. I cannot help thinking that if these good monks, and others like them, had been properly backed up, a vast deal more might have been done for the West African negro. It would be always impossible, from the deadliness of the climate, to keep any large staff of priests of any denomination there. But I must break off, getting on dangerous ground, only saying that the negroes of those times were evidently intensely eager to embrace the Romish form of the Christian religion; apparently preferring it to the higher and more intellectual forms of Christianity which have since been offered to them. None of them, of course, so early as that time questioned the *legality* of slavery, though on occasions they protested against slaves being acquired by mere violence and without due bargain.

It was late in the year 1667, when they at last set sail for Congo, and the S.E. trade being almost exactly foul for them, did not fetch the coast of Africa under 29° south (Pernambuco being 8° south), below the Orange River. They then coasted up to Benguela, getting into Portuguese and Christian territory at Cape Frio, in latitude 16° 10'.* The captain had great alarms here, mostly fearing that the native magicians would sink his ship for him by their enchantments. The good Fathers were neutral on this point, declining to express an opinion on the subject, only giving us the results. One result, and that the most remarkable, which acted in a most singular way on the captain's internal organization, we are unable to give. The Philistines wouldn't stand it at all, and so human knowledge must suffer.

The Father Superior and he went ashore, and he

* Possibly this is as good a place as any other for acknowledging my obligation to Mr. Stanford, of Charing Cross, with regard to his loan of the as yet unpublished map of Africa. It is the finest map I have ever had the luck to see.

preached in Portuguese; and his account of Benguela reads like a description of a hell upon earth. Drinking the water of the country was death. The whites who lived there "looked as if they had been dug out of their graves. Their voices are broken, and they hold their breath, in a manner, between their teeth" (low fever and ague one would suppose). Socially, again. "The courts at Lisbon, as a punishment for some heinous crime, banish men to Angola and Benguela, as the most wretched and infectious countries under their government. Therefore the whites are the most deceitful and wickedest of men." Heaven help the poor blacks!

Arriving at St. Paul de Loanda on Twelfth Day, they met with a most enthusiastic greeting. The town they describe as a handsome one, with 3,000 white inhabitants and an immense black population. There seems to have been *no* free negroes at all; the whole of the black population being held in slavery by the whites: some individuals among whom held as many as 3,000. They were a great source of wealth, as they were hired out, and brought the proceeds of their labours to their masters.

They found the Jesuits to be the most important, the wealthiest, and busiest Church people here, doing (in their way) wonders. In addition to a considerable grant (nearly £300 a year) from the King of Portugal, they had the rent of many houses, and no less than *twelve thousand slaves!* many of whom being skilled artisans, were sources of enormous profit to the good Fathers—bringing in a crusado (two shillings or thereabouts) a day for their labours.

There were also some Carmelites here, and some Franciscans.

The account of the circulating medium in this place, and at this time, is quaint and strange enough to be written down; and, what is more, to be remembered. "Zimbi" (or, I think, cowries), were useful in dealing with up-country tribes, who adored the sea, and who put a fetish value on them as coming from the sea. The coast-folk dealt in other "coins:" maccutes, biramese, and "Indian pieces," which latter were otherwise called "muleches." Maccutes are pieces of straw cloth, a yard long, worth ten "reys" apiece. Birames are pieces of coarse cotton cloth, five ells long, worth 200 reys the piece. Now, what are muleches, or "Indian pieces," the highest coin of that realm? You would never guess. Young blacks about twenty years of age, worth about twenty mil reys apiece.* If they are younger, they are valued by competent folks, and had cheaper. Young women the same price as young men, and no dearer; thanks, I suspect, to the Jesuits, who have done their work, and gone to their place.

The mission of these two monks was to Bamba (which is 120 miles north of St. Paul de Loanda, two-thirds of the way between that town and the mouth of the Congo). I find, now, that space is short, and that it would be a perfect waste of labour to inflict on the reader the miserable squabbles and politics of the

* Taking a mil rey as the tenth of a pound sterling, or two shillings, this would make the worth of a human body about two pounds. Birdofredum Sawin might have qualified himself for President without any subscription, had niggers been so cheap in his time.

black dukes, most of them subsidized by the Portuguese Government; such, for instance, as the gallant resistance to Portuguese arms by the Prince of Songo (Sogno in Merolla). Human intellect and human memory are too small for such things. Carlyle himself would hand them over to Dryasdust; and if one went into them, one little book would swell into fifty. I have taken all the pains I could. We must now follow these two monks: the only people we came across worth following.

They went on board, and were two days getting north, thirty miles, to Dante (Dunde), just north of the Bengo Bay of Andrew Battel. Their letters to the governor of the fort procured them thirty blacks to carry them in nets or hammocks, as Grant is depicted coming from Rumanikas. Barefooted friars could not walk in those parts: and so they went on northward from "Libbate" to "Abbatee," as they call the straw-built villages, being courteously received by the "Maco Conte," or native governor.

Their principal work was baptizing. They, the Capuchins, had had this mission now for thirty years, and the Jesuits seem to have respected their vested interests, for most of the younger children had to be baptized. The "surplice" fee was either two palm-tree handkerchiefs, or else 3,500 little shells; or else a pullet. But pullets were scarce, the dovecotes having been terribly harried by the wars. If no surplice-fee was forthcoming, the children were "christened for God's sake." At the end of the first day's journey up the country Fathers Michael Angelo and Denis christened thirty—fifteen apiece.

Next day they got put up a church of boughs, on an eminence, and had mass, having the necessary things with them in a box. Father Michael Angelo performed mass, after which they baptized ten more children. Then they catechized through an interpreter; one can only hope satisfactorily: and then the blacks, having had enough of it, fell a-playing upon several instruments, a-dancing, and a-shouting, so that they might be heard a league off. Few of us, nowadays, thanks to the great influx of American thought, are unacquainted with African music; but on this particular occasion it seems to have been of somewhat special quality.

These two defenceless friars went on with their journey, utterly unarmed; they were pleased with the monkeys, but much terrified with other animals; so much so, that they at one time regretted they had not brought a gun, though I very much doubt if either of them knew how to fire it off. Animals which they took to be lions frightened them at night; a boa-constrictor and an elephant in the daytime (the latter could not have been what our Indian brothers call a "rogue," or he would have exterminated the whole party). The way began to be very long, and at last Father Michael Angelo agreed to push on and send back assistance to Father Denis.

So Denis remained behind alone, attended only by a young negro, the son of a marquis, and with nothing at all to eat but kidney beans. He had no money or goods, of course, and there were no children to be baptized here, and therefore no fees. He got so weak as not to be able to stand. In this pass he, to a certain extent, broke through the rules of his order;

Father Denis and his Negro Guide. P. 89.

at least he apologizes for his conduct. He sat in front of his straw hut, and began threading a few beads he had, which soon attracted the attention of the natives, and they begged some of him. He promised to give them some if they would give him a chicken, which they did, "being little acquainted with giving of alms for God's sake," mourns the good Father.

At length, foot-sore and worn with fever, he heard through the tropical forest the sound of the convent bell ringing for mass: and soon after rejoined his beloved Michael Angelo. It was but a poor place, this convent, and now threatening ruin; only four cells of mud thatched with straw for dwelling-places: but the garden delighted and astonished him from the beauty and abundance of the fruit. Now they set to work arranging their monastery, and selecting their servants from among the negroes: gardeners, cook, sacristan, water-carrier, treasurer; the old monastic machine, every part of it carefully fitted by centuries of experience in Europe, was soon set running again in the wilds of Africa.

Going on a visit to a brother Capuchin at Panba, a cell about fifty miles off, he had an opportunity of seeing the King of Congo. He was a young black about twenty, clothed in a scarlet cloak and gold buttons. He commonly wore white buskins upon carnation silk stockings, and was said to have had new clothes every day. He was surrounded by young dukes and marquises, all in long blue cloth cloaks. His umbrella was of fine coloured silk and gold: his chair; also borne before him, was of carnation velvet, with gold nails. He was exceedingly kind to Father Denis, thanking him for entering his kingdom, and desiring him to attach himself to his person at San Salvador, which Father Denis humbly declined, urging the necessity of the work at Bamba. He was a Christian and very pious; and, although handsomely dressed and rich, evidently inferior in wealth and magnificence to his predecessor, Alphonso III., who, in 1646, received the Capuchins, sitting on a throne under a canopy of crimson velvet, having a splendid crown of diamonds and other stones upon his head.

Their life continued peaceful for some time, though they were nearly starved. They baptized from eight to twenty children a day, a great many of which were brought from a long distance; and so, after a consultation, it was thought better that one of them should save these poor negroes the pain of coming to the monastery, by going to them. Father Michael Angelo volunteered first to go a journey into the bush for the purpose of baptizing, and Father Denis was left behind, to await his turn at the same work, in the meantime spending his time at the convent "in administering baptism and keeping school." Among his pupils were two young black noblemen, sons of a religious negro duchess of those parts. These young fellows were, according to our good Father Denis, perfect gentlemen, "with a genius suited to their rank;" which was in reality very high, and was practically acknowledged by these Italians as being as great as that of people with the same titles in Europe. We must remember that the black, *quâ* black, was by no means a down-trodden person at that time. The theory of the moral and intellectual inferiority of the negro as a negro was not known to these simple Churchmen at all events.

This simple monk, **Father Denis**, was now left alone, and began to feel the effects of hard Church work with utterly insufficient food. He was well in health, he tells us, but had much to do to stand on his legs, being so spent with living upon that food (kidney beans) with which he was forced to be satisfied in those parts. "So I commended myself to God, that it might please him to preserve my health, for the sake of these poor blacks; not so much, to say the truth, because I found myself incapable of undergoing very long the fatigue of our continual employment, as because of the little likelihood there was of seeing any other missionary come into that country to succeed us, and to ease me of that employment which I found above my strength." I do not envy the man who cannot revere and love this blinded young papist. We Protestants have done great work; but where will be the balance when the books are made up, supposing they were to be made up to-morrow? For the future I dare not speak.

Michael Angelo came back to him at the appointed time. He seems to have been a gentle and kindly youth, with a courage not of this world. Coming back, a doomed young man, to their little convent, he set himself to work at the garden, and made all the poetry that was in him, not a little I suspect, flower out in that way. He had been baptizing the people about an iron mine, and had taken his surplice-fees out in iron tools. He set to work with these tools to make the desert flower like a garden, and his noble young friend, Father Denis, went his round into that wilderness, on his errand of baptizing and catechizing, leaving Michael Angelo, weary, weak, drawing day by day nearer to the newer knowledge and the clearer light, trenching in the foul African forest land, among his oranges and his grapes.

Then Father Denis set out in his turn; sometimes baptizing as many as a hundred in a day, "taking from such as could give, and bestowing my charity for God's sake on those who had nothing." He took presents of the Macolontes. What presents, think you? "Beans, and kidney beans, to maintain those who went with me, who were satisfied to attend us, provided we maintained them." This greedy Churchman was also much plagued with sorcerers and enchanters,* as was Merolla twelve years afterwards. But I let go any fun which might be made out of that circumstance, for the sake of the honest respect which I have for Father Denis. He went his round among those pestilential west-coast African woods, and came back again to their poor little convent at Bamba, and saw his brother and friend of his heart, Brother Michael Angelo, wasted lean and wan, trenching their precious garden, or showing the negroes how to do it.

Brother Michael Angelo was getting very weak. The clock was running down. So young, so bold, so devoted, so noble. There was the soul of a soldier—

* "As there are heretics in Europe," says the good Friar.

of a soldier among a hundred thousand—there, but the physique was wanting. An Italian gentleman and scholar, with an ambition which reached beyond the grave, longing to live, yet longing to die, was there in that garden, digging among his negroes, when Denis came back from his expedition. It is true, sir! think of it.

Fra Michael Angelo told Fra Denis one day that he was much spent, and then fell into a fever. At this time their superior, Fra Philip, happened to come to Bamba, which was a great relief, because he knew the way of treating sick persons in that country. But Fra Michael Angelo told Fra Denis that the disease would be fatal to him, for that it prevailed against him. Fra Denis comforted him in this manner; that his disease, being but a double tertian, he might hope to recover; at the same time advising him to leave all to God. But simple, double, or treble tertian, Father Michael Angelo died, and his young companion Denis was left alone among the ghastly cold green African woods, wringing his hands for his lost friend, even as Jonathan would have wrung his hands for David.

Fra Philip stayed by him a little while, for Father Denis himself lay dying now, and Fra Philip thought that he might as well stay and bury him. But the Father lingered longer than he expected, though now reduced to a heap of bones, and it was for the good of the mission that Philip should depart. He confessed Father Denis, gave him the Viaticum, and left the dying monk among his negroes, believing that he should see his face no more.

I suppose that the original idea of a book of adventures would be one which should describe men in situations from which there should seem no escape. If that is what is meant by an adventure, Father Denis certainly claims a foremost place among adventurers. He had brought his affairs to such a pass, that the odds were a hundred to one against him. When Father Philip left him, he had only just strength left to bend his body, and to ask that Father Michael de Orvietto might be sent to him (who never came). Then he was left to the mercy of the blacks, who stole what they could (little enough from him, I doubt), and, *when they thought of it*, brought him a porringer of broth.

Like a little ray of sunshine on the twilight of the fast dying Capuchin—a twilight fast gathering into night—came one day a brisk, lively, dexterous Portuguese Jesuit, as vivacious and cosmopolitan as any of his countrymen: as worldly-wise as any of his order. Can the human mind, knowing of Portuguese somewhat, and of Jesuits somewhat, conceive of a combination of nation and faith which will give one a greater amount of highly-educated cunning than a Portuguese Jesuit? Your Greek? No. Your Greek is only a very dexterous rogue. Your Portuguese Jesuit is not necessarily a rogue at all: if he is, he is a rogue with a difference.

The Portuguese Jesuit was not unprovided with the goods of this world, and he gave the simpler Capuchin some fowls. They confessed to one another, " he," the Jesuit, " declaring that it was a satisfaction to him to be thus provided," in consequence of the danger of wild beasts. Then he left Father Denis and went his way, and Father Denis saw him no more.

Dying always, he did not die at last. Being held up in bed by his blacks—one of them holding the book, another the basin—he baptized ten or a dozen children a day; receiving what alms they gave him. He also married some of the chief people; but marriage by the Church was not a popular business. Marriage was one of the predicates of monogamy, whereas polygamy was the fashionable failing. However, one of the young couples gave him, as surplice-fee, a she-goat, and the milk of it did him good.

He mended so far as to lose the immediate dread of death; but, with his new hope of life, petty vexations—lost in the dread of that great shifting of skin, with which we are all familiar, and yet which we all dread—began to grow once more into actual evils. The rats ran over him in his helplessness, and the negroes stunk. He felt himself forced to keep his blacks sleeping close around him, for there were scandalous tongues to be met even then, and there, even about a man in as hard a case as was he. The rats cared nothing for the smell of the negroes, and ran over their prostrate bodies to nibble and bite the holy Father's toes, as Madame Tallien (by courtesy) said that they did hers.

In an extreme difficulty of this kind, in the present day, one would hardly think of writing to a Duke for a remedy; one would sooner write to the *Times*. Father Denis, however, now somewhat convalescent, sent his hard case about the stink of the negroes and the ravages of the rats to a Duke (black) who lived near; and that Duke, a good Christian, at once provided a remedy, and, with a most comical apology for having forgotten such a trifle hitherto, he sent him a little tame monkey, who stunk so much worse than the negroes, that the lesser result was lost in the infinite greatness of the larger. The good Father is careful to let you know that the little monkey is not to be confounded with the civet cat. However, he smelt so very musky, that the "buck nigger" smell was lost; he also frightened the rats by blowing at them whenever they appeared; and, furthermore, combed the good Father's beard better than any of the blacks could be taught to do it.

One night, as he lay between life and death, his little monkey leaped in terror on his head, and the negroes began crying, "Out! out! Father! the ants are upon us, and there is no time to be lost." As he was utterly unable to move, he made them carry him into the garden; and they were only just in time, as the ants were already on his body. After some time, by burning piles of straw, they got the upper hand of them; but the stench left was so horrible that Father Denis had to hold his monkey close to his nose, and retreat again into the open air. These are, I suppose, the same ants described by M. du Chaillu. There is little doubt that they would have devoured Father Denis. He says it is not uncommon for cattle to be destroyed by them, and their bones found picked quite clean. Why the cows did not run away is one of the things we shall never know.

He, after a time, finding his circumstances desperate should he stay where he was, determined to get himself carried to Loanda, and applied to the Duke for bearers. The Duke sent him all that he had, but they were not enough to carry all his luggage, and so he abandoned some, and started in a hammock on his almost hopeless journey.

He was so ill as to be unable to speak in the heat of the day, and the blacks often stopped to see if he was still alive. But he had such confidence in St. Anthony of Padua, whom he saw visibly before his hammock, that he never feared reaching his journey's end. Once the clumsy bearers let the poor young fellow down by the run, and the pole of the hammock broke his head; but he bound it up quite silently, fearing that, if he complained of being badly hurt, they would desert him and seek safety for themselves in flight.

At length he reached the first Portuguese settlement, and saw white faces once more. His appearance was that of a corpse, and they wondered that a man with that face was actually alive. They crowded weeping around him, expecting his immediate death; but by their affectionate care he rallied a little, and ultimately got back to Loanda, where he lay unable to leave his hammock for six months more: when on the arrival of the Superior he was sent to a pleasant house a little way up the river Coanza to try and recover his health.

The priests were dying in all directions. Highly-trained ecclesiastics from Italy, brought with great pains from that country, men who being lost were not easy to be replaced, were being lost almost before they had had time to put their hands to the plough.

H

At last a ship was loading for the Brazils, whose captain would be honoured by receiving on board a man of such proved piety as Father Denis for chaplain.* The cargo consisted of ivory, and no less than 680 slaves, men, women, and children.

It was pitiful to see how these poor wretches were bestowed. The men were *standing* in the hold, fastened to one another with stakes; the women were between decks, those in the family way in the great cabin; the children packed in the steerage like herrings in a barrel—causing an intolerable heat and stench—all going over to be "civilized" in the Brazils in the way we saw above.

The time generally allowed for this middle passage from St. Paul de Loanda to Bahia was from thirty days to thirty-five. On this occasion they were fifty, and having passed the Island of Assumption, and having neglected to get fresh provisions there, found themselves toward the end of that time becalmed under the line, without provisions, and with 600 helpless blacks on board.

The captain's remedy was to set up the image of St. Anthony against the mast, and tell him that he should stand there until he sent them a fair wind, reminding one very much of the black sergeant's treatment of his fetish in the cruise of the *Midge*. He still had an eye to consequences however. There was a penal statute against the introduction of un-

---

* Merolla tells us that the law about ships' chaplains at this time was:— *Capuchins* are to have only their table free, whereas a priest or other religious person was to have not only his diet, but a stipend of so much a month, and three calmos a day, and a house while on shore.

baptized blacks into the Brazils, and so the captain got Father **Denis** to baptize those who had last come on board; which he did, "instructing them in the doctrines of the Christian religion." Had the good man no sense of humour? How strangely puzzled the poor negroes must have been at their new religion!

The captain came again to Father Denis, and told him that they were all dead men. Father Denis was lying in one of his worst attacks of illness, with a basin before him of blood from which he had just parted. He quite agreed with the captain, but told him to look in the stern lockers, where he would find some provisions which had been put on board for his (the Father's) use, to which he was welcome. With these he advised the captain to keep the whites alive: as for the blacks, *he* (the captain!) "must have patience." There was still water on board: he told him to give them plenty of that. The Friar seems to have had the best head on board the ship after all.

Meanwhile the dreadful news got abroad among the six hundred and odd miserable slaves who were festering in all the unutterable filth and horror of the between-decks of a slave-ship. They could have had little to live for one would imagine; but life is very dear in very desperate circumstances. The confusion and uproar which ensued *cannot* be imagined. The children began the wail, it was taken up by the women, who were afterwards joined by the men. There arose

"A cry that shivered to the tingling stars,"

the death-cry of 680 unhappy savages, brought out here to die cooped up, so far on the desolate sea, under the burning sun of the equator.

The monk was equal to the occasion. He got them quieted by the hymns to the Virgin and the saying of *eighty* masses—forty for the souls in purgatory, and forty for St. Anthony: then he made the captain give them water; but they began whimpering for their food; so that Father Denis, having nothing for them, in sheer sickness of heart went back to his miserable bed again; abstaining from eating such fare as he had, lest it should annoy the poor wretches to see him eat.

He was aroused from it by hearing some of the crew talk of eating man's flesh; and he came forth and severely reproved them: but so far yielded to the dreadful necessity, as to tell them that, if the worst came to the worst, and a victim should be necessary, that he, Father Denis, was to be that victim and no other.

No such victim was necessary. They had been three days without food, the water was spent, blacks were beginning to drop, when they made Bahia. The people there, when they heard that they had been fifty days at sea, concluded that all the blacks were dead, and were agreeably surprised to find that the death-roll was only *thirty-three:* it often happening that half of them died in that passage. Father Denis got himself carried in a hammock to the Franciscan convent, which, though not of his order, received him courteously, and gave him rest.

After a short time, apparently improved in health,

he took passage with a Genoese captain, a friend of his, whom he had met here at Bahia, on his arrival, and set sail for Lisbon. She was a large ship, carrying fifty guns, a good fighting merchant-ship, and was consequently ordered by the Governor, in the King's name, to convoy the other merchantmen. She was, says Father Denis, like a Noah's ark: and, indeed, one could agree with Father Denis about the likeness, had Noah's ark been freighted and commissioned by Avarice and Cruelty, and commanded and sailed by Cowardice and Superstition. Let us look for a moment on this queer Portuguese Indiaman; she seems to me a ship worth recovering from the dim past.

She was so crowded with passengers that one could scarcely hear oneself speak. Her lading was: a thousand chests of sugar, three thousand rolls of tobacco, dye-wood, veneer-wood, and ivory; steward's stores for the passengers—wood, coal (charcoal), water, wine, brandy, sheep, hogs, and turkeys. For other live stock, ventures of the home-going passengers, monkeys of several sorts, apes, baboons, parrots, and the birds of Brazil which they call Arracas. For the passengers, they were as motley a lot as the live stock—Italians, Portuguese, English, Dutch, Spaniards, and Indians, slaves who followed their masters. One Amaro (a man who in his treatment of Father Denis belied his name) had given a thousand crowns for the great stern-cabin, and had laid in two thousand crowns' worth of provisions (of the "medical comfort" sort doubtless) for the voyage. This Amaro and his wife being religious people, shared their cabin with

Father Denis; though the good monk was so *répandu* that he had to bargain that he should only breakfast with them sometimes after morning mass, the rest of his time being promised to the captain. Father Denis was not ship's chaplain on this voyage, but captain's friend. He said mass every day in the great cabin; the ship's chaplain on deck.

One would guess that there must have been fearful accidents at sea among these Portuguese ships—accidents which, if ever reported, are now lost to us; for, to judge by the silly cowardice and foolish superstition of these Portuguese sea-captains, no ship's company was safe with them. This present ship bumped on a sandbank, not, according to Father Denis, six miles from the anchorage at Bahia; and the whole of the intricate arrangement of this wonderful fighting-ship of forty guns was thrown out of gear at once. The officers and pilots got out the boats and jumped into them (they were still confessedly in harbour), and the sailors and passengers began to cry aloud, "We are all dead! we are all dead!" They began to pitch the sugar overboard to lighten the ship, and the captain "sat still like a statue, without being able to speak or to stir, though he had fought six Turks in this same ship." The animals, hearing the noise, began to add theirs to the general confusion: a fine clanjamfry of parrots and monkeys. Father Denis had now got out of bed to see to things, and whites and blacks began to throw themselves at his feet, crying for confession and absolution (they were close to the shore, in harbour, and in calm weather). Father Denis made them give the **sign of contrition,*** and gave them all absolution generally, wanting time to hear them singly. Father Denis then met the chaplain **of the ship in** his **shirt,** looking ghastly, though, "as he had often made it appear," one of the bravest men aboard, having fought the Turks on several occasions. The poor wretch **had lost all** nerve, and increased the confusion. **Father Denis,** who **really** believed that there was danger, gave him confession and absolution, but leaves behind no word of the scorn which he, the **brave** Italian gentleman, arriving from more fearful dangers, must have felt for **him.** One might claim the position **of a** gentleman for Father Denis for that, if for that only, as I would claim it for **Mr.** Draper, the Dissenting minister who **went** down **in** the *London;* though it is quite possible that neither of them had a coat-of-arms **to** show.

But we are telling of adventures, of human courage, brought to its mettle in hopeless circumstances ; **not** of exhibitions **of** human cowardice. There was nothing on earth the matter here ; **and** I would not have told this episode, had it not **been** to show the unutterable cowardice of the Portuguese, and to show also that this wandering **Italian** Capuchin kept his

---

* The sign of confession is holding up the hand. **Merolla** once, in a gale of wind, gave absolution to a sailor who had fallen overboard, and whom it **was impossible to** save, but who had not yet drifted so far to **leeward but what he could** see and understand the movements of the monk on the poop. **We must** remember **that there are** 120,000,000 of rational human beings on the earth who agree **with them** for coming in this way **between the** creature and the Creator **at the** last moment, and whose **exit from the** world is rendered easy and happy by the motion of **a** priest's hand.

head and his judgment after that of every one else was gone. The ship got fairly off this bank and sailed away for Pernambuco, and from that place to Lisbon.

The internal economy of this great ship is worthy of notice. Awful pack of stupid cowards as they were; terrified into abject fright and superstition by the first cold, cruel look of Old Mother Nature in her frosty and inexorable mood; distrusting the beneficence of the first cause, her Master, as they did; trying to propitiate the Being who hurled Saturn and Jupiter into space, by offerings unworthy of an old African fetish; nevertheless these fellows showed considerable power in their industrial organization. Every tradesman worked at his trade as though he had been in his shop. "When the weather permitted, other vessels bore up to us and gave us a concert of drums and trumpets, and the captain exercised his men in firing volleys." It seems lucky, considering the quality of the courage of his crew, that these volleys were only fired blank. Everything went on smoothly save for an internal dissension, caused, I regret to say, by "my countrymen."

Our good Father Denis is wilder than M. Assolant in his account of the Englishman. He, it seems, was put into the bilboes, and also another who had made himself drunk with two bottles of brandy, and was not sober again for three days. He was so strong that they said he had cleft a man with a cutlass. A somewhat strange old picture, these blonde great Englishmen, the men of Blake, going Berserk among the brown little Portuguese.

Landing at last at Lisbon, he bade farewell to the companions of this part of his adventures. His face was now set eastwards, and he soon found a ship which wanted a chaplain. He accepted the post; but so many Benedictines, Dominicans, and other religious men came on board also—idle people, one doubts, wanting a free passage—that one sailor was heard to murmur, "We were afraid we should want a chaplain; here are enough for a choir." They were all of them landsmen and cowards, however, and never once showed after the vessel got to sea, admiring the contempt which Father Denis, although ill, felt for the sea. During this voyage Father Denis succeeded in converting a heretic Irishman.

After a frantic chase after a salt-fish ship from Nantes, which they mistook for a Turk, they came to Cadiz. He was highly delighted at the noble show of ships in that port; galleys, barks, caravels, tartans, &c. Landing here with some Spanish gentlemen, he saw a strange disturbance which had a strange ending. There was a dispute with the Custom-house officers which ended in swords being drawn. The dispute heated itself: Father Denis considers that there were a hundred blades out: but the singular part of it was that, in spite of flying dust, furious oaths, and clashing rapiers, no one was in the least damaged. They kept the points of their swords up, striking one another with the pummels. At last, (*teste* the Italian priest, a bystander,) four drunken English sailors found this clanjamfry between them and their ship, and it growing to be a nuisance to them, being probably pressed for time, sent the whole business right and left, "every man thinking himself happy that his legs were sound enough to run away."

Before setting his face steadily for his beloved Italy, he visited several places, going from convent to convent, among others the church of St. James of Compostella. Hearing there was a ship at Finisterre which would be likely to take him on his way, he went thither, and by that means met with a new and splendid adventure.

Here, for the first time, he met with an English gentleman. This ship was an English seventy-four, going after our fleet of frigates, which was beating up the Turks' quarters, with stores of ammunition and so on. It was a great chance for Father Denis; and so, just as the English captain was going into his galley, the simple monk in his simple habit stepped up to him, and "knowing him to be a heretic," asked him for his passage to Cadiz, "for God's sake." The captain, not understanding Spanish, motioned him into the boat, and told him in Portuguese that he was welcome.

They were well out at sea, when Father Denis observed the English captain examine two distant sail with his telescope. The next symptom he observed was a council of all the officers in the cabin; the next the drums beating to quarters; then studding-sails set, and the ship flying through the water like a shark. The good Father was going to look on war face to face.

In an hour they had overhauled the chase, and fired a gun to bring them to. They were, as was guessed now and known afterwards, a Christian ship in the hands of a Turk. The Turk evidently considered himself by far the stronger party, and to his Majesty's summons replied by a shotted gun: in another moment the English broadside came ripping and tearing into his sides, deafening poor Father Denis and terrifying his companion: and so the terrible game began.

The Turks fought like furies: our captain had the weather of them, and so they fought blinded with his smoke and their own; yet he had done little with them in an hour and a half, and seeing that the death grapple must come, he gave the order to board; and as the blue-jackets went swarming over the bulwarks, the quiet monk, soothing the terrors of his companion, could hear for the first time, in the comparative silence, the cries of the wounded who were now lying thick around on the deck.

The assault was furious and the resistance ferocious. Few experienced officers, I believe, deny even to the "Turks" of the present day the quality of an almost savage courage; our fathers used to speak of fighting like a Turk, and the expression is almost alive now. These Turks (probably Arabs would be a more correct name for them) were utterly outnumbered on this occasion, when it came to hand-to-hand work. Their force was divided between the two vessels— between the man-of-war which had captured the prize and the prize herself. Our English captain having boarded and taken the man-of-war, and the captured Christians assisting him, had an easier task with the prize, whose crew tried to make off with her. The captured rover, followed by the English man-of-war, soon overhauled her, being deeply laden, and the sea-fight was over by the submission of the Turks.

The Christian captain of the prize, "a lusty man, half stripped," told our English captain how his mischance had occurred, and the Christians knelt and thanked his Majesty's officer. The recovered ship was of Malaga, laden with wine, and was off Cape St. Vincent when attacked by the rover. She resisted, but was overpowered, by what one may suppose was a Sallee rover. The English captain put the Christians (among whom there were Spaniards, Neapolitans, Milanese, and Flemings) in possession of their ship again, and gave them convoy to Cadiz.

Father Denis seems to have been perfectly cool during this rather hot little affair with the "Turks," but was a little uneasy in the white squall which happened soon after, the next experience which Providence offered to his calmly expectant and unwondering soul. It was a very heavy and sudden squall undoubtedly, but to the credit of our sailors, sudden as it was, the captain had time to make all snug, for Father Denis makes no mention of lost canvas. The words of command, roared by Teutonic and Celtic lungs, from post to post, heard above the strange scream of the wind in the rigging, which some of us have heard, gave the good Father an idea that death was impending.—

"Hark the boatswain hoarsely bawling."

But the English captain found time, amidst the anxieties of a lee shore, to tell the two friars, penniless papists as they were, not to be frightened, for that he would bring them through; whereby I came to the conclusion that the captain of that ship was a gentleman. The monk who was with our good Father Denis was evidently in a miserable state of fright. His miserable little conscience began to trouble him; he told good cosmopolitan Father Denis, "that we had done ill in going aboard of these heretics, who are always under excommunication." Father Denis, who seems, as far as I dare generalize, to have possessed all the makings of a first-rate Jesuit, except the dishonesty, replied that "those who travel about the world must make a virtue of necessity." The two monks (I suppose, there is no mention of the fact, but they always did so) *confessed* to one another and gave absolution. After which they found themselves in fine weather off the coast of Barbary, in that part now called Algeria; and the English captain finding himself dangerously near that whilome Turkish, now French, wasp's nest, called Algeria, bore up immediately for Oran, then in the hands of the Spaniards.

Father Denis was much impressed by Oran. The civilities which were carried on between the English captain and the Spanish governor were, to say the least of it, excessive. Our captain received the thanks of his most Catholic Majesty by deputy; his Catholic Majesty probably never hearing a word of the matter. Father Denis says that Oran was the only place held by Christians at that time on the Barbary coast to which Christian ships might run.

His kind captain carried him to Cadiz, and afterwards insisted on his taking passage with him in a bark he had hired up the Guadalquivir to Seville. Here this quaintly-assorted pair parted from one another, the monk thanking the English captain for the many favours he had received from him, and the captain giving the monk to understand that the Capuchins were well *répandus* among the English; whether out of complaisance or not I cannot say.

Father Denis now, his wandering licence as a "Missioner" still holding good, wandered on from monastery to monastery of his order. He gives one quaint and shrewd notices of the places he saw, which it would be almost useless to produce here, as far as my judgment goes, at any length. The "Dome" at Seville would be equal to that at Milan, he thinks, were it only of marble (the detailed work of the pinnacles can be hardly so fine one would guess). The canons of the city are very rich, and go in coaches drawn by four mules. From hence he started on foot to Cordova, through a wretched country without house or tree, nor so much as water, which made him provide a bottle of wine which a gentleman bought for him, "there being no hopes of having it given to me for God's sake by the innkeeper" (too many professional religious persons there evidently, even in the year 1667). Being in a town where there was no convent, he begged some bread, but the baker stood in amaze, and Father Denis left him so, praying of God soon to remove him from a country where there was so little charity. But one would really think, considering what Spain has suffered by ecclesiastical persons, first and last, that it was hardly a place for a penniless monk, and he a foreigner, to get much private charity.

From Cordova he went to Alcala la Real, where some Spaniards told him that Andalusia was the "Garden of Spain," whereupon he said to himself, "God keep me from the rest of Spain if this be the garden. I had better return to sea." Next he went south-east to Granada, and saw the Alhambra; southwest to Anteguera; and then south to Malaga; having made the tour of south-western Andalusia cheaper probably than it was ever done before or since, by any educated man (having done it indeed for exactly nothing at all), leaving behind him as good an account of what he saw and heard as another in his time was likely to do.

At Malaga he was set on his legs by an English physician, and then got taken on board a fleet of galleys by a Spanish nobleman, as chaplain to the fleet and confessor to his Excellency. He did not like these galleys at all, having been used to more commodious ships. They were to him as our ironclads are to our more old-fashioned sailors. One could have wished that he had given us some sketch of the internal economy of one of these floating hells, as he did of the slave-ship; but he is, unfortunately, dumb. They overhauled an English ship, "like a mountain upon the waters," and with their newly-reviving impudence, "Annus Mirabilis" being over and finished, and certain unfortunate things of which it is unnecessary to speak having happened since, "gave her a gun." But it all ended in civilities, and Father Denis, with a compliment to the English for cruising against the

Turks, and as much of a sneer against other Christian princes as his good heart was capable of giving, was carried on to Carthagena, "now the most wretched place in Spain; for after the inhabitants had stoned their Bishop," (what had *he* been doing?) "they had no rain for seven years. But it seems that God took compassion on them after that, for it now rains twice or thrice in the year." Here he landed and went on "the tramp again, through Murcia, Alicant, Valencia, Castile, Tarragona, to Barcelona in Catalonia," and so from town to town, on and on through the south of France, by Monaco, to the beloved old monastery at Piacenza, and to rest at last.

"Be it all," he says, "for the glory of God, whose judgments are incomprehensible, and the means he uses for our salvation—various and wonderful in all respects—that we may all meet together in our desired port in the kingdom of heaven. Amen."

PETER CARDER.

In Drake's voyage to the Pacific, by the Straits of Magellan, in 1578, a singular and astonishing accident happened to one Peter Carder, of St. Verians, seven miles from Falmouth, of which there seems but little doubt. It holds well together, and apparently was taken down from the man's mouth. One part of it seems incredible in *my* narrative. The reason for this is, that some of the details in the original are too horrible for publication.

Sir Francis Drake ordered Carder, Burrush, Cottle, Arthur, a Dutch trumpeter, Gidie of Saltash, Pitcher of London, and one other, to get into the pinnace, which was only five tons' burthen, and stay about the ship. They lost her one wild night, and never saw her again.

They were now loose on the wildest sea in the world, between the Straits of Magellan and Cape Horn; they had but one day's provisions on board, and no compass. In two days, however, they made the coast of Terra del Fuego, and found oysters, mussels, crabs, and roots. They landed here in two places, and in a fortnight had got north of the Straits, and were on the mainland of Patagonia.

Here, as before, they got shell-fish and water, and saw some savages, who however ran away. They then made for Penguin Island in the Straits, and having caught and salted many penguins, they proceeded very prosperously to Fort St. Julian—where Drake had just previously beheaded Captain Doutie—feeding on this miserable food.

Not that they thought it so. The sailors of those days would eat anything. In Sir Richard Hawkins' voyage of 1593, he describes these islands, and gives full directions for preparing this food. Nay, that gallant gentleman, Sir Richard, also tells us how he caught albatrosses, and what dainty food they were. Nothing particular happened to our adventurers until they had passed the great mouth of the river Plate; here they put into a small river on the north side of the estuary, and began to look for food.

They were probably close to the town now called Maldonado, in the Banda Oriental, when the Indians of the country, whom he calls Japines, suddenly attacked those who were in the woods with bows and arrows. Four were at once taken or slain, the others fled to their boat, and after a hard fight, in which they were all wounded, the four remaining ones got to sea, and made a little island a few leagues off, probably Isla de Lobos.

Two of the others soon died here of their wounds, and the survivors, Peter Carder and William Pitcher, were so exhausted, that they were unable to manage the boat, and so she got broken to pieces in the surf, and these two men were left alone on the little island, only three miles long, nine miles from shore, with absolutely nothing whatever, not even water.

There were however some small fruit, crabs, and sand-eels, and on these they lived for two months, in the most horrible shifts for water, until a large piece of timber floating out of the river landed on the island, with which, and some other pieces, they made a raft, and in three days and two nights they reached it, and found a delicious stream of fresh water.

Poor Bill Pitcher, "mine onely comfort and companion," would not be restrained from this water. In spite of his more experienced comrade's expostulations, he drank and drank, until in half an hour he died, leaving poor Peter Carder all alone, bewailing him upon the lonely shore.

This Peter Carder must have been no ordinary man, not one whit brutalized by the hideous and indescribable sufferings which he had undergone; when time was precious, and a hundred howling savages might be on him at any moment, in spite of all, he would not leave the body of his faithful friend to bleach upon the wild, strange coast unburied. He laboured until he had laid him decently to rest, and then shouldering his target, with his good sword upon his thigh, he strode off across the sands, between the Pampas and the ocean, towards Brazil. An Englishman against the world.

One day only had passed, when there came across his path dark, dancing savages, with tabrets and rattles, which they played before him as he went, keeping a musket-shot from him. But at last they ceased their dancing, and hung up a white cloth—

going away from it. He having approached it, taken it down, and hung it up again, they approached him and led him away, dancing round him, until they came to the place by the river where their hammocks hung, and fed him with the best they had.

These Indians of the Banda Oriental, among whom he lived so long, appear from his own account, which, as they were kind to him, may be considered as favourable as he could make it, to have been but a poor, tipsy, cruel, cannibal lot of vagabonds as ever disgraced the earth. Sentiment is thrown away on such people. A great question must be heard at the Judgment Seat some day, between the blacks and the whites, between the Indian and the European. Yet who can doubt that it is not better for the world that such people as these, if they refuse civilization, should cease to exist?

Their employment was war and plunder. The chief of the village had nine wives, every other man only two—one to mind the children, the other to follow the husband to war. The captives taken were put to death, broiled on the coals, and eaten. And this not in a country where cannibalism could be excused by want of animal food, but in a country where it was plentiful. Nothing will ever induce me to believe in that old excuse for cannibalism, put forth by the apologists for the Maories. The cause of it is lust of good living, lust of the belly, and something more; read Eyre's account of the Australian cannibalism, and you will see what that something is: it is a demoniac possession, whatever that may be. A police magistrate in London has to deal with it once a day; the sort of devilishness in the face of which the old Berserk madness becomes tame and calm. We hang, guillotine, garotte men now for crimes not half so horrible as these gentle Indians committed every day; it may become necessary, sometimes, to execute a race.

The Americans, with all their gentle and just dealings with this race, have been nearly driven to it, and will ultimately be driven to "put it through." In spite of all our gentle petting of the Maories, they must go or submit. No savage race ever had more gentle treatment from a conquering one than the Indians have had from the Americans, or the Maories from the British. About the Australians I say nothing, knowing too much. The end will be just the same, but it will come more slowly, and by the hands of English, not by Spaniards, the nation who even now are revelling in the sight of mutilated cab horses, while their brothers and cousins are fighting for what might be liberty in another nation. Of Bart. Las Casas, that noble monk, and his glorious protest against his countrymen's cruelties, I will speak again.

Peter Carder invented targets of bark for these people, assisting them greatly in their wars, learning their language, and noting their manners. Once, it is said, that in a competitive examination the question was put, "Describe the manners and customs of the Africans." The answer given was, "They have no manners, and their customs are beastly." An old story which may do duty again here. It must serve, because now one-half of the world not only does not know how the other half lives, but furiously abuses anybody who tries to tell them.

Among these innocent Indians, who had no religion save the observance of the full moon, and whose "men and women do drink at their feasts till they be as drunke as Apes," Peter Carder stayed some time, helping them in their wars; but at last some Portuguese and negroes advancing from the north to see if the report was true that some of that Devil Drake's men had been cast ashore, got into an ambush of these Indians; two Portuguese and "certayne negroes" (the number of that kind of cattle not particular) were taken, and on confession of their purpose were brained with clubs, broiled and eaten.

Peter Carder had a tough stomach, but this turned it. He demanded of the Cacique that he should be sent to some river of the Brazils, not settled by the Portuguese; and the Cacique consenting, he started with an escort of four Indians, who had orders to provide him with provisions. With these four companions he started on a walk of about five hundred miles.

I honestly confess that when I came to this part of his adventure, I was very much inclined to throw my manuscript into the fire, and to treat this story, as I have treated others on examination, as a sailor's lie. But no; this story holds water. If the man had been lying, he would have made the Indians bring him to Rio. On the contrary they brought him to Bahia, four hundred miles north, having passed in the rear of Rio de Janeiro.

He says distinctly Bahia de Todos los Santos. He means evidently St. Salvador, called now by our sailors Bahia, or as they say, Bayhee; and our Englishmen call the Bahia of St. Salvador "All Saints' Bay." There is nothing astonishing about this walk, unless the fact that his accompanying Indians passed unquestioned through so many tribes. But this fact should be taken as a *fact*, establishing that the South American tribes would allow the passage of some members of another tribe under certain circumstances,—such, say, as the possession of a white man. This is surely no special pleading, and with regard to the length of the walk there is nothing astonishing. He walked through nearly the richest country in the world, for, say, six hundred miles, with four attendant Indians. Eyre walked for seven hundred miles, without water, save such as he could scrape from the sand, through land apparently given over to the devil, with murder waiting on him at every footstep. When one comes to think of it, there is nothing incredible in his avoiding Rio and coming out at Bahia. This present compiler, who certainly does not pretend to be a traveller, walked two hundred miles between Monday morning and evening church on the next Sunday evening. The late Edward Irving walked sixty miles in the day and preached in the evening, holding his Bible stretched out in his left hand, and that same Bible was put into the present compiler's hands one evening after prayers, and he could not hold it up for three minutes. There is no improbability in this part of Carder's narrative if you compare it with others.

He was within four miles of the town of Bahia, when, meeting a Portuguese, he surrendered himself to him at once, and inquired if there were any Englishmen in the town. It appeared that there were not, but that one Antonio de Pavia spoke English and was a lover of that nation; to him Peter Carder repaired, and found himself once more in civilization. What became of his Indian guides he does not say.

But the mere fact of being in Portuguese dominions was a crime punishable by imprisonment, deportation to Portugal, and services in the galleys for life. The Governor was very sorry, allowed that it was a sad accident, and that he was perfectly blameless, but nevertheless sent him to prison.

Being brought to trial, it was determined that he should be sent to the house of Antonio de Pavia until the King of Portugal's pleasure should be known; this took a year, and then the only reply was that they would send further instructions. Meanwhile Peter spent a not unpleasant or unprofitable life, his friend Antonio having made him overseer of his plantations, tilled by both negro and Indian slaves. Here they grew cotton, white and red pepper, sugar, cut down Brazil wood, and planted ginger, which last, he says, "is a forbidden trade to be transported out for the hindering of other places;" a piece of political economy which, even taking "trade" in its West-country acceptation of "stuff,"* puzzles me entirely.

Antonio also, finding he had been brought up to the sea, made him skipper of a little coaster, in which

---

* Thus, to a Devonshire ear the line,

"Hangs one that gathers samphire, dreadful trade,"
means really—

"Hangs one that gathers samphire, *horrid stuff.*"

he made pleasant voyages even as far as Rio Janeiro; but this was not to last. On returning from one of his voyages, his good friend Antonio advertised him of his doom; he was to go to Portugal next ship, and he could save him no longer, but would give him the means to escape. He gave him a boat of his and five negroes, and with these Peter coasted to Pernambuco, and dismissing the negroes secretly remained behind himself.

Here he found a Portuguese ship, in which were some Englishmen, bound for England, and gladly shipped himself. All went well until they were off Teneriffe, when they were overhauled by two English ships, commanded by Raymond and George Drake of Exeter; and now learned for the first time that the long bickering squabble between England and Spain had broke into open war, soon to end in one of the most deadly conflicts of all time. One of these ships landed him safely at Chichester a few months afterwards, in the end of November 1586. His troubles had lasted nine years and thirteen days.

Lord Howard, our admiral, introduced him to the Queen, who saw him at Whitehall, and listened more than an hour to his adventures, more particularly to the execution of Captain Doutie, having possibly only heard the other side of the question before. After she had satisfied her curiosity about the latter strange matter, of which he provokingly tells *us* not one word—one would have liked to hear his account of it—she gave him twenty-two angels, and many gracious words. And so he departed, thanking God.

THE PRESERVATION OF THE "TERRA NOVA."

It is an ascertained fact that the very last form of shipbuilding is almost, if not quite, the most dangerous which the world has ever seen. The caricature of the "clipper" ship, which is now coming into vogue, sacrifices everything for mere useless speed: stowage, comfort, safety. The extremely long and narrow ship is, to begin with, very wet; she goes through the water and not over it, consequently the misery of her decks is terrible, in some latitudes they are rarely dry; next, in going before the wind she rolls in a fearful manner, particularly when, as is nearly always the case, she is over-sparred. Another fault is that it is extremely dangerous to lay her head to the wind in severe weather; and another, that she will miss stays time after time. I heard a pilot say to a captain once, on board the *Gauntlet*, which either won or nearly won the race from China afterwards, "*I* can't get your ship about; if you can't do it yourself, she will be ashore in ten minutes." The skipper took charge again and *just* managed it, with about as ugly a surf bursting half a mile to leeward as any one would wish to see.

Every resource of modern shipbuilding science was supposed to be wasted on the *London* by Messrs. Money Wigram: the result was a coffin as dangerous as an old ten-gun brig; she was simply unable to float in a gale which the tiniest of her boats weathered; she sank from the water which slopped on board of her. Neither must we forget that the very ship which was to defy nature and nearly annihilate danger, the *Great Eastern*, fearfully misconducted herself on one occasion. I remember once being in one of those horrible weltering sixty-foot seas, which one, I believe, only gets in the Southern Ocean, when I saw a tiny cockle-shell of a brig, about 200 tons, faring on her way, at one time as high up over our heads (or so it seemed) as our mainyard, in about another minute after sinking slowly, slowly down in the hideous grey valley beneath our feet: yet she was floating comfortably like a cork—making, as the mate said, much better weather of it than we were. Once when she was below, as I held hard by the rigging and looked down on her, there were two men at her wheel and a man in blue, I suppose the captain, standing comfortably by them, and a little dog, who ran to and fro and seemed to bark at us, though if he had barked within three feet of your ear the sound would have been lost in the wild rushing and raging of the winds and the waters around. No dog could have run about much on our desolate storm-washed deck. We must have been a splendid spectacle to them, hurling our magnificent length at every conceivable angle, and in at least one-half of all possible positions before and through the following sea; yet I doubt they did not envy us. For "spectacle," however, an enormous American steamship, with roaring steam-pipes, tearing her way furiously and defiantly through a Cape Horn gale and a Cape Horn sea, is a sight so awful and so majestic that it lingers on the eye for ever.

The sea is as wicked and as cruel in its anger now when the English and Americans love it, as it was when the old Greeks hated it. All things have changed but that—earth, man and his works, even the seasons to some extent, and even, sailors have told me, the trade-winds, but the sea is the same. The ways which man has invented of doing battle with this all-devouring monster have changed almost more than anything, particularly within the last 300 years. Let us take a tale of nearly 200 years ago, and see how our forefathers acted, and how they fared, when it came upon them in wrath and fury.

Of all the ships about which I have ever read, the two which appear to me to have been in almost the worst case, and to have survived, with an authentic account of their state, are the *Mary Ann*, of Wilmington, about which you may read in Reid's "Law of Storms," and the *Terra Nova*, Peter Daniel, commander, homeward bound from Virginia, in 1688.

You must at once dismiss from your mind all the ships you have ever seen, and imagine a small, three-masted ship, of only 180 tons burthen, with a very high square poop, and a rather low and round bow, what would be called now a very clumsy-looking ship, yet one which, in a dumb ox-like way, would fight it out to the last with her enemies the winds and the waves. She carried, like all ships then, a goodly number of somewhat small guns; a ship not much altered from those of Blake, still less from those of Monk and Rupert. She had three masts, I think all square-rigged, and an ensign-staff on her taffrail, so large that it afterwards made a mast. She was evidently, to begin with, most dangerously "tophampered."

In the year 1688, this ship, the *Terra Nova*, arrived homeward bound at Port Royal, in Jamaica, and while she was loading there, the Duke of Albemarle,* then Governor of the island, fell sick and died, and the Duchess determined to go home at once. The *Terra Nova* was requested by her to take fifteen of her men-servants, who, with two brothers they had before, made seventeen passengers. She sailed on Christmas day, well loaded with sugar, logwood, Jamaica pepper, hides, indigo, and sarsaparilla, besides other freight of a very different sort, viz. my Lord Duke's costly furniture, rich hangings, curious chairs, and large looking-glass. There was also a large chest, so heavy that six men could scarcely drag it along the deck, "full of pigs of silver, bags of pieces of eight, and some gold," which might give good reason for a cynical man to say that Duke Christopher had inherited the family virtue of his sainted father, Duke George— that of looking after his own interests; for a man does not carry pigs of silver to Jamaica, whatever he may fetch away.

The wealth of their freight was not unknown to some gentlemen of the Bob Singleton school in those

* My younger readers will forgive my reminding them that this must have been Christopher, second duke, son of the great George Monk, by the ex-milliner ex-blacksmith's daughter.

parts, for on the very night of their sailing a ship hailed them, and proposed to them the very stale old trick of asking them to send a boat on board. This being declined, the strange ship made the rather cool proposal to lay them aboard on the larboard quarter. The skipper, however, by dint of "threatening them hard," in what language we do not hear, caused them ultimately to sheer off, and give up their tempting enterprise as a hopeless business. And so the *Terra Nova* sailed away past the Caymans, to encounter the wrath of nature, instead of the fury of man.

Sailing on the 24th of December, by the 8th of February they had passed the Azores, not a very bad passage for a tiny sailing ship even in these days. In fact, the rapidity of sailing passages are only increased by two improvements, the superior speed of the ships and the system of great circle, or to be more correct, "composite" sailing. Will the younger readers wait while I rudely explain this?

If you will take a terrestrial globe, lay any two places on the meridian, and then draw a pencil line from one to the other, you will come to some very startling results. You perceive that by doing this you arrive at the *direct line*, the shortest way between any two places; so far much is gained, but not all.

I was not a pupil of the great American Maury, —only a pupil, and but a poor one, of a pupil; but I believe when those lectures of his were given, and those splendid "sailing orders" distributed, his most familiar illustration of great circle sailing was the route from London to Melbourne. The straight line, the great circle, carries you, if my memory serves me, through the Brazils and part of Patagonia, so close to the Antartic pole, three thousand miles south of Kerguelen's Land, and then up to Melbourne This short route is obviously unavailable, until you can get a ship which will sail over land.

To make a good passage, however, you must approximate to it as closely as you can; you must follow this line nearly. A sailing captain who could get fair winds on this route would take his ship clean across the Atlantic to Pernambuco or Bahia, run close down the coast, and then go down, down, down into the southern ice. This, however feasible for a steamer, is not quite agreeable for a sailing ship, for the winds, both regular and irregular, have as far as possible to be studied; therefore, grand circle sailing in its perfection is only to be accomplished by a steamship.

Maury, following Reid, saw that God had thought it good to reveal certain laws about the winds of heaven to those who chose to look for them. Fitzroy followed, and thought that he could read the whole of the business like a book, but he could not quite, though he did much good. Maury, adding his wonderful researches on wind currents to the strangely simple discovery of the great circle principle, produced the theory of composite sailing, and made him one of the greatest benefactors of the human race.*

A ship, nowadays swift, large, and strong, with the last results of human knowledge to guide her,

---

* In the last American revolutionary war, he was on the losing side. One would be inclined to hope that when matters are quite quiet again, the nation which produced him will not be ashamed to be proud of him.

may manage to make a very bad passage. She may be becalmed on the outside edge of her expected winds, on the line, and elsewhere. So in old times a ship may have, and sometimes did make, a smart passage: this one promised far from badly. They were in 48° N. early in February, well north of the Azores, when their troubles began.

They had had a gale, through which they had got charmingly. They had been forced to send down their top-masts,—I read nothing of top-*gallant*-masts, —and had made everything snug. The weather however moderated, and they were enabled to "sway up" their top-masts again, and set their topsails. However, one day at noon the weather began to look extremely foul, and they had to send down their top-masts again; and reefing sail after sail, hauled the foresail, and sent the yard close down "a-portlings;" then reefed the main-sail, and lowered the main-yard "snug, close down a-portlings." The expressions of old seaman- ship which I have put in inverted commas, are those which are beyond my knowledge.

After this they lay her to; that is to say, put a sail on her which had the effect of keeping her head to the wind. I believe that this is generally done now by spreading a fore-and-aft sail on the mizen- mast, and putting the helm a-port,—so making a weather-cock of the ship,—making it perfectly certain that she will lie with her bow in the wind's eye; under which circumstances nothing can hurt her, unless she goes ashore. I must be careful, however, as a landsman, not to make some very foolish mis- take. I have heard a sailor describe a very safe ship by saying that you could lay her to, by putting the captain's cocked hat in the weather rigging. The *Terra Nova* was lain to by a "main bonnet;" and what that is, I am not sailor enough to say.

In this way, head to wind, offering no obstacle to the wind, a ship may lie comfortably in the most furious weather. It is said, I know not how truly, that a clipper-built ship will lie to better than another; but that if she ever does, by accident, broach to, present her broadside to the weather, and get into the trough of the sea, the disaster is only greater than it would be in the case of a short tub of a ship like the *Terra Nova*. I have never had the luck, or ill-luck, to be in a ship which has got into the trough of the sea whilst lying to; but twice, singularly enough, I have been in disasters in ships which have got into the trough of the sea while trying to make passages, by scudding before great gales of wind. On the last occasion we ran 1,000 miles in 92 hours, under a close-reefed main topsail and a rag of a foresail. During the full rage and fury of the storm, while the pressure of the wind on the sails was sufficient to keep her before the ever-accumulating and ever-following seas, all went merry as a marriage bell; but when the weather slightly moderated, when the seas began to grow in strength, when it got impossible to get the vast length of the ship round and lay her to—then, I think, that the captain, although noted for his suavity of manner, began to get short, sharp, and peremptory with those passengers who seemed inclined to amuse themselves by staggering about the deck, falling into the lee-scuppers, and getting handed over to the doctor with severe

K

scalp bruises, and a very puzzled expression of countenance. At this time I thought I noticed that the captain looked old; and, moreover, he had to stand behind the two men at the wheel, with his arms in cleats; he had two hundred souls to answer for, this captain, with the pay of a ten-year Home Office clerk, and his wife and children on board, beside.

The last time I saw the thing itself, a similar thing to that which ruined the *London* and that great man Bowen Martin together, I saw the senseless fury of the wall of green water which leaped on our deck.

Those who have once been on board a ship when struck and damaged by a heavy sea, are not likely to forget it. If going before the wind she rolls deeper and deeper (the sailors say three times), the last roll goes down deeper, deeper yet, till you think she is actually upset, and then recovers herself with a sickening jerk; at which time *it* happens. Before she is fairly level, or just after, there is a concussion accompanied by a *bursting* sound. Then many sounds of innumerable kinds of ruin, from the crashing of crockery to the thundering fallings and thumpings of heavy and dangerous things on deck; then a heavy leaden feeling in the ship, so different from her late mercurial boundings and divings; mixed with a swashing and pouring down of waters, the water making another miniature sea inside the bulwarks, which, fighting to get free, hurls every loose matter on deck to and fro to the danger of life and limb: above all, you can always hear the hoarse roar of the officer in command, fighting the brutal inorganic savagery around. The next time you go on deck you find boats gone, bulwarks burst out by driving spars, or far worse mischief according to the extent of the disaster.

The *Terra Nova*, being comfortably laid to, for what reason is scarcely apparent (most likely having broached to by some shift in the wind, for her spritsail was blown away at the same time), took a tremendous sea on board, which carried away a boat. This was immediately followed by another, which washed an anchor overboard, and did a deal of small damage which would be almost tedious to follow in May's sea language: after which disasters were in some sort put right, all hands having worked like horses from six till night, May and the captain went to get some breakfast, and found the Duke of Albemarle's sixteen gentlemen most comfortably in bed, apparently not aware that anything was wrong. They, however, had such breakfast as there was, *apparently* in bed.

Our friend May the mate having had his breakfast, stood looking out at the steerage door, which I think corresponds to the door which opens from the grand cabin into the waist of most modern ships,* when the great disaster happened. A great sea burst over the ship, and, laying on her beam ends, set them all swimming for their lives, not knowing whether they were in the ship or out of her. This sea sent every moveable thing flying to leeward, broke away the starboard (stroke side) gallery, and staving in the

---

* The term "steerage" and "steerage passengers" seems to have got into its second intention. "Steerage" passengers are generally berthed forwards.

cabin windows, and filling it with water, hurled a quantity of moveables (May says a chest of drawers, the cabin table, and a quantity of chairs. My dear sir!) on to the captain, who was all the time under water; the passengers fared but little better, being likely to be drowned in their beds; they, however, all got out, as did also the captain, in spite of May's chest of drawers, which I must persist in thinking unnecessary.

The ship now lay on her beam ends, with the water up to the loaming of her main hatchway. That is to say, for the use of any reader not acquainted with the sea, she was so far upset that a man might walk upon her side. If you will think of the last steamer you were on board, and conceive her lying over so far that the base of her funnel was in the water, and the funnel itself lying over so much that it was nearly parallel with the level of the sea, you will appreciate the position of the *Terra Nova*. If a ship lies like this for long, she is nearly certain to founder from the water she takes in through her deck.

Such was not the fate of the *Terra Nova*; a short, cork-like ship, she in the hurly-burly hoisted completely round, so that the sea got under her larboard (bow-side) bow and knocked her upright again, the water poured off her deck (as well it might, seeing that her starboard bulwarks were gone), and they began to examine the extent of the disaster. They had got their ship; but they had got little else.

The starboard side, on which the sea had struck them, was gone as clean as if it had been sawed off close to the deck, so that the sea had leave to wander about the deck as it would, and it was a matter of great personal danger to get from one part of the ship to another.

Next, the ship had performed that curious feat which I have heard some sailors call "whipping the sticks out of her!" That is to say, that in her sudden jerking recovery from her position on her beam ends, her masts had been broken nearly short off to the deck, as you may break a reed by waving it to and fro, and then jerking your wrist. In addition, seven powder-chests washed overboard; the longboat staved to pieces in the bits, with all the live-stock in her, hogs, sheep, goats,—all the live-stock went utterly; two "minions," two "falconers," and a "paterero," none of them guns of any size however, sent overboard; and lastly, "thirteen turkeys sitting on the guns in the forecastle were drowned." An unlucky number of a very foolish bird!

The captain cleared himself from the lumber, and gave orders to clap the helm a-weather, but the tiller had fallen into the gun-room, and May dashed in after it, being up to his knees in water; he was instantly covered all over his body with the drowning rats; making his escape from here, he made for the rudder, and had just time to see it break from its remaining gudgeon, and float away. The ship lay in the trough of the sea perfectly helpless. The sea kept pouring into her hold through the broken bulwarks, and the wreck of the masts was driving and thumping her sides on to leeward. It seemed as if *nothing* could save her.

But now began a fierce hand-to-hand desperate fight between the captain, the mate, and the boatswain on the one side, and all the fury and ferocity of the sea on the other; and the three men beat the great sea, and brought their ship into Plymouth harbour, and beached her by the Barbican.

One thing must be done, and done instantly: it was a matter almost of minutes. The sea must be prevented from breaking freely over the deck and pouring into the hold. There was no vestige of bulwark between the forecastle and the poop on the weather side, and they expected the other bulwark to go every moment from the inside, by the water which poured over the breach, and fell on it to leeward. It was necessary at once that a weather bulwark should be made, with the ship rolling furiously for want of anything to steady her. It reads like one of the most awful passages in the "Travailleurs de la Mer."

They got a stout rope stretched from end to end of the breach, and then the mate, May, and the boatswain, with ropes round their waists, crept onwards through the water, at their dangerous task of stretching a bolt of sail-cloth on the rope, and nailing it down to the deck: this was done, as I understand it, by hanging it on the rope as one hangs a towel on a horse, double. The ropes which were round their waists were attended to by two men, while the captain served out the iron hoop with which they fastened down the canvas. In two hours this wonderful piece of sailors' dexterity was completed, and the mate and boatswain, blinded by the long exposure to the beating sea, had time to rest.

Meanwhile the captain had kept his sailmaker busy; two long canvas hose were by this time ready to carry the water overboard, and the pumps were got ready. If those pumps had been carried away by the fall of the masts, it would have gone ill with them yet, but they were there, and in working order. The captain now said a few words to the men, exhorting them to stick by him and by one another, and then sitting himself down with the half-hour glass between his knees to relieve the men, they went to work to pump the ship dry. After eighteen hours' steady work at it the ship was nearly dry, and men looked at one another with brighter eyes.

Next to lighten the ship. Out went my Lord Duke's curious chairs, rich hangings, and unopened cases, probably of priceless bric-à-brac, to float or sink upon the weltering sea. Conceive a part of the sea on one of the great highways dry: heavens, what should we see there! Then went hogsheads of pepper, sugar, and indigo, which last fell about the deck, and spoilt all their clothes. When this was done, it became necessary to see after their provisions.

All the live-stock, as we have seen, were drowned, and, besides, half their bread was spoilt by salt water: it therefore became absolutely necessary to retrench in the way of provisions. For two days they lived on the drowned cocks and hens; but this dainty fare did not last long: they had to begin on the spoilt bread, which they made the cook heat, after which they ate it with sugar and some good bread which they had found. This lasted for twelve days, after which they were reduced to still harder allowances; for the wet bread having mildewed, they cast it overboard, and had recourse to very small quantities of the food. May had hitherto kept the key of the bread-room, but observing that some men grumbled, believing that he helped himself, he at once gave it up to the captain, who ultimately arranged the allowance at two pounds a week for every man and boy in the ship, including himself. They now also began to live on the fodder (Indian corn) which was put on board for the live stock, but which was "damnified" by the salt water, sometimes boiling it and sometimes beating it up with sugar. They had of course stock fish and the usual salt provisions, though even these were served out in small quantities, but boiled in salt water. It was perhaps as well that there was not too much salt provision, for the allowance of water was now reduced to half a pint (one tumblerful) a day.

The carpenter and the mate had a thirteen-gallon cask of lime-juice, which they secretly broached, and drank privately with sugar, lest any one should see them, for if any one was ever seen eating or drinking others would beg so hard for some of it that it was not pleasant.

May, the mate, had opportunities which others had not, and in the madness of hunger took advantage of them. He was sent to assist the steward in stowing the dry provisions, and he found peas, spoilt with salt water, in the scuppers, which he secreted, and greedily ate in private. Also he used to assist at scuttling the casks of beef, and had an opportunity of slipping any loose pieces he could find into his pocket, which he afterwards ate raw in bed. He also deluded the steward into putting his head into holes and bulkheads in the bread-room, and while he was so engaged May would, I regret to say, slip some bread into his boots. However, his friend the steward found out these malpractices, and, although he *said* nothing, took care that they should not occur again.

The Duke of Albemarle's footmen had many parrots on board, which they would sell to the sailors for a biscuit a-piece. Some of the sailors bought them, and actually brought them home. May had given five dollars for a bird in the West Indies, and actually (with filched peas, I doubt) brought it home. He says that that bird cost him more trouble to keep than he has since found a wife and two children.

They mended their poop cabin with ox-hides, and so for just three weeks they lay in the trough of the sea, drifting utterly helpless, the weather scarcely improving. On the twenty-first day they sighted and spoke a Portuguese ship, to their short-lived satisfaction.

The mate and the captain boarded the Portuguese, and begged of him to give them any spar to make a jurymast, and to lend them a compass. They saw spare spars which would have been their salvation lashed under her bulwarks, but he would give them neither spars nor compass. Captain Daniel offered to pay for them, but the answer was no. All that the Portuguese would do was to offer to take the *Terra Nova's* company, provided they would leave the ship and bring their own provisions. Now Captain

Daniel and Mr. May had resolved to stick by their ship, and declined, whereupon the Portuguese sent them on board again in his boat, without asking them either to eat or drink.

Getting on board, Captain Daniel had together all hands, and told them of the Portuguese offer, pointed out to them that the boat was still there, and that as many might go as chose, and be soon safe on shore. The answer, in spite of their desperate condition, was a singularly unanimous No—very pleasant to hear. The Duke's chief gentleman, speaking in the name of his brother servants, informed him that they would stay and share his fortune; and the crew made exactly the same resolution, and all hands saw the Portuguese sail away with equanimity. One gets from this passage a dim suspicion that Captain Daniel was one good fellow, and that the Duke's first gentleman was another.

But now came for the first time fair weather and a smooth sea. The rudder had, as we know, been torn away, and the rudder bands had given so much that they made a very serious leak. May and a black man were now lowered over the ship's side with hammers and spikes to see if they could make these tight. They drove in thirty-two spikes, although the band was a foot and a half under water; and so tightened it up that the ship became perfectly tight, and the men were entirely relieved from the pumps. The black who assisted in this work was evidently a first-rate man. Having dropped a piece of very necessary wood overboard, he immediately leaped overboard after it, and got it.

Now to get her head before the wind and get her to sail. It would be tedious to tell of the shifts they went to before they got up a mainmast seventeen feet high, with a topmast of a piece of the old crossjack yard, and a mainyard of two tillers spliced; but they hammered away till they got up such a mast with three sails on it; and then they set to work on their foremast. The carpenter was found to be utterly inefficient, and the whole direction of the work was by the captain.

May noticed in the gun-room a beam which was neither bolted nor kneed, that is, formed no real part of the ship's frame; and mentioning this to Captain Daniel, he had it cut down and brought on deck, and having done many mysterious things with it, for an explanation of which one would have to consult Admiral Smythe,[*] they made a foremast of it; they made a small bowsprit also; and lastly a mizen-mast of the ensign staff—a rather considerable spar according to old pictures, now only to be seen on Monitors and pleasure-boats. And having done all this, they found they could make about one knot and a half an hour, and that the ship would not steer; sometimes turning suddenly round with her head to the wind, and taking all hands three hours to get her round again. They first tried to steer her by her headsails, but this was useless; then by towing a grapnel overboard with a buoy to prevent it sinking,

---

[*] May writes "Sidnet" for "Sinnet," which brings us much nearer the root of the word; invariably "boltsprit," "gunnel," "bittacles" for binnacle: and many other variations from the spelling of the present day.

and hauling hard upon it for sometimes three hours before she would come round; and, alas! six minutes after would be round again. At length Captain Daniel hit on a plan of his own, which I have tried to understand, and make out to be this. A flat cross was towed overboard about sixteen fathoms from the ship, offering resistance to the water (and lessening her very small speed, although it rendered her manageable): to each end of this cross were ropes, which, being hauled upon, produced exactly the same effect as a rudder. This is all I can gather out of the deluge of practical seamanship which May pours over one in explaining it.

Provisions got shorter and shorter: they tried eating boiled hides, but it was no good at all—"a mere thong." A storm burst upon them, carrying away their main topmast; but the wind was fair, and although laid-to,* she made some way to leeward in the right direction. The storm was followed by a brisk fair gale, before which they stood, going from a mile and a half to two miles an hour—six to eight miles in four hours, but homeward. A great dog they had now went out of his mind for hunger, and tried to attack the men, so they cast him overboard.

They now considered that they must be coming near soundings, and getting out the deep-sea lead struck ground in a hundred fathoms, only six hundred feet from the earth after so much wandering in soundless waters! The captain instantly made a powder-barrel half full of punch, and gave to each man a cocoa-nut shell-full.

* "Laid a try:" May.

The next night, steering E.N.E. they came by an adventure. As morning broke one of the passengers descried rocks ahead of them. The captain came up, and declared that they were the Bishop and Clerk rocks of Scilly, and that they were lost after all. He had a violent altercation with May, whom he accused of having been to sleep; but fuller morning light showed the truth. These were no rocks, but the British war fleet of sixteen men-of-war with their tenders, bound for Bantry Bay, under the command of Lord Torrington. From these they heard the news of the revolution. They begged assistance, lest the wind should turn easterly, and drive them to sea again. It so happened that a son of Lord Bath, whom they had carried the year before from Smyrna to Constantinople, was commanding one of the ships, the *Advice*. He, hearing that the wrecked ship was commanded by none other than his old acquaintance Daniel, begged leave to tow them into Plymouth, which, being granted, he did. And on April 11th, after two months of almost unequalled suffering, she was run aground under the Barbican at Plymouth, an object of wonder to the thousands who crowded to see the shattered bulwarks and fantastic rigging of what they called "the wreck ship."

SPITZBERGEN.

THE island of Spitzbergen may not unfairly claim the title of the Arctic Italy. Although the highest land yet reached by man, lying between the 78° and 82° parallels, yet the mean winter temperature is only 20° of Fahrenheit, or twelve degrees of frost; while at Winter Harbour, in Melville Island, some four or five degrees further south, the winter temperature is 0°, or thirty-two degrees. Nova Zembla, again, lying much to the south, is a miserable desert, producing no kind of herbage, while in Spitzbergen grow wild celery, scurvy grass, endive, watercresses, and some flowers, ranunculus, saxifrage, mouse-ear chickweed (cerastium), and a few others; and at the same time there is sufficient grass and moss to support numerous herds of reindeer.

The reason of this is very plain. The furthest point of the Gulf Stream just washes the east side of Spitzbergen, and this tongue of warm Florida water is sufficient to raise the mean temperature some ten degrees. Millions of sea-fowl, auks, grebes, gulls, terns, and the eider-duck, naturally select such a favourable spot, situated in the midst of a teeming polar sea, for their breeding grounds; but strangely one of our own land-birds has actually been tempted so far into the land of night. The Great Brambling hops innocently about among the moss hags and limestone boulders before the feet of the wandering sailor, who is astonished and gladdened to see so homelike a bird among those melancholy Arctic mountains.

Although the climate of the east side of the island is probably in some degree the milder, yet it is utterly unfrequented. The west and north coast, washed by the Arctic current, is far more popular with whalers. On this coast the whales in winter used, as late as 1780, to approach so near to the shore that the Russian garrison told Rackstrom that they frequently killed them from shore with a gun. This west or cold side of the island is a perfect emporium of Arctic wealth. Whale-blubber, whalebone, white bear skins, white fox skins, eider down, unicorns' tusks, ivory, and smoked tongues were the cargo which the above-mentioned keen-eyed surgeon found the Russians preparing for shipment to Archangel.

Lord Mulgrave, who saw as much of the island (or rather islands) as most men, describes it as a country abounding in black mountains, the glens between which were filled by glaciers, such as once filled Glen Roy. These glaciers end in an abrupt wall, over which cascades pour in summer-time from a great height. Masses are detached from the edge of them with a sound like thunder, and float away. One mountain which he measured, close to the Black Point, was 4,500 feet in height. Rackstrom the surgeon, one of the sharpest observers, and one of the *neatest* narrators I have met with, seems to have been impressed very much with two things—the vivid light and the awful unbroken silence.

Very early in the seventeenth century commercial people began to be aware of the importance of the island, and to perceive the advantage which would be gained, were it possible for a party to winter there; that to collect the treasures of the northern sea during the later autumn and the earlier spring, when ice prevented the approach of ships, and so gain eight months on the inexorable Arctic winter, was most desirable. The first attempt, so far as I am aware, was made by the Dutch Greenland Company. The attempt appears to have been partially successful at first: how many times before 1633 I am unable to say. But the events in Spitzbergen that year are certainly worthy of a place in this little collection of adventures.

Andrew Johnson (Jansen?), of Middleburg; Cornelius Thysse, of Rotterdam; Jerome Carcoens, of Delf; Tiebke Jelles, of Friesland; Nicholas Florison, of Hoorn; Adrian Johnson, of Delf; and Feltje Olters, of Friesland, volunteered to pass the winter here, evidently succeeding another party who had done so successfully. The account of the matter in Churchill's collection gives us no idea on which part of the islands they were left; but Lord Mulgrave puts it at Smeerenburg Harbour on the north-west coast. Both he and our clear-tongued friend Rackstrom—the first in 1773, the second in 1780—mention the ruins of the Dutch boiling-down establishments near Huckluyts headland. Rackstrom saw open coffins at this place, the crosses on which bore dates corresponding to the time of which we are speaking.*

These seven men, as one is forced to conclude, had been terrified by the accounts of their predecessors. The fellow-countrymen of Ruyter and De Witt, the men whose younger brothers and sons burnt Chatham, were no cowards, yet the clockwork order and punctuality to which they had been used among the tulip gardens of the United Provinces, was hardly the best preparation for spending a four months' night in a hideous solitary country, so dreadfully far from home and from order. What was done so easily by the irrepressible and younger Russian race, accustomed to fight winter from their childhood ; what was done easily enough by your headlong, happy-go-lucky British sailor-boy of the seas, was not so easily done by these sons of whitewash and order. From the very first we find them in a state of melancholy: melancholy in those latitudes produces scurvy, and scurvy death.

There is one circumstance about these seven Dutch sailors which it would be worse than wicked to omit. They were men of deep and tried piety. When the wild Arctic night closed in on them amidst whirling snowstorms, it seems as though there were eight of them instead of seven, and the eighth like unto the form of the Son of Man. I say no more for fear of offence. One could have wished that they had been

---

* Surely I have seen a picture of the very place in the *Illustrated London News*. The author of the "Birds of Spitzbergen" will perceive that I have not used his book, valuable as it is.

less melancholy—nay, sometimes one could wish that they had sung and danced, told stories, and sung songs, as a British sailor would have done. But then, again, when one is in a certain kind of mood, dancing Jack of Wapping Old Stairs seems but a poor brute beside these melancholy, pious, square-headed Dutchmen. It requires Trafalgar to cure one of such sentimentality.

The whole business was an utter failure. In September, after the ship had left them, they saw plenty of whales close to the shore, but could not manage to take one. The Dutch are not good in these adventures—you want a Briton or an American for them. They now began hunting, but made no hand of it, not even finding scurvy grass. On the 21st of October the sun left them, and the hunting after fresh meat and green herbs grew more hopeless. In less than a month the scurvy made its appearance, as a matter of course; and then—Heaven help them!—they began doctoring themselves, and talking about their symptoms. They mark the 2'd of December (of all days in the year), in this manner: "Nicholas Florison took a dose of scorbutic medicine, *after which they went out and set traps to catch foxes;*" who, however, declined to be caught—neither Cavaignac, Changarnier, Lamoricière, Bedeau, or any of the rest of them.

"They went often in quest of some refreshment, but found none, and so recommended themselves to God's providence." On the 12th Cornelius Thysse did likewise take a medicinal potion against the scurvy. It is hard to go on; when folks in difficult situations begin thinking about their health and talking about their insides, it is all up with them. The United States were not founded, India was not conquered, nor Australia settled, by such men as these. The Dutch had the chance of doing all these three great works, and have done neither. They were before us everywhere: see how far they are behind us now, through wanting the one quality of recklessness.

The quality which is wanting in the Dutch, and which has prevented them to some extent from being the most successful colonists on the earth, is that adaptability to new circumstances which is found in the highest degree in the Scotchman, next in the Irishman, next in the American, and lastly in the Englishman. No other nations seem to have it in any appreciable degree. The Frenchman must carry France with him; and the only thing which has prevented Holland from being the outlet of the swarming Teutonic nations of the Continent, is that the Dutchman is dazed and lost as soon as he has left his Dutch respectability. The world swarms with O'Donnels, Macdonnels, MacMahons, and McClellans; but almost all the Dutch names written in geographical history are those which tell us that the Dutch nation could discover and could fight, but could not hold. No better place could be found to make these remarks than the present; that is my apology for making them. This is a story of Dutch failure and of Russian success.

So we return to our poor Dutchmen, locked up in their hut in the bleak Arctic winter. Any one who knows Dutchmen, knows their sweet imperturbable temper. These men had two hundred years ago the same temper which makes Dutchmen so loveable now. Men coming from fiercer races would have perhaps quarrelled, at least have grown petulant with one another. Not so with these gentle Dutchmen. That they must have been wretched company cannot be denied, but they tended one another with the greatest care and patience.

On the 14th of January Adrian Johnson died, the others being now in a deplorable condition, suffering horrible agony. The next day Feltje Olters followed him; and the day but one after, Cornelius Thysse, "being the man of all the rest in whom they had most put their hopes, went to God." The others could hardly stand; yet they contrived to make coffins for these, and laid their bodies in them; soon after which they took entirely to the hut. Jerome Carcoens was still somewhat better than the rest, and was able to get about and get them some food and some fuel. The others were beyond helping themselves.

On the 24th of February, the sun rose once more upon their misery, and on the 26th they wrote thus in their log: "The four of us that are still alive lie flat upon the ground in our huts. We believe we could still feed were there but one among us who could stir out of the hut to get us some fuel, but no one is able to stir for pain. We spend our time in constant prayers, to implore God's mercy to deliver us out of this misery, being ready whenever He pleases to call us. We are certainly not in a condition to live thus long without food or fire, and cannot assist one another in our mutual afflictions; but every one must bear his own burdens."

When the ships arrived in June, one Middleburg, a baker, ran swifter than the others, and got to the hut first. No smoke rose from the chimney, and on opening the door there was a silence as of death. The frightened man ran over the house, but at first only found the carcases of the two dogs. At last, opening the door of the front room, he fell in the dark over the body which lay nearest to the door; and light being procured, they found all of them dead together in the same room.

Adrian Johnson, Olters, and Thysse were in their coffins; Nicholas Florison in a bunk, Andrew Johnson, Jelles, and lastly Carcoens were, one in a bedplace, and the other two on some old sails on the floor, with their knees drawn up to their chins. The time must have come when they could no longer move about, but lay down to die. They would talk and pray together till voice after voice became silent. Sometimes one of them would say, "Brother, are you asleep?" and no answer would come; and last of all, Jerome Carcoens would find himself alone in a solitude and a silence too terrible to be contemplated. Let us leave this subject: God save us from such a death as that!

"These were the last," says the writer in the Churchill collection, " who pretended to spend the winter in Spitzbergen." But he was wrong. The fathers of the men of Eylau and Inkerman accomplished the adventure without difficulty under the most unfavourable circumstances.

In 1743, Jeremias Ollamkoff, of Meisen near Archangel, sent out a vessel with fourteen hands to the west side of Spitzbergen to fish for whale and morse. When within two miles of land they became enclosed in ice, and seemed in such a hopeless condition that they sent four men across the ice to the shore to look for a hut which some of their fellow-townsmen had built there on a previous occasion.

These men's names were: Alexis Himloff, boatswain, and three sailors, Ivan Himkoff, Stephen Sharapoff, and Feodor Weregin. These men took with them a musket, a powder-horn with twelve charges of powder, a quantity of lead, an axe, a small kettle, a stove, a piece of touchwood, a knife, a tin box full of tobacco, and each one his pipe. Heavily laden with these, they managed to cross the ice; and by means of these things, and these only, they contrived to exist for the astonishing period of six years, during which time they received no external assistance whatever, and never set face upon their fellow-men. Borodino!

They very soon found the hut, a most spacious and comfortable one, and passed the night in it. It blew all night, and in the morning, ice, ship, and all were gone, a clear sea was sparkling everywhere in the sunshine, and they were left alone on this desolate shore without provisions.

Their grief and dismay were beyond bounds; they well knew the extreme improbability of a ship's passing that side of the island, and knew also the rigour of the winter which was approaching. They looked in vain for the ship in every direction, but they never saw her again. She never reached Meisen, and undoubtedly foundered at sea. After the next winter, the folks at home gave them up as lost, and Himloff's wife put on her widow's weeds, and submitted to her situation, often wandering, however, about the quays and bridges with the other sailors' wives, full of sad thoughts about her poor lost Alexis.

Meanwhile he and his three companions were left standing utterly at a loss what to do next. The very first thing, naturally, was shelter and warmth. The hut was in tolerable order, and with their axe they very soon mended the hut, and stopped the crevices with moss, of which there was great abundance in that part. The fireplace was a square elevation in the middle of the principal room, from which the smoke ascended to the roof, and lay there in a dense strata. The advantage of this form of fireplace seems to be that the hot air is not drawn up a chimney and wasted, but is diffused around. The cold air is supplied by a line of little windows the length of a man's hand, which, in cases of extreme cold, can be closed. The air is always perfectly clear of smoke below these windows. From first to last they never wanted for fuel. They found a wreck close by, which lasted them nearly a year, and besides this there was plenty of driftwood. Another traveller mentions in one of the north isles of Spitzbergen a beach almost composed of it; sometimes trees marked into lengths by the axe are cast ashore in considerable quantities. It is hard to say whence they come; looking at the set of the Gulf Stream, one would guess from the east coast of Iceland, though possibly from the Hebrides, or even from Norway.

Next came the all-important question of food. Their twelve charges of powder procured them twelve reindeer; when these were gone, and their muskets only so much old iron, they would have been not only without food, but also entirely without protection against the Polar bears; but while they had been living on these reindeer they had been working with a degree of skill and pluck which fills one with the very profoundest astonishment, and by the time the powder was exhausted, they were fully armed against all-comers.

The first thing to get was a hammer, and this was the worst of all; for every hammer requires another hammer to make it; so there must have been a succession of hammers from the time of Tubal Cain. But they had broken through the succession, and found it necessary to make a Nag's Head hammer as quickly as possible. They found a large hook on a piece of wreck heavy enough for the purpose, and in this hook there was a little hole. By heating this hook, and patiently and slowly enlarging the hole with a big nail, they at last made the aperture large enough to receive a handle, and their hammer was made. If any of my readers have ever done a turn of blacksmith work, they will the more readily appreciate the ingenuity and patience required to do this without either tongs or a hammer. And we must remember, moreover, that it was a match against time with them: they had but twelve charges of powder, and an Arctic winter settling slowly down on them:

everything depended on this hammer, and the hammer was done in time; if it had not been, we should never have heard of them. Professor Le Roy saw all their wonderful manufactures after their return, but provokingly makes no mention of the all-important Thor's hammer of theirs.

The hammer being made, matters grew better with them. A stone, moved by a hand-barrow made of reindeers' horns, was their anvil; and, yielding to their greatest necessity, the first things they forged were spears with which to kill the Arctic bears. Le Roy says that a bear may be killed by a pike or halbert by a man possessing "resolution." It requires a good deal of "resolution," however. An old friend of mine who lived eleven years in Russia, a perfect prince among sportsmen, has often told me that even the brown bear is exceedingly dangerous, and that it is considered a great sporting feat to kill one single-handed with a well-tempered spear, with a cross on it to prevent the bear hitting you with his paw; the butt of the spear being of highly seasoned wood, and held firmly against a tree till the bear is dead. "If you waver for a moment," R. D. has told me, "you are a dead man." These four sailors habitually attacked and killed the Polar bear, a much more terrible animal, with spears of their own manufacture; the shafts made of brittle deal.

They lashed on the heads of these spears with the fibres of the reindeer, and with two of them attacked and killed their first bear. They ate his flesh, and thought it better than reindeer venison. Lord Mulgrave, who, as a British peer, may be supposed to know a haunch from a neck or humbles, don't agree with them at all. However, they ate their bear, praising God, and, in doing so, made a most important discovery. They found that his fibres would divide into cords of any degree of fineness or coarseness, and of vast strength and toughness. A large and tough fir-bough, strung with a cord of these fibres, made a bow of fearful power; they had wood and feathers, and they forged some arrow-heads, binding them on their shafts with bear sinews; and thus they had arrows of a large size, fit for any game. In the six years of their exile they killed no fewer than two hundred and fifty reindeer with them.

The white bears were their greatest enemies; they frequently attacked our sailors in their hut, sometimes they would be driven away by the shouts which our sailors made during their preparation for attack, but often would bring matters to a bloody issue, in which they were, of course, worsted: ten of them were killed in this manner.

From the cordage of an old wreck they made wicks, and they had an abundance of reindeer fat, but their great difficulty was with their lamp. They could not at first make one of clay, which was not too porous to hold the fat when melted. They, however, remedied this in a most ingenious way by dipping their jar, after it had been baked in the fire, into a paste made out of some of the little bag of flour they had brought ashore. From this time they had continual light.

One great necessity remained, the supplying their clothes as they wore out. They had skins, they had deer and bear fibres, and, lastly, they made a needle piercing the eye with the sharpened point of their only precious knife; some skins they regularly dressed, soaking them in cold water, others they wore green: breeches, waistcoats, pelisses with hoods, were all made in this way. One has only to remember seeing a sailor at sea making a pair of canvas trousers, or fashioning some elaborate piece of inutility with his knife with the greatest diligence, to see how deeply busy these sailors were over a work of such utility and importance. One can see them trying on their pelisses, and talking about the set of them with all the eagerness of a young lady at Madame Elise's.

The poor Dutchmen, left with every luxury, died in six months of idleness and ennui; these busy Russians, left with only a week between them and starvation, lived for six years. The cold was practically as great on their side of the island as the other. They had no antiscorbutic potions, except energy, hopefulness, and the fresh blood of reindeer, which last seems but a doubtful remedy. .They were just as pious as the Dutchmen, keeping their fasts and festivals carefully. This one element of "pluck"—I know no better word—was the only thing which the Dutchmen lacked, and which brought our noble Russians out of their trouble triumphantly, with one exception, to be noticed presently.

They were all bachelors, with the exception of Alexis Himloff, the pilot. He had a wife to whom he was very deeply attached, as was she to him. This is the woman I have spoken of before as frequenting the bridges and quays, with other sailors' wives, in her widow's dress, and talking of her poor lost husband. Alexis used to get very low about this wife of his sometimes in the five long winter nights of four months each. If these Russians were as good-natured and gentle as those few I have made acquaintance with, it is not difficult to believe that they cheered him and condoled with him over their busy sewing: no doubt they did; for we find their good-nature and patience exhibiting itself towards one who needed it more than poor Alexis Himloff.

Feodor Weregin was a big and loutish man, of a plaintive and despondent nature—somewhat lazy, withal; his inside, like that of many heavy men, was weak, and he could not stomach the deer blood: it may have been this, or it may have been his habit of staying almost always in the hut and brooding, but the result was the same—he very soon fell ill of scurvy.

He had to be nursed like an infant, but they nursed him tenderly; and when he died, nearly at the end of the sixth year, they missed him and mourned for him, and looked at his vacant place at their narrow and dismal hearth with regret. This is in no way surprising to any one who has seen the wonderful, almost feminine tenderness which the better class of sailor always shows towards a sick messmate; one only mentions this and similar circumstances, which may by some be considered sentimental, to show that the sailors of Archangel, in the middle of the last century, were, some of them at all events, a very high class of men indeed.

Feodor's death had a very depressing effect on them. They now began each one to brood on the two questions: Who would be next? and on the still more terrible one, Which of them would be left last? To which one would fall the lot of staggering out into the darkness and the whirling snow to lay his last comrade beside those who had gone before? Which of them would have to return some night to the empty hut and the desolate hearth, only to sit down and brood and sicken, until death came to him all alone under the blackened rafters, beside the expiring fire?

But while they brooded, help was coming to them from that East to which they had always turned in their prayers.

One Vernisobre, "director of the offices of pitch merchants," was about to send a ship to Nova Zembla, but for some reason persuaded his captain to go to Spitzbergen. He had great objections, to which objections Le Roy gives no clue, but ultimately was persuaded to do as his masters wished. He not only was so obliging as to do this, but made the island exactly at the point where our friends were. When they signalled him, and were taken on board, it was found that they, with their axe and knife, had done something more than live. They carried on board with them two thousand pounds' weight of reindeer fat, a large number of deer and fox skins,* ten bear skins, and agreed to pay eighty roubles for their passage.

* They must have been white and blue fox-skins, worth, I believe, at present prices, some ten shillings. The invaluable black fox is not found in Spitzbergen; their skins are worth fifty guineas apiece. There used to be a story in St. Petersburg of the late Emperor Nicholas. He, so the story goes, took a common droschky in that city once, and ordered the man to drive to the back-door of the palace. When he got there, he had no money, and told the driver that he would send some one out to

And so they came back to Archangel, after all:

> "We drifted o'er the harbour bar,
> While I with sobs did pray,
> Oh let me be awake, my God,
> Or let me sleep alway."

Mistress Himloff, the boatswain's wife-widow, whom we have mentioned two or three times before, was standing on the bridge at Archangel, along with other sailor women and fishwives—let us suppose with her two hands under her apron, or else with her arms akimbo, scratching her elbows (sailors' ladies generally do stand like that when a ship is being warped in)—on the bridge at Archangel, watching a whaler coming up to the wharf, when she saw her husband, our old friend Alexis, who had pined for her and his little ones these six years, standing on the deck. In the madness of her unutterable joy she forgot everything. "The man she loved was on the deck." She forgot where she was, and the terrible drop between the bridge and the ship, and, before the other sailors' women could stop her, had leaped headlong over to get into his arms. By God's mercy she missed the

pay him. The driver, who had not recognised the Emperor, replied, that many people went into that place who forgot to pay him, and insisted on a pledge for good faith. The Emperor good-humouredly threw his *schube* across the droschky, and went in. His back was scarcely turned when the driver pulled the coat open to see with what fur it was lined, and so judge of the quality of his fare, and his chance of his copecks or roubles, or whatever his due might have been. He saw at a glance that it was lined with black fox, and gave himself up for lost. He made a wild dash at the gate, and was in time to throw himself at the great man's feet. The Emperor declared himself, praised him for an honest man, and gave him a handsome donation. The story was told me by a man who had been a tenant of the Emperor Nicholas at Alexandroski for eleven years. *He* believed it.

ship, fell into the water, and was rescued. It seems to me a pretty incident and worth relating; leading also up to this conclusion, that there were, judging from internal evidence, in Archangel, about the year 1749, certain people whom one would uncommonly liked to have known.

These sailors were **dependants (serfs, I** suppose, in some degree) of **Schuvaloff, to** whom the Empress had given **a charter** for whaling. Le Roy, a member of the Petersburg Academy, wrote the **account of** their adventures in German. He got Count Schuvaloff to send them over to him **from** Archangel, and he closely examined the implements which they so ingeniously made to carry on their fight against the Arctic winter. When he saw them, soon after their **return, we** may, from M. Klingstross' **account,** place **their ages thus :**—Alexis Himloff, fifty years; **Stephen** Sharapoff, forty-two; and Ivan Himkoff (Himloff?), thirty-five.

They had only lost their reckoning, **in these six** years of Arctic winter, with four months' night, by *two days*. Alexis Himloff **was very** indignant at the accusation. "What sort **of a pilot** should I be to make such a mistake?" he asked. But he undoubtedly **had.** Until the matter was referred to the Wessen Schaften, or club of the wise men **of** Gotham, he was **inexorable.** But at last **it struck one of** the wise men **that they** had been at Spitzbergen six years, or two *leap years*, **and** that Alexis **had forgotten** them both. **At which explanation Alexis** had nothing to do but to scratch his head, **and leave** the room in silence.

One more circumstance seems worth mentioning, as exhibiting their wonderful diligence and ingenuity. They had made a box to hold their needle, and made it with such sailor-like perfection, that when Le Roy showed it to a number of savants they all insisted that it was spurious, and had been turned. One Homann, a great turner, accidentally came in, and Le Roy reversed the question between them; *he* maintaining that the box had been turned. Homann's sense of truth was stronger than his sense of politeness to his host, Le Roy. He said, "Sir, this box has never been turned: it is a piece of bone scraped round with a knife."

Let us conclude with a piece of Russian self-glorification on this affair; which, however justifiable, will, I think, make us laugh—at least, all except the last sentence.

"The English have a fabulous history of Robinson Crusoe" (they knew that wondrous book even then and there, and took it *au grand sérieux*). "*This* history" (the Russian) "is *certainly* true" (doubts about the veracity of Robinson). "The first is represented in a warm climate; but our sailors were in 77° of latitude. The Englishman was enabled to make a kind of punch with the raisins which grew on the island" (is not this a new fact about our dear friend?); "but our hardy and sturdy Russians were under the necessity of contenting themselves with water. Robinson lost almost all knowledge of Christianity; but our adventurers, at all times as I am assured, preserved their faith, and unceasingly placed their confidence in God."

D'ERMENONVILLE'S ACCLIMATIZATION ADVENTURE.

THE French are not great travellers; it is possible that they, like the rest of the world, find their own country too pleasant to leave. Yet, when you get a highly educated French traveller with a distinct object before him, he equals the best of the nations in zeal and in enthusiasm; in reckless audacity, in rapidity of motion, in untiring good-humour, he surpasses them: in his power of imitating foreign customs he is nearly equal to the Irishman, though they both, like some Jews, overdo the business. The power of *becoming* foreign, and really understanding and feeling with foreign nations, seems to be limited to Scots, Jews, and one class of Americans. The Irish have not this faculty, at least in the first generation. They act too much: look, for example, at the ridiculous caricature which the whitewashed Irish make of the real Americans.

I think that I am justified in saying that his intelligence, good-humour, *élan*, and splendid courage, make him as good a traveller as any other, when he is once started. Unless he is a very highly cultivated man indeed, he is very apt, more apt perhaps than any one except the Irishman, to deduce results from an insufficient number of facts; M. Assolant, for one instance, among many. Moreover, he is very apt to be taken ill on the road-side with an *idée*; but if you will only let him—well—bring it up, let us say—he will go on as fresh as a lark the next minute. He soon gets better again; and besides, there are some nearer home than France who habitually say the first thing which comes into their heads, and call it thought.

D'Ermenonville has his ideas and his sentimentalities—is even obliged to take the world into his confidence in a scene in which he resisted temptation and enacted the character of Joseph; is obliged by his muse to tell you that when Justice and Peace, tired of living among mortals, ascended, on the authority of Fame, to heaven, that Fame as usual lied; that Justice took refuge at the village of Dommguello, at the junction of the Rio Grande and Vueltas in Mexico, *because* the alguazil of that village had prevented his being cheated out of three dollars. There is but little of this nonsense, however, and his adventure is worthy to rank with the best in this book. If there were such a thing as a Cobden medal for those who have faced personal difficulty and danger for commercial objects, he should have one. I do not compare his expedition to that of Clement Markham's, because Markham's expedition, in its objects, was immeasurably higher; nay, when the books are all summed up, it is perfectly possible that Markham, by his acclimatization of quinine, may be found to have done as much towards the alleviation of human misery as any president or emperor of the lot. I only allude to his expedition beside that of

D'Ermenonville, because they were both botanical, and attended with great difficulties. Markham went for a drug, D'Ermenonville for a dye. "There is a river in Macedon, and a river in Monmouth, and there are salmon in both."

M. D'Ermenonville, who was botanist to King Louis XVI., in 1777, made the determination to attempt the introduction of cochineal from the Spanish colony of Mexico to the French one of St. Domingo; an enterprise fraught with enormous difficulty, and with no little danger, but of very great commercial importance. When I mention that the duty was paid in England on no less a quantity than 489,988 pounds in the year 1839, the reader will perceive that it was as important for the Spaniards jealously to guard their monopoly of it, as it was for the French to try and destroy that monopoly by introducing it into the French colonies. Since the year 1839 I regret that I have no statistics, but that is sufficient for our purpose. The retail price of cochineal is about 24s. per lb. which would give the value of the quantity imported as (very roughly) 586,000*l.*

In my translation of D'Ermenonville, he speaks of an appendix, in which he gives an account of these beloved cochineal insects of his, which must be deeply interesting. I have not got it, however, and am forced to more recent sources; for it seems to me that some little account of the insect will render the following story not only more intelligible, but more interesting.

The Spaniards first discovered it in their invasion of Mexico under Cortez, at which time they found the natives using it for staining ornaments and patterns on their houses. Such assertions about it as that it was the dye of Hiram, King of Tyre, or of the Imperial purple (and such are made), are of course only made by good people who never heard of the Murex. It is, however, a most important article still, and the *habitués* of water-colour exhibitions would miss it were anything to happen to the crop. An absent friend of mine once told me that there would be no more Madeira, for that the vines had got the potato disease; he might also say that if the cochineal insect were to get the rinderpest, there would be no more lake or carmine, and what would become of —— and ——? But we must not be personal.

In addition to its use in these very important pigments, it has many others of which one can read in Ure and in Pereira. The dregs of it, after the paints have been made, are used by the paper-stainers. Medical qualities have been attributed to it, which are treated, however, with utter scorn by the best informed of the faculty, with Pereira at their head. The thing is a dye, and nothing but a dye. It is used for colouring pickled cabbage and apple jelly; mixed with levigated French chalk, it makes *rouge*. Theatrical readers may be glad to know that they get theirs very cheap and very much adulterated, the price being 10s. an ounce, while the real article would be between 3*l.* and 4*l.* the ounce. Gentlewomen of the *haute noblesse* might like to know that "Lady Dungannon's mixture is composed of carmine, with a little ammonia and water." This scandalous, Pereira!*

* Pereira's Materia Medica, p. 2217.

The insect which makes this wonderful dye is the apterous female of a very beautiful fly. She fastens on the leaves of a large arborescent cactus, the nopal, or, scientifically, the Opuntia cochinelifera, where she is visited; she dies before the young ones are born, her empty body serving for a cocoon. The best cochineal of the shops is composed of the dried body of the young females, just fecundated, which are carefully brushed off with a squirrel's tail, killed in warm water, and dried. I have one in my hand now, like a small grey sweet-pea of irregular shape. I put it on the white mantel-piece with a little water, crush it with a glass rod, and forth comes a stain like the blood of a murdered Montezuma or Maximilian. Such is this wonderful Mexican insect.

The principal, nay, the only place where the best sort was produced, was at Oaxaca, a district and city lying about 200 miles S.W. from Vera Cruz. D'Ermenonville's voyage to the last-named place, *viâ* Port au Prince and the Havana, has but little to do with us; we will begin with him at Vera Cruz.

He was to have had 6,000 francs, but Necker, the new broom, "financed" him out of 3,000, on the very probable grounds that there really was not the money in hand. With this and his books he landed at Vera Cruz in the character of a French physician and botanist.

He soon became very popular and famous. In one of his very earliest walks out of the town he saw growing the Convolvulus jalapa;* he dug up some of the roots, and taking it to the druggist's in the town,

* *Ipomæa* ja'apa it is called now.

got it verified for true jalap, and then showed the astonished governor enough of it to freight a ship growing under his own nose. In their idleness and ignorance they believed that it was only to be got at Jalapa, six-and-thirty miles away, and were actually giving three reals, or eighteenpence a pound for what was all around them like a weed. He now heard that vanilla was also grown by the Indians at Oaxaca, and determined to smuggle some of that also.

His scheme now was to get a passport either for Mexico or for Orizava, and use it for Oaxaca. M. Fersen, his friend (son, I think, of Count Fersen of the Varrennes business), actually got him one; but the Governor,* whose suspicions were thoroughly aroused as to D'Ermenonville's object with regard to cochineal, sent his secretary the next day and took it away from him. His walks were now confined within the district of Vera Cruz: this thunderbolt was hurled at his head by the Viceroy of Mexico, and was followed by another ordering him to leave the country.

We will spare the reader his frantic appeals to himself, to his father, to destiny, his friends, to the king, to everything short of the Nine Muses, as soon as he found himself alone. He was a Frenchman in a state of distraction, generally an absurd object to an Englishman. Wait a little before you laugh; there are various ways of doing things; we are quite as absurd to the French in their caricatures as the French are to us in ours.

* This gentleman's title was, "El Excelentissimo Señor, y Beato Fraile, Don Antonio Bukarelly y Ursua, Jemente General de los Reinos de Nueba España."

He passed the morning in tormenting reflections, swallowing three quarts of lemonade, but without the least appetite for food; and having thus "blown off his steam," he began to reflect.

1st. He was still at **Vera Cruz.**

2d. There was no ship to sail for three weeks, so they could not turn him out before then.

3d. His father and his friends had made him advances for this adventure (to supplement Necker's deficit, I suppose), and he wanted to pay them back.

4th. He was not going to be made ridiculous by a failure before Frenchmen by any Spaniards under the sun.

5th. He meant to do it.

How?

Why, just to step out of the town some dark night without any luggage, and *walk* to Oaxaca, three hundred miles *by road*, with a liability to be stopped and impugned at every mile, and a perfect certainty of being fetched back in irons at either of the four cities on his route. He began to put his difficulties together.

He had no passport.

He was not dressed as a Spaniard.

His colloquial Spanish was miserable.

He was so utterly ignorant of the road that he did not even know by which gate he had to leave the town.

He would have to go with merely the clothes he stood in, without even change of linen; and the distance was three hundred miles.

He had his money, and would pay his way. He

would avoid the highroads, and sleep with the Indians as much as possible; he would be dressed neatly, and wear all his trinkets, and look thoroughly respectable; finally, to account for his bad Spanish, he would be a doctor from Catalan, in some parts of which more French is spoken than Spanish—a shaky "platform," but the best under the circumstances.

He fixed upon a Friday night for his plucky but almost ridiculous venture, "after setting aside about 300 gourds in quadruples." What *does* this mean? I believe that a "gourd" was the slang word for a small Mexican coin, say the sixth of a real, or a penny; but why set them aside in quadruples? I cannot help thinking that it means mesmer-caliogstro hanky-panky, the more so as our friend was not satisfied with Christianity, but was decidedly encyclopædist. If so, the spirits had rapped wrong; for after stepping out over the low walls of Vera Cruz, and blundering about all night among the sand-dunes surrounding that city, he was glad to knock up an Indian, and, climbing the walls again, go home.

The next night at three o'clock he made a fresh and permanent start, and guiding himself by the constellation Virgo, held steadily westward, parallel with the road, but a little distance from it, so as to avoid being seen; and having made some cautious inquiries of a muleteer, found himself in the afternoon nine leagues on his road, crossing a wide plain, with the glorious white peak of Orizava, behind which lay the object of his hopes, straight in his path, thrusting up its sharp straight peak into the summer air, snow-white, awful, with a little cloud of smoke crowning the topmost crater.

The plain was long and wild, not a house or habitation to be seen, and the sun burning him into a fierce thirst, yet there was no water. He managed to get along by picking and eating the common prickly pear, which grew wild; but peeling them in a hurry, he got those agonizing little spines into his tongue, and was rather worse off than before. Few pains are more exasperating than this. Stay-at-home travellers may produce a slight imitation of it by eating the seeds of the wild rose without taking out the stones.

At length, when nearly spent, he came upon a shepherd's hut, and cast himself upon their hospitality, which was promptly accorded. After having drunk a quart of water, two quarts of milk, and, regardless of colic, topping up with two quarts of lemonade, he ate some roast turkey, paid four reals (2s.), and felt a man again. This host asked him whether he was not a European Spaniard, for that he took such long strides in his walk, as the Creoles are not used to do. Ermenonville, to account for his bad Spanish, said that he came from Catalonia.

Slipping away in the darkness of the morning without awakening his host, he came to the river Jamupa, about 200 yards broad; he was just stripping to swim, when he caught sight of a canoe with no one near it, and getting in, ferried himself over triumphantly. When he got to the other side, he saw a negro, of whom he facetiously demanded a real for doing his work. He gave the poor negro his fare, however, and went on his way.

He found afterwards that he had escaped a great danger. The real passage was lower down, where there was a picquet of soldiers; without passport, with nothing but his walking-stick, he would certainly have been arrested, sent back, and ruined. He had fortunately taken the wrong road.

For the next six leagues he did not see a single human being, only many wild turkeys and rabbits; but at the end of this distance he came to a rancho, where there was no one but a very old negress, who was impudent to him, and would give him nothing but bad beans; so, leaving this aged witch, he passed on over torrent-bed after torrent-bed, holding no water, but delighting him with their botanical treasures. Yuccas sixty feet high were on them, and a gigantic arum of great beauty. This night he reached the rancho of Calabuca.

He passed that night with a suspicious host, drenched to the skin by a shower which came sweeping from the hill like a water-spout; but the morrow was bright, Orizava loomed higher and higher across his path, and he went hopefully on across the desolate, torrent-furrowed plain, and came to the end of it. The first range of mountains, covered by hanging woods, was before him, and in front of it rushed a very swift torrent. Crossing this and another river by bridges, he met with but very few adventures until he arrived at San Lorenzo; and having refreshed himself, started on at once for Cordova, having succeeded in hiring a horse, and having passed a guard-house unobserved in the rain. After one night more upon the road, he reached the city of Cordova. It was a noble city, principally of stone, with large places in it, some as big as the Place Vendôme, surrounded by Moorish arcades, and with magnificent fountains. Here he was not noticed at all, and spending one night, pushed on to Orizava, a similar city to Cordova, which he was also allowed to enter unmolested.

Orizava must be one of the most beautiful places in the whole world. It is a handsome town of some 5,000 inhabitants, of exquisite temperature, and deluged everywhere with crystal springs and fountains. The vegetation is so luxuriant that it bursts up everywhere in the streets; the scenery also is amazingly fine, the town being surrounded by a palisade of jagged, wooded mountains. But there is one thing at Orizava which overpowers and crushes everything else in the place: there is a perpetual presence and awful *thing* there which keeps in a stranger's thoughts before anything,—its mountain; 15,000 feet above the house-tops towers the great crystal peak of Orizava, a nearly perfect cone. One thing struck and intensely delighted D'Ermenonville; while the town was still buried in darkness and sleep, aloft the topmost peak of the mountain was blazing in saffron-coloured morning before the coming sun.

After deep thought our worthy doctor pursued the following course of action: going to a convent of Carmelites, he obtained audience of the sub-prior, and told him confidentially his tale. He was a physician and a botanist, who had been travelling now for three years, and one day, during a storm, had made a vow to go on foot to the shrine of

Nostra Señora de la Solidad at Oaxaca. Now he would be deeply indebted to the good father if he would advise him whether or no he could not, by charitable deeds, get a dispensation from foot travelling for the rest of the journey.

All this was by way of bringing on a discussion about the distance and the route. After a learned discussion, the good monk gave it as his opinion that the doctor might certainly acquit himself to our Lady by alms, whereupon the doctor pulled out 7*l.* 10*s.* and offered it to him. He would have none of it, however, saying that it was three times too much, and so extinguished all the doctor's hopes of bribing him. The sub-prior introduced him to some of the other monks, and they showed him their garden, the doctor greatly delighting them by pointing out the names and uses of their plants. They were about parting, the doctor having gained nothing, when, as a last resource, he asked if there were not a convent of Carmelites at Oaxaca, and expressed a wish to visit it. The sub-prior's tongue was loosened at once, and he unsuspectingly gave the enraptured doctor a full and careful account of the route to the place of his hopes.

He left the door of the convent and walked away instantly towards the mountain. Crossing the river which bathes the town, he was stopped by the Customhouse officers at the *tête du pont*, and asked where he was going. Seeing only a well-dressed gentlemanly man, with a walking-stick, they were perfectly unsuspicious; and finding he was a doctor, got him to doctor their chief, after which he walked away, and soon left the beautiful town of Orizava behind him.

According to his description, the Mexican Indian of the Spanish times must have been one of the most simple and affectionate beings in the world. He stayed the next night in one of their huts, and they treated him with great kindness; but what struck him as most noteworthy, was the extraordinary amount of domestic affection which they exhibited towards one another. The host was a half-starved Indian, who came home dog-tired with work, yet the affectionate welcome which he received, and his gentle demeanour towards his wife and children, seem to have impressed the kind-hearted Frenchman profoundly.

By two o'clock in the morning, in an intensely cold mist, he was passing along the scarped and terraced road which leads over the shoulder of Orizava into Tecuacan. Although the mountain was so near, it was quite hidden, and at last topping the shoulder he found himself among oaks, and in a new country, the temperate country of Mexico;—geraniums, heliotropes, mistletoes, fuchsias, *tradas cantias* (? *Tradescantia errata*), all blooming around him, while the road was covered with beautiful turf; and at seven o'clock in the morning he arrived in safety at a village called Clapulco, famous for the manufacture of a drink (Pulque) from the Agave Americana. They cut off the crown of the aloe, and having scooped out a hollow in the lower part of the stump, put it on again; into this the sap from the crown drops. When the plant is exhausted, it dies;

fresh plantations are kept always in bearing by propagation.

Crossing now the splendid plain of Tecuacan, with six cities, and innumerable villages and farms, bearing every kind of grain known in Europe, and irrigated like Lombardy, D'Ermenonville came to the city of Tecuacan, but did not go in. Having stripped to cross the river and avoid the town, he no sooner got into the water than an innumerable number of small turtles, which he had not observed, jumped in also, frightening him terribly. He touched at one of the suburbs and bought some bread, and struck out once more for St. Francisco, and meeting with no noticeable adventure slept there, and by six o'clock in the morning was at St. Antonio, where he expected to get horses.

Here he was very much impressed by the high altar in the cathedral. The two larger candlesticks on each side of it are real growing plantains, thirty feet high; he describes the effect as superb.

Here he got a mule, and riding pleasantly along, passing many bignonias, passion flowers, and Cerie (a large cactacean, in English torch-thistle), thirty to forty feet high and fifty feet in diameter, the fall of one of whose gigantic leaves would be fatal, he came to St. Sebastian, where, getting horses, he pursued the valley of the Tecuacan to Los Ceres. He was now comfortably mounted, and began to get over the ground; reaching Aquiotepec by the valley of the Rio Grande de Tecuacan, which had now narrowed itself into a gorge.

At length even the gorge came to an end, and

D'Ermenonville sees the Rio Grande.

he had to ascend the barrier by a path two feet broad, and extremely insecure, with the roar of the Rio Grande in his ears. He could not bear to sit on his horse, but getting giddy, and finding himself trembling in every limb, he dismounted and led it. The precipice below them he calculates at 1,800 feet, and in some places the zigzag was so sharp that the horse could barely turn himself; at some of the most slippery and awful places there was nothing but the branch of a tree to save them from destruction. It was, however, the highway of the country, and the only route to Oaxaca. After five hours of terror and danger he reached the summit. With the still tortuous Rio Grande on his right, stupendous mountains all around, and a peak only eighteen miles from Oaxaca straight before him, he continued his route.

He now got to Truccallan, an old and beautiful town, planted thickly with fine trees, and bubbling with cool fountains and rills brought from the mountains, in which the population bathed continually. The church was a fine one; and in the evening at the inn he made the acquaintance of a very jolly friar, who agreed to go on with him next day if he would only wait till he had said mass.

It was a source of consolation to the good monk that he waited to perform his devotions, for the passage of the Rio Grande next day was a very uncomfortable business. It was 400 yards in breadth, and breast deep. A naked Indian led their horses, while they lay on their backs, the poor brutes trembling and feeling their way, and the doctor giddy with the swift rushing current. They now left the Rio Grande of Tecuacan, and entered the deep gorge or cañon through which comes the tributary river, the Las Vueltas. In some places it is 100 yards broad, in others not a dozen; and before they were through it at Asletlanca, they had crossed the river seventy times. There was, however, another route over the mountains, for they had seen a Government courier, who told them that he was going over the mountain, and should be in Oaxaca early the next morning; passing still along the Las Vueltas ("the river of turns"), he came, on one of the most memorable days in his life, to Galiatitlan, where to his boundless delight he saw the cochineal feeding upon the nopal which supported it.

Topping now the last mountain, that of La Costa, by an ascent almost as bad as that of Aquiotepec, he looked upon his promised land, the great plain of Oaxaca. It begun at his feet and stretched away in boundless beauty towards Guatemala. Fifty villages were in sight, built with dazzling white stone, and roofed with red tiles as in Lorraine; the extent of the plain he puts at about 120 miles.

But what took his attention almost beyond anything else was a glorious lily, the lily of St. Jago, the *Amaryllis formossimus*, which covered the hill with splendid blood-red blossoms. Neglecting his more useful botany in a devout contemplation of this superb flower, he descended on the end of his journey, St. Juan del Rè.

The first sight almost that his eyes rested on was

a plantation of nopals, and his good luck was in the ascendant. The negroes in these Spanish times, although allowed to fill municipal offices, were treated socially with the greatest contempt. Now this plantation belonged to the Alcalde of the town, who was what Strewel Peter would call a Kohlpeck Rabenschwartzemohr—an intensely black man, with an intensely black wife; to them enter an elegant French gentleman, bowing and kootooing, hat in hand, apologizing and flattering, and you may conceive the result. The unsuspecting and delighted negro laid his whole secret bare before the Frenchman, and in the openness of his heart took him into his garden and explained everything to him.

Starting from here after his dinner, on a wretchedly bad horse, with a terror of certain banditti before him, he came, in the mysterious twilight, on a religious procession; passing into Attetla with them, he made his way to the rectory there, and kissing the sleeve of the rector, got directed to the Casas Reale, or post-house. What Attetla is like since the Revolution I have no idea, but the main square of it, dominated by an enormous Dominican convent, must have been extremely fine and curious. The buildings, he tells us, were a mixture of Roman and Arabesque.

Starting on once more in the morning, his mare, heavy in foal, gave out, and he discharged her and his "topith" (post-boy), once more proceeding on foot. The country road through hedge-twined convolvuli was charming beyond measure; and as he approached Oaxaca the plantations of nopal got more thick and frequent. At length, with the air of a man who had been out for a walk, he sauntered into the city, and up to an inn close to the convent of Nostra Señora del Solidad; his journey half over, but nothing whatever done.

This splendid city, of about 6,000 inhabitants, is 3,200 yards long, and 2,000 broad. The beauty of the buildings, of the domes, pinnacles, and arcades, was very great; the streets wide and well paved; the suburbs planted with nopal and many kinds of productive shrubs. The slope below the town is bathed by a beautiful river, and the town is deluged with fine water by aqueducts. The temperature was 68° above freezing (Fahrenheit) in the morning, and 81° at noon, giving it the climate of perpetual spring: "an actual paradise," he says, "were it possessed by any other race."

The morals of Oaxaca were not to our good Frenchman's taste, the more particularly that his whole soul was taken up with the importance of his enterprise. He could scarcely believe in his good fortune on being allowed to go unmolested so far, and determined to profit by the occasion. He needed repairs to his watch, and going to the watchmaker's, after a slender flirtation with his wife, made acquaintance with him, and through him got directed to a trunkmaker's.

Here he bought eight trunks, two feet long and fourteen inches wide, for four shillings a-piece; they were well and strongly made, and he says that he could not have got better in Paris. He took the keys of them, and walked out into the city as though in a dream.

Wandering into the suburbs, he came to a very beautiful market-garden, in which were rows of nopals running east and west, four feet high, and other beautiful productions. He stepped in and asked to buy flowers. While his flowers were getting ready, he feasted his eyes on the "grana," the cochineal; looking at one plant, he considers that you could not have broken off a leaf without crushing hundreds of insects.

Leaving the garden he went to visit an apothecary, a Don Antonio Piba, who had a garden. While he was here, he was annoyed by a great Spanish lady sweeping into the garden, in a black mantle with gold fringe, and looking at him. She had come to set eyes on a Frenchman out of curiosity. However much D'Ermenonville might have been annoyed, we thank him for telling us this trivial incident. For a veiled Spanish lady, in a black mantilla with gold fringe, standing still in a bright, hot, sunny garden, among a dazzle of flowers, makes a picture worthy of the brush of Mr. Walker.

He found an inn kept by a Frenchman, and enjoyed himself much, going to bed early, for on the morrow he had determined on the great venture. Before daylight he was up, and taking two Indian servants of the inn, he went quickly to the market-garden where the day before he had bought the flowers. The negro proprietor, whom he had not seen the day before, was barely awake, and D'Ermenonville represented himself as a physician wishing to buy some nopal leaves with the cochineal on them as a plaster for the gout. The case was urgent, he said, and they would not quarrel about price. The negro instantly gave him as much as he wanted for two reals, and D'Ermenonville, throwing him a dollar, wrapped his treasure gently in towels, and posted homewards, meeting not a soul in the street. He says that he would have sung with joy, but was afraid of being overheard. It was not long before he had packed the cactus leaves in the boxes.

Wonderfully stimulated by his success, and hearing that vanilla was to be procured close to the town, he determined to attempt the smuggling of that also, and so, disguised as a Spaniard, he went at noon on horseback, with one attendant, and after a ride of twenty-four miles, succeeded in bringing back a fagot of stems of the vanilla plant, rolled up in arum leaves and linen, without having excited the suspicions of a soul.*

Quietly also, and without consulting his French host, he got five post-horses to be ready for him early the next morning, and having broken his sudden departure to his surprised landlord, he spent half the night packing the cochineal and vanilla in his boxes; and at daybreak, mounted on one of his horses, with the others led before him, he was rapidly pacing on his way to St. Juan del Rè.

He was there by eleven o'clock, and went at once

---

* The vanilla which he got must have been the kind known now among druggists as *Vera Cruz* vanilla. It is a pod of the *Vanilla satroa*. The scent and flavour are well known to the eaters of chocolate.

to his friend the negro Alcalde, with a view to buying some more cochineal. He was away, but his wife was in, who at the mere sight of a dollar let him have as much as he would, and he continued his rapid journey. The mountain of La Costa was passed, and he had looked on Oaxaca for the last time, and slept that night at Galiatitlan. Here he opened his boxes for air, and took a moonlight ramble in the church, where, after digging up some Amaryllises from the grave of a dead Spaniard, he says that he felt forcibly reminded of that beautiful passage in Young's "Night Thoughts:"

> "Let us, while through the vale we speed,
> Cull every floweret by the way."

Which is interesting in two ways: first, as showing that this book was read in France in those days; and secondly, as showing that the habit of quoting twaddle because it is written in a foreign language is not confined to the English nation.

Here he secured some more nopal, and singularly enough this supplementary quantity was the only part which he preserved during the exasperating delays which followed. From the Indian gardener here also he gained information about the culture of the cochineal, almost as valuable as the cochineal itself.

All went well; the good-humoured Frenchman won his way rapidly back, and indeed met with the kindest of treatment from the Indians. The three races, Spaniards, negroes, and Indians, seem (when free) to have been on an absolute political equality; indeed the Alcaldes of the villages seem more often to have been Indian or negro than Spaniard. They were most just in their decisions, and he got on admirably with them; but at Tecuacan he came across his first Custom-house. He had been able to pass round it on his inward journey, but now, loaded with baggage, he was forced to pass through.

The town seemed nearly deserted, and he was nearly through it, when he was brought up by a mounted Custom-house officer, who ordered him to come back to the Custom-house. His heart was in his mouth, but he put a bold face on it and swaggered in; he was most courteously received, and on his saying that he was merely a French botanist, was politely told that he could proceed. One of the officers seeming still suspicious, however, he opened his boxes and showed them the vanilla. They did not know what it was! But on his opening the box with the cochineal they at once exclaimed, "Acqui sta grana" (There is cochineal). They were quite satisfied at being told that it was wanted as an unguent for the gout, and laughed heartily at seeing a collection of the plants and seeds of the commonest weeds in the country.

Going to the Alcalde for horses he saw a mirror, and was horrified at his personal appearance, wondering greatly at the politeness shown by the courteous, high-bred, Spanish gentlemen to such a tatterdemalion as himself. Matters were still prosperous, and at Clapulco he was delighted and refreshed with the cool snows of Orizava, and without mishap arrived at the gate of that fine city.

The guard-house was shut up, and in the darkness

he hoped to slip by. Suddenly, however, his bridle was seized, and he began his usual peroration, "Gentlemen, I am a travelling French physician, collecting——" He was interrupted by a cry, "Ah! great heaven, Señor, where have you been so long? you are he who snatched from death the superintendent of the other guard-house; for the love of God come and see my wife." So saying, the unhappy young man clasped him in his arms and persuaded him. The Frenchman went of course, but he had to tell the husband that his wife's days were numbered. They did not talk of searching his boxes now; he went away to walk about the city of the great mountain.

At Cordova was his next danger; but the lazy Spaniards examined his boxes so very lightly that, little dreaming what they were doing, they let the smuggler pass. This took place no less than three times between here and La Punta, one fellow recognising the *grana*, and calling our friend fool for going so far to get what he could get abundance of at Vera Cruz. D'Ermenonville left this pretentious gentleman quite in the dark.

No other interruption, except countless squabbles about horses, took place until he came sneaking up to the walls of Vera Cruz, like a truant schoolboy whose father has believed him at school. What if the Governor should discover that he had been beyond the limits of his jurisdiction? And the Custom-house also? And suppose the two ships for which he was hastening should have sailed?

It was before daybreak that he found himself before

the Orizava gate, and thinking that his appearance would attract attention, scaled the walls in a quiet place, and running home changed his clothes, coming up to the *inside* of the gate when he had done so. What was his horror to find his horses and his treasure gone! They had only, however, been sent round to the Mexico gate for examination, and by running he got to them before the officers had got hold of them. The guards wished to send them to the main Custom-house, and he rallied them. " Did they not remember the French physician ? " he asked ; " and were they not men enough to examine his trunks themselves ?" The sleepy soldiers did so, and after a few objections bade him depart in God's name, which he was not slow in doing. Scarcely a soul was about in the streets, and he was soon, after his three weeks' anxiety, safely locked up in his bedroom, planting his nopals.

He soon sallied out to find out how the land lay. He was perfectly unsuspected ; every one believed that he had been at the baths of Madilina. Don Antonio Uloa, the most inquisitive of his friends, was at Mexico. M. de Fersen, his fellow-countryman, was sly about his not having been all this time at Madilina, and D'Ermenonville confessed to him that he had been a little trip as far as Orizava, at which M. de Fersen professed profound astonishment, thinking he could not have got so far in the time. He also informed him that the ship of M. de Harisson, in which he meant to sail, did not go for another month. He was so far safe.

How were the nopals to be preserved on board

ACCLIMATIZATION ADVENTURE.

ship, and got through the Custom-house, as he expresses it, "in the sight of all Israel?" Two terrible problems.

While going about the streets and seeing after the necessary boxes, he heard to his great delight that a ship was to sail that very week for Cape St. François, the captain of which he had known, but unluckily had cut and quarrelled on this account: Captain D—— had the habit of coming into his room and talking in such a free and easy way about politics and religion, as made D'Ermenonville laugh at first, but after his persistence in it made him suspect the captain of being a political spy. The botanist of the eldest son of the Church here got into buckram directly, and drily and officially informed him "that it by no means suited his station to meddle with affairs which naturally belonged to the civil and ecclesiastical powers, to whose imperative decisions and superior intelligence it were better that he should submit."

That was all very well and very discreet at the time, but it was rather unfortunate now.

But it all came to a good end. His friend had forgotten and forgiven, and the cochineal was triumphantly carried away to the French islands, and acclimatized.

THE OLD SLAVE TRADE.

I HAVE heard it stoutly maintained that the horrors of the Middle Passage were increased very much by the efforts of our cruisers to put down the Slave-trade. Of this I do not believe one word, and for these reasons. We made the negro more valuable, and therefore it was worth while to treat him better; and he could not have been treated much worse and live. Besides, it is an abomination so iniquitous that it can only vary slightly in degree.

I once got a great deal of information on the interior economy of a slaver from a man in my employment. The details, however, were so inconceivably detestable that I am unable to reproduce them. The man was a rambling young Portuguese sailor, who had now been to sea so long that all countries and all peoples were alike to him, and would as soon have chucked his kit aboard Captain Kydd's ship or Captain Avery's ship, and sailed under the skull and cross-bones, as he would under the Union Jack or the stars and stripes. He was captured on board a slaver and condemned to two years in the road-gang at Sierra Leone, which he took with a sailor's philosophy—as one of the things which *occur* like gales of wind or short commons; but of the life on board the slaver he talked with no philosophy at all. He spat when he spoke of it.

Let us see how it was in the year 1693 by a man who seems to have been a tolerably good fellow, and who claims for himself an exceptional degree of humanity.

One Captain Phillips, while doing his business on the great waters, had the misfortune to come across three French men-of-war, who seized his ship and carried him into Brest a prisoner. How long he was detained he does not say, but after a time he got back to England, exceedingly out at elbows, and for some time, like Major Pawkins, rather loafed away his time than otherwise.

There existed at this time a company called the African Company, which traded to Guinea for gold, ivory, and negroes, carrying, of course, the negroes to America, and fetching the gold and ivory home. A certain worthy, "John Jeffreys, Esquire," was at this time sub-governor, and his elder brother, Sir Jeffrey Jeffreys, was the beloved friend and patron of the needy, but not for those times unscrupulous Captain Phillips.

Things seemed to suit very well. Here was this agreeable young Captain Phillips to be provided for and kept out of mischief. What could Sir Jeffrey do better than use him in a slaving adventure? He had been at it before, and it would almost certainly bring money. Sir Jeffrey put his hand in his pocket, and bought him the *Hannibal*, of 450 tons, giving her to Captain Phillips, and inducing his brother and several other merchants to go shares in the cargo, and to allow him to sail for the African Company.

He was now fairly on his legs again. He got everything in order and sailed away, making one of a goodly squadron enough. The *East India Merchant*, Shurley, 30 guns, was the leading ship—Shurley having seen a good deal more of this rather dirty work than any one else. Then came the *Hannibal* (our ship), Phillips, 30 guns; *Mediterranean*, Daniel (probably he of the *Terra Nova*), 24; *Jeffrey*, Simes, 12; *Fortune*, Captain Hereford, 12; and lastly the *Eagle* packet, Perry.

Off the South Foreland in a fog the *India Merchant* got ashore, and as Sir Jeffrey Jeffreys had a large share in her also, Phillips dashed to her assistance in a boat with his best men, carrying an anchor to warp her off with. He found Captain Shurley in a state of distraction, his men refusing to obey him, which leads Phillips into a discussion about the treatment a captain should give his men, in which he strongly hints that Captain Shurley had a temper. He, Phillips, always treated his men well, he says, and pointedly declines to make any accusation against Captain Shurley to the contrary. But he gives us two or three instances of old ship life which are interesting, as are all events showing how pirates were manufactured. One captain used to wear out his cables by keeping his men passing it through the hawse-holes and coiling it away, merely to prevent them having a moment's relaxation, or, as he said, to plague the dogs. Another man he knew would throw a chip overboard and make a crew lower a boat to pick it up; he would then make sail and keep them rowing for six or seven hours after him, in pure "spleen." Things might be mended now, without keeping our men in cotton wool, but things were infinitely worse then. My brother's buccaneer sings:—

"Likewise the merchant captains, with hearts as hard as stone,
Who flog men, and keel-haul them, and starve them to the bone."

The only result worth getting from the first part of his voyage is this; he consulted his officers on the subject of bearing up for Plymouth, after an accident, showing that the captain of those times did not always consider himself utterly and entirely an irresponsible person. He would not listen to a word they had got to say, but he certainly consulted them.

Sailing on the 5th of October, by the 21st of November he came in sight of the Peak of Teneriffe, computing it to be seventy-five miles distance. All he saw of it above the horizon was the last peak of the crater with its broken lip to the left; about as far as I can make out one-fifth of the whole peak, or some 2,400 feet, leaving over 9,000 feet buried beneath the horizon at seventy-five miles distance. An intelligent reader may compare the results of the calculations of this rough sailor with those of the great Humboldt about the same peak. I think that he gives the extreme distance from which it is visible as 180 miles: by allowing a little for refraction, this would make our captain about right.

Here Captain Phillips went near to making another unwilling journey to France. Sailing to the east of

Teneriffe, he became aware of two ships under the land, one of which, the largest, instantly made for him. He tacked at once to the north, not to fly, but to get ready. He did what was usual in such cases, things which must be read with respect by a landsman, grotesque as the language may appear. An idle person may laugh at hearing Captain tell us how he "clapped on our stoppers, our puddings, our plattings under our parrels," but the idle person must remember that had it not been for such men as Phillips, calculating chances, he, the idle person, would never have been born. And also to consider, that by twelve o'clock this very valiant Welshman was ready for anything which might happen, and perfectly ready to give an account of any one who dared to stop him on his Majesty's highway. He lay by for the ship which was so earnest to speak with him. We are obliged to quote Shakespeare:

> "And though it seemeth somewhat out of fashion,
> There is much care and valour in this Welchman."

It was above twenty-four hours before the mysterious stranger, in consequence of light airs, could manage to get within gunshot of our valiant Welshman, who all this while, as he says, jogged quietly along under his fighting sails, rather wondering what the stranger was, but "ready, aye ready."

She came up quietly with the English ensign flying, and only one tier of guns visible. What was she? for she was now within pistol shot. What is that? She is hauling down the English ensign.

Down went the red flag suddenly, and in its place there leaped up a round white ball, which, expanding in the breeze, showed itself to be the broad snowy banner of France; a lower tier of guns was run out, and Captain Phillips found himself suddenly and unexpectedly in the presence of a splendid French frigate.

It was four o'clock in the afternoon when the dance of death began, and they fought confusedly and furiously until ten at night. At that time the Frenchman's fore topmast came by the board, and he hauled off, being towed by his boats. So the havoc slackened and the glorious British pendant was left to droop in victorious peace above the half-ruined ship.

When they had time to draw breath they found that they had had a really great and terrible fight, and that they had won it by the English tactics of pounding steadily and rapidly into the enemy's hull, and for the main part leaving his rigging to take care of itself. The Frenchman, on the other hand, had cut the rigging of our ship to pieces, but had only killed five men and wounded thirty. Shortly after his return to England, Phillips was intensely interested by meeting a skipper who had been captured by this very French ship which he had beaten off, very shortly before the engagement, and who was actually on board the Frenchman during the fight. She was the *Louis*, of St. Malo, of 52 guns, and the *Hannibal*, of 36 guns, had beaten her off, killing seventy men. This accounts for Phillips noticing that when they hauled off "there was such dreadful howling and screeching on board of him as I never heard."

The night was a terribly anxious one. "Would he

have any more of it, or had he got enough?" If he came again he would very likely get the better of them, and then farewell to all poor Phillips' high-flown hopes. His brother was wounded, some of his best men killed, his whole crew dog-tired, and in such a state of reaction, after six hours of concentrated fury, that, even with as much punch as they could drink, they would scarcely knot the rigging. Morning was dearly welcome, and, thank God! the Frenchman *had* got enough, and was standing away to the northward, three leagues off.

The canary merchants at Orotava had watched the fight with the deepest interest, and had Phillips put into that roadstead they meant to have given the gallant fellow a present; but he sailed away, glad to have escaped, the poor ship looking miserable, as full of chips as a carpenter's yard, four shot-holes under water, chain pumps going, nothing to eat but bread and cheese—for poor cookey's coppers were knocked to pieces, and the armourer was tinkering them up—a whole suit of sails utterly ruined, surgeon, carpenter, and sailmaker all as busy as bees.

He now stood for St. Jago, doing such things as "woolding three large crows to his foremast," and in the midst of it had another alarm from a large ship. If all human experience did not point to the direct contrary, one would have thought that his men had had enough fighting for the present; but no! the men were more eager for the affray than ever, and the deck cleared in a shorter time than before. It is certain that the love of fighting grows on those who have once tasted it

A few days' prosperous sailing in the pleasant northeast trades, over the joyous, sparkling sea, under the bright, gently-moving clouds, brought him to the snug harbour of Praya, in St. Jago, the most southerly of the Cape Verds, where he intended to refit his shattered ship.

They were a little surprised at their reception, for gun after gun was fired to make them come inshore, and at last a shotted one, after which Phillips thought he would go on shore and save their powder and shot. A few miserable-looking soldiers, armed with lances and swords, more like skeletons than men, received him and led him to their commandant, who seemed to Phillips to be much too gentlemanly for a Portuguese. Indeed he was not, but an old "Flanderkin," deluded here by Portuguese promises, and desirous of getting away again. He told them that, seeing so many shot-holes in their sails, he had thought them pirates, who often came here under English colours, which was the reason he had fired at them. Phillips, like a real sailor, the instant that he found the old gentleman wanted to "run" offered to smuggle him away, but the old man said wearily, that it was no use, he was too much watched. The deputy-governor, a mere boy, galloping up soon after, was supercilious to Phillips, who paid him in his own coin, and treated him with extreme contempt. Sailor as he was, he had hung about Sir John Jeffrey's house long enough to know how snobs were treated.

Sunday was spent at the town of St. Jago, some seven miles away, with the governor of the island, a fantastic little Portuguese of fifty, with a black wig down to his waist. All that Phillips got out of him was some Madeira, so hot and muddy that it nearly made him sick; but out of Phillips this dexterous governor got a good clouded cane with a silver handle. To make things pleasant, and get some provisions out of the little man, Phillips asked him to dinner on board. The little fellow frankly stated that his people would never permit it. It was, as it appeared, the custom for English pirates to seduce governors on board their ships and keep them there until they were supplied with provisions, for which they paid in bills payable in London, but drawn on John A. Nokes, the "Hookey Walker" of those times; nay, the much too celebrated Captain Avery, whose very improving biography I hope soon to write, had even gotten goods out of the deluded governor of the island of St. Thomas and paid him with an order on Aldgate pump. The governor would deal for nothing but cash.

Next day, however, the market got brisker, the sailors buying all manner of fruit, poultry, and of course monkeys, for old shirts and drawers. He began laying in a fine store of fresh provisions and water; careened his ship and stopped the shot-holes, and began mending her rigging. His account of the island is not uninteresting; and he gives us the history of it. At this time its principal trade was salt, the Newfoundlanders going there to load salt for the curing of their fish. This bay contains the most enormous quantity of fish, much of which the sailors salted and carried away; you could catch them as fast as you could haul them in.

In six days he had refitted and sailed away past Fogo, which was in eruption then as it is now, towards the coast of Guinea, which he made in a fortnight at Cape Mount; and coming in fourteen leagues to Cape Monserrado (Mesurada,* close to Monrovia in Liberia) he, to his great astonishment and pleasure, just as he was clearing for action, found his old friend, Captain Shurley of the *East India Merchant*, in a mess as usual, praying for help, just as he was when they got him off in the Downs; he had got struck by lightning now, and had his foremast and fore-yard broken to pieces with it.

Here they stayed over Christmas, wooding, watering, and buying provisions. Here they found a loose Scotchman among the natives, who said that he had been shipwrecked and was the only survivor, offering to ship himself with Phillips. Our captain, however, did not at all like the looks of him, thinking him only a pirate; and when from other sources he found out the real tale, he had good reason to congratulate himself on his refusal. One would have liked to hear this gentleman's account of the matter from his own mouth, it is so entirely horrid. He had belonged to a small pirate brigantine commanded by one Herbert, and while on this coast the crew had quarrelled, and had fought until there was no one unwounded left to manage the ship except this man, who drove her ashore at the

* Both, one would think, mere corruptions of Montserrat, or Monte Serrato, a name which is like its near relation Montague. But I think that Campbell (Fairfield) is a more frequently recurring family name than even Montague.

end of the bay and escaped, leaving all the others to die of their wounds. The imagination can picture to itself few things more unutterably horrible. Under the scorching African sun the internecine fight between men who had utterly forgotten God and had abandoned themselves to their own lusts took place; think of their frightful language; think of the pauses in the strife, more horrible than the strife itself; think of the dread uncertainty about the time of its renewal, of hell's breaking loose once more; of the final cessation, when no one could fight longer, and there were only the wounded wretches crying out in the burning heat, like Dives, for a drop of water to cool their parched tongues; until there was only one man left, who moaned feebly and intermittently— and then silence. Think of what those men's lives had been, and what their deaths must have been like, and say whether a more ghastly crew was ever steered by human hand, than this steered by the solitary Scotchman towards the mangrove swamp of Monserrado.

Of course that man Shurley was not ready again —enough to tire the patience of a saint, keeping us waiting here with all our stores on board in the burning sun; however, we wrote our letters and sent them by other ships—among others, one to our agent on the gold coast, telling him to get as many negroes together as he could, for that we were coming. Even when we did get to sea, this left-handed Shurley was instantly taken violently ill of a fever and ague. A most tiresome fellow.

At Satos, 100 miles from Monserrado, they made

another halt, but not for long. Sailing on they came to Sangreni, which makes in a heap of high trees, and which is the beginning of the grain coast.* At Sino, which is known by a tree making like a ship with the topsail loose, he bought, for a bar of iron, 1,000 pounds' weight of pepper to mix in the messes of his negroes, and keep them from the flux, as well as from the dry belly-ache; for the inside plenishing of these cattle must be studied if you are to make them pay, and have a comfortable pew at Limehouse church in your old age. He did not buy Malagetta pepper enough, this good Phillips, or the niggers were perverse, like Mrs. Prig's patients, who went off dead, and kept her waiting for her tea; or the stars in their courses fought against him: one way or another, not to keep a secret from my readers longer than is necessary, this voyage was not successful, and our captain had to worship at his native Brecknock, instead of the aristocratic Limehouse.

We were not very particular, even according to the lights of those times, but we loved our brother dearly. Our brother had fought well by our side in that action with the French frigate, and had got wounded, and now our brother died, like the brother of any negro whom we were going to catch. We, Phillips, were very sad and miserable. He was only sixteen years old, and we were very fond of the pretty plucky lad. We rowed

---

* The "Grain Coast" (roughly speaking, conterminous with the "Liberia" of which we have heard so much), was first called so, I believe, from the fact of the Malagetta pepper being the main article of commerce there. It lies at the lower point of the great shoulder of West Africa.

the corpse a mile to seaward, and the prayers of the church having been read, we committed his body to the deep in twenty-five fathoms of water, not without tears. The *Hannibal* fired sixteen guns at quarter minute's time, the number of years which our bonny boy "had lived in this uncertain world;" and that blundering ass Shurley fired ten. He was buried off Growa, this boy, bearing N.W., and ten leagues east of Cape Palmas, near which the land is high and hummocky. After this we sailed sadly away to get our niggers.

Coming now to the ivory coast, he found the negroes very shy; as he thinks, from some tricks which "Long Ben" (Avery) had been playing on them. They even jumped overboard when the ship's dog barked, but they would do but little business at all. Trade was very slack all along the ivory coast, but a little more brisk along the gold coast. The gold brought to him was mainly in the form of wrought fetishes or charms.

As they drifted deeper eastward into the Gulf of Guinea, the weather grew less brisk and healthy, and a steaming fog enveloped them, the wind dying quite away, and making them extremely anxious about the health of the crew (Captain Shurley fell very ill at once, of course); and at last came to Axem, the Dutch fort on the slave coast.

The colonial policy of the Dutch seems to have failed by its very severity. The monopoly which they had conceded to their own Guinea Company was inconceivably exclusive. All Dutch ships not belonging to the Company trading in these waters were treated not merely as enemies, but as actual pirates; the ship and goods were confiscated, the men sent to the mines, and the officers put to death; the powers of life and death being vested in the governors of forts, without appeal to Europe, without any appeal home—probably the most ferocious commercial code which the world had ever seen. It was inoperative, however, for interlopers abounded, and both men and officers fought with such terrible resolution that the Government ships were loth to meddle with their own countrymen driven to desperation.

The factors of the Dutch Guinea Company were also used to cheat their own masters by dealing with the interlopers; and so the chief fiscal was always rowing about the coast to take them unawares. Should any goods not supplied by them be found in the fort, the unhappy governor was instantly sent to the mine either to be imprisoned, or made to act as a common soldier in that dreadful climate. The Governor of Axem was getting drunk with Phillips and Shurley on board their ship, when he was suddenly stricken speechless with horror at the sight of a large canoe with many men in it. Captain Phillips, in his capacity as host, offered to blow it in pieces if it gave any annoyance to his guest; and, indeed, had run out a gun with that intention, when his guest begged him to desist, and, leaping into a little canoe, hurriedly went on shore, lying on the pit of his stomach. He thought it was the fiscal, and that he was a ruined man: it, however, was not.

Coming to the English fort of Succandy, they found the unhappy factor raving mad, and cursing in his bed, and his second, a young Christ's Hospital lad, in command, who told them the pitiable story of his chief. He had, it seemed, brought up a beautiful young mulatto girl, and had fallen in love with her. Just as they were on the eve of being married, her mother, bribed by the commander of the Dutch fort at the mine, spirited her away. The poor man went mad, and his Dutch rival, not contented with that, incited the negroes against him after this; who, taking advantage of his unhappy condition, plundered his fort and cut him in pieces.

Passing the chief Dutch settlement of "the Mine," they came to their own castle of Cabo Corce, or Cape Coast Castle, the English capital of those parts,[*] which he describes, with its great tank and its orange gardens, where they sat drinking pleasantly with the factors, firing eleven of the ship's guns at every health. Here they landed thirty soldiers in as good health as ever they were; but in the two months they stayed one half were dead, and the other half hardly strong enough to bury their dead comrades. A duel here between one of his trumpeters and a sergeant of the force leads Captain Phillips into a digression on the former, in which he gives a slight sketch of that gentleman's life, which had been so outrageously and consistently disreputable, as to be actually laughable.

Passing on from fort to fort, and ever drawing nearer to that evil corner, the bight of Benin, they began to fall sick, Phillips being unable to sleep, and Shurley getting worse. At last, at Acra, poor Shurley made his last mistake—and died, to Phillips'

[*] Miss Landon died here.

great grief. Of course he had refused to make any will.

They were now fairly off the slave coast, which is backed by the kingdom of Dahomey, of evil reputation, and very soon began to hear of the chattels they had come after. A canoe came out with three women and four children to sell; but they were mere skeletons and unable to stand—damaged articles, which so old a hand as Phillips would not look at, particularly at the money. Moreover he was off the Alampa coast, where the negroes are esteemed the worst and most washy of any that are brought to the West Indies. Those most in demand, he tells us, were gold coast, or Coromantine,* which he had passed, and which are worth 3*l*. or 4*l*. more than the Whydah or Papa negroes; these again are preferred before the Angola (10° S.); and, as we said before, these Alampas were worst of all: so he arrived at Whydah.

This wicked place is the most beautiful on the Guinea coast: beautiful champaigns and small ascending hills are diversified with ever lovely groves of wild orange and other trees, among which wander fair rivers filled with fine fish. Swift death lurks in the swamps by the sea, however, and in the hills behind it are enacted the abominations of Dahomey.

Our factory at this time lay in a swamp, so that scarce any white man sent down to it from the higher lands lived to tell the tale. Had fever not

---

* Is it not Marryat who gives us the wonderful negro refrain, beginning,

"Father was a Coromantee,
Mother was a Mingo"?

been sufficient, the musquitoes would have, in time, killed any one for want of sleep: "the cursed spight of this little flie" was enough to make a strong man ill. A few mud huts and a trunk for slaves completed the building, and close by was the enclosure for burying the dead whites, horribly called "the hog yard." To this place, garrisoned by brave and faithful gold coast negroes, one of whom could have beaten ten Whydans, the slaves were collected from the upper country, and sent in boats to the ship, as the weather served, sometimes a hundred at a time.

The next movement in this creditable business was to be carried, some eight or ten of them, in hammocks up to the king's town inland, and bargain with that filthy old vagabond. They found him drinking brandy, most ready to trade, and had a dinner with him, which I will spare the reader; greed will swallow anything, and Phillips says that he was not a squeamish man (and indeed I think he speaks truth), but this dinner was nearly too much for *him*. The king asked for poor Shurley, and on being told he was dead, broke into loud lamentations, declaring that he had promised to bring him mortar guns, silks, and I know not what. Mr. Clay, the new captain of the *British Merchant*, told him that there were no such things on board; but he insisted that Mr. Clay was keeping them for himself. At last the old thief was pacified by large promises, and the following iniquitous bargain was struck.

They were to have warehouses and lodgings assigned

The Old Slave Trade.

to them; a man was to be sent out with a bell to summon all men who had slaves to bring them to the trunk for sale, and Captain Phillips was to buy one day, and Captain Clay the other. The price for a good man slave was about 100 pounds of small cowry shells, or 3*l.* 15*s.* They were not always paid for in shells, however; many other goods were taken, especially brass basins to cut up into ornaments.

So the trade began. There follow here details impossible to give, unutterable, abominable, yet exactly tallying with those given to me 150 years after by my Portuguese servant. Four hours a day of it was enough to reduce Phillips, who was no girl, to a fearful state of ill-health. Verily, they that make haste to be rich, compass themselves about with many sorrows.

The king's slaves, ever the worst and dearest, were always forced upon him first, after which he could buy what he would. Each one was most strictly examined by the surgeon, one very particular matter being to examine their teeth, there being no other way of guessing the negroes' age but by their decay, as the people who sold them cunningly shaved their heads and beards, so that the buyer could not detect any grey hairs. As soon as a slave—man, woman, or child—was passed by the surgeon, it was branded with a hot iron with the ship's letters in order that it might be known when finally handed over. A few days after the goods agreed upon were paid, and the slaves sent to the trunk.

When about fifty or sixty were collected, they

were marched down to the shore, and got through the surf into the longboat, and so to the ship. On their arriving on board the men were at once put in irons, two and two together, to prevent mutiny, swimming ashore, or even more desperate and certain efforts for liberty. "For," says Phillips, "the negroes are so 'wilful' and loth to leave their own country, that they will leap out of the ship and stay under water till they are drowned sooner than go to Barbadoes, 'which they dread worse than we do hell.'" Twelve committed suicide in this way, while others, with still greater resolution, starved themselves to death, "believing that after their death they would return to their old homes."

It was the custom, it seems, with some commanders to cut off the legs or arms of the most wilful to terrify the rest, as they believe that if they have not lost a member they will return home. His officers urged him strongly to pursue the same course; but he strenuously refused, having, one would suppose, quite enough upon his soul already.

These slaves are all prisoners of the wars, which are made expressly to obtain them, which wars are often most bloody—resistance being, of course, desperate. Phillips had seen nine or ten bags of men, women, and children's heads brought to the king's town at one time, which they would contemptuously kick about. There is, however, another source of supply, a very singular one, and only resorted to when others are very scarce. The old king had no less than three thousand wives up and down the country, and when slaves ran short he would make nothing of selling three or four hundred of these.

The whole complement of slaves being now made up, the shark-surrounded ship sailed upon her ill-omened voyage. The *Hannibal* (450 tons) had on board 700 blacks,—480 men and 220 women,—besides her crew of at least 80, probably more. Now a splendidly-found ship of 1,300 tons, in a state of perfect purity and ventilation, carrying 200 highly civilized beings, will be found quite full enough under the line, in a calm, as I can testify; and here were 750 creatures, nearly all savages, in a ship of 450 tons,—say very little bigger than the *Prince Imperial* or the *Samphire*, the Dover mail-boats. To make the matter still more startling, the *Warrior*, the largest frigate in the world, of *six thousand* tons, carries *six hundred* men; the *Hannibal*, of *four hundred and fifty* tons, carried *seven hundred and fifty*.

The sailing also was very slow: drifting along under the blazing line, he had only gone 750 miles (as I roughly compute it in a straight line) in eleven days. On the morning of the eleventh the long white sand, "the grote white Pleken of the Dutch waggoner" which marks the mouth of the melancholy Gaboon, the river of the gorillas, was under his lee; his negroes were dying very fast, and the confidence of the sharks in following his ship was amply repaid.

To reach Cape Lopus (Cape Lopez, at the mouth of the Ogawai), where he wished to wood and water, was hopeless with these winds; so he turned his ship's head along the line towards the island of St. Thomas, 120 miles distant, which he reached in three days, sailing along the equator at the rate of 40 miles a day, with this mass of festering humanity on board.

The deadly beauty and wealth of St. Thomas must be very great. It lies under the equator,* and is crowned by high mountains wrapped in perpetual mist. Here are wood, water, and every kind of provisions in the greatest abundance, but the climate is rapid death to a European constitution, though healthy for the negro. There were but two hundred whites on the island, and they looked like ghosts :

> "And if his fellow spake,
> His voice was thin, as voices from the grave."

No Portuguese would come here voluntarily. These were men who had histories, who had been forced to fly their country, and whom their Government left alone, as being sufficiently punished. None ever reach the age of fifty years. Here Phillips fell sick, and three or four of his slaves died every day. After a fortnight's delay, he sailed away once more across the ocean to Barbadoes.

He got down upon the south-east trades, and ran upon them, and after six weeks of mostly burning heat and slow sailing found himself not two-thirds

* They showed Phillips a rivulet with a bridge over it, and told him that you crossed the line by crossing the bridge. He does not endorse this story himself, and he is right. The stream they showed him must have been at Sta. Anna de Chaves, on the north-east of the island, whereas the equator runs directly over a small rock, the Isle das Rollas, near the shore at the extreme south point of the island.

of his distance; and it became necessary to put his men on short allowance and two quarts of water a day. This was the 4th of October, 1694.

They were kept baffling about in search of the north-east trades for a long time, and meanwhile they took on board a passenger they would have been glad to part with—cholera, in its most frightful form.

There were scarcely any recoveries. When a man was seized, they gave him up for dead; and they were right, for he died. At the same time the small-pox was busy; but it was cholera which was king and lord over that floating charnel-house. For two months and eleven days the plague was not stayed, and on their arrival at Barbadoes the tale of death was made up—14 of the crew and 320 negroes. The sharks of Whydah were wise sharks.

It was a ruinous speculation; the dead loss was £6,500 sterling to the company and the owners. Those left alive (bought for about £3 15s.) were sold for about £19, no very large profit even if all had lived, considering the cost of their keep during such a very long passage. Nevertheless, with short and healthy passages, there is no doubt that large fortunes were made at it. When one considers the build of these ships, and their very slow rate of sailing, and contrasts them with the slaver of the day, the swiftest and most beautiful craft in the world, one must come to the conclusion that a larger proportion are brought to their destination. Looking once more at the fact that the price of slaves, such few as are sold now, is nearer £90 than

£19, one can see how vastly profitable the modern slave trade must be, and cease to wonder that there are still found desperadoes to embark in it.

The way in which Phillips gets pious and sentimental over *his* (Phillips') dreadful bad fortune at the *negroes* dying of cholera is something too wonderful to be thought out. It is Defoe's "Bob Singleton" entirely. Of course, there is a degree of moral obtuseness and depravity about it, deeply shocking to every well-regulated mind; but, at the same time, like all other utterly incongruous things, the effect of it is laughter. We will shortly take leave of our good Phillips and see how he fared.

Barbadoes was at this time most fearfully afflicted by the plague. Captain Sherman, of the Queen's ship *Tiger*, had buried *six hundred men*, his complement being only *two hundred*, he having impressed every merchantman he could lay his hands on as they arrived in different ships, to fill up his vacancies, until he had reached this horrible amount. This plague, among many other victims, carried off Mr. Gordon, Captain Phillips's surgeon, to his great grief. Gordon had been a faithful friend to him; not only had he stoutly gone through the loathsome details of the slave trade, but he had also given the most careful attention to the physical well-being of Phillips himself, doctoring him, after the manner of those times, with so many drastics, setons, blood-lettings, blisters, and other remedies, of which he gives us a rather particular account, that Phillips got to be very fond of him, and quite unable to get on without him.

He had had but little luck on this voyage, and all that little deserted him now. He fell dreadfully ill on the voyage home, and attributes his last catastrophe to the absence of his favourite doctor. Fever set in, followed by convulsions, which ended in his being stone deaf, and utterly unable to navigate his ship, which ended in his having to hand it over to "my old drunken beast of a mate Robson." Things went well enough with the ship, though ill enough with poor Phillips, until they came into the Channel; when, off Beechy Head, Robson, in sheer brutal drunken obstinacy, ran her into another ship coming down Channel, and poor Phillips, crawling from his bed to the cuddy door, saw his faithful old ship with her bows stove in and her decks a tangled ruin of spars and ropes.

It was the last ounce which broke the camel's back. The great loss he had brought upon her owners by the failure of the slave venture was bad, his deafness was worse, this was the last. He held up his head no more. He got his ship into Portsmouth, and giving up the command of her, this right valiant Welshman, who only acted according to the light of his time, after all, wandered away, deaf, broken down, and ruined, to end his days among his native hills, and his place knew him no more.

MILES PHILIPS.

"A DISCOURSE written by one Miles Philips, Englishman, one of the company put on shoare north of Panuco in the West Indies, by Mr. John Hawkins, in 1568, containing many special things of that countery and of the Spanish Gouernment, but specially of the cruelties used to our Englishmen, and among the rest to himselfe, for the space of fifteen or sixteen yeeres together, vntil by good and happy meanes he was deliuered fro their bloody hands, and returned into his own countery. An. 1582."

The squabble between the Spaniard and the Englishman, between Protestantism and Popery, was now getting towards red heat. It is almost an impertinence to notice that the last date quoted, the date of my "Breeches" Bible, is just six years before the affair of the Spanish Armada. It is within the bounds of possibility that Miles Philips, in his clumsy, straightforward narrative, may be able to explain to us the fury, amounting to ferocity, with which the Spaniard was met in the Channel.

It was a terrible fight, and it was very much thrown on the hands of the English. The other Protestant nations of Europe could do but little to help us.

The land of Luther had no fleet; Motley tells us how Holland was tied; France was not in earnest either way; and the duel between the Papacy and mankind had to be fought out on the sea by Spain and England.

England won, and the world is free. England is at this present moment the most potentially powerful state on the face of the earth, not even excepting our wonderful sister America. Where is Spain with her priests *now?*

The English language, the language of Shakespeare, is now spoken by very nearly 90,000,000 people, and will soon be spoken by 200,000,000.

The story which follows is confirmed in every important particular by one Job Hartop, who was in the same scrape, and who was, as he pathetically says, like his great scriptural namesake, born unto trouble: and indeed this may fairly be predicated of a man who was, off and on, in the Inquisition in a hot country for three and twenty years. But I have preferred the narrative of Miles Philips, because Job Hartop sometimes draws on his fine imagination; " monstrous, venomous wormes" with two heads, who turned the Captain's sword "as blacke as ynk," not to mention mermen who rose out of the sea, off Bermuda, "with the complexion of a Mulatto or tawny Indian," savour much too strongly of our good friend Sir John Mandeville for reproduction in a modest little book like this. Yet his narrative is still more spirited than that of Miles Philips; and in the case of the battle of Vera Cruz I shall use it without troubling the reader to distinguish it.

On Monday the 2d of October, 1567, Captain John Hawkins, of famous memory, hoisted his pennant on board of the ship *Jesus*, with Robert Barret for sailing-master: with him went five other ships—the *Minion*, Captain Hampton; the *William and John*, Captain Bolton; the *Angel*, the *Swallow*, Captains' names forgotten in sixteen years' misery; and last, not least by any means, the *Judith*, Captain Francis Drake.

They were to go the round then so common, to the west coast of Africa, and so across on the northeast trades to America. The object of Captain Hawkins was first and principally negroes.

Accordingly, having rendezvoused at the Canaries, they crossed to Cape Verd, and tried their hands on the Gambian negroes, with great ill-success. The savages beat them off with heavy loss, hurting many of their men with poisoned arrows, who died with every symptom of lock-jaw, so that they had to put sticks in their mouths to keep them open. In another account I read that Sir John Hawkins himself was wounded, but was taught by a negro to draw the poison out of his hand with a clove of garlic: quite incredible. Then they departed for the coast of Guinea to see how they would fare there.

They were here much more fortunate; the negroes were, as usual, at war among one another, and Sir John Hawkins assisted one side, and, after a little sharp practice on the part of one of the negro kings, got as many as 500 slaves, with which he sailed away.

With very slow sailing,* but prosperous for those

---

* One does not wonder at any amount of scurvy when one examines times, they made St. Domingo, and were sailing and trading about till May, meeting with considerable opposition from the Spaniards, who looked on them as interlopers, but were evidently afraid of them, but with no open violence until they came to Rio de la Hacha, where the governor positively refused to have anything to do with them. As it was absolutely necessary that they should have provisions, they assaulted that governor and took his town, with a loss of two men; after which a peaceable trade was made up, and they sold 200 of their negroes (which unhappy wretches must by this time have been festering under hatches for four months). After which, sailing northward, they encountered a gale of wind off Florida which made them take refuge at Vera Cruz in an evil hour.

The moment of their arrival, the principal Spaniards taking them for the Spanish fleet came on board, and so put themselves entirely in Sir John Hawkins' power. He, however, courteously entreated them, and only kept two hostages, men of substance, Ulloa and Riviera, and did not do what he certainly might have done without getting into any terrible trouble at home—sack and plunder the plate-ships in the harbour, which had just then above 200,000*l.* worth

these voyages: salt diet and small beer, and a rate of sailing, even in the trade winds, extremely slow. In the log of a ship before me now, a hundred years later, extending over two months and a half, the greatest day's work is 140 miles, and this with a gale of wind on her beam. The *White Squall,* or the *Red Jacket,* would in all probability have hurled themselves over or through some 300 miles of water under such circumstances. In Maury's sailing orders 401 miles is, I think (I quote from memory), claimed for the *Flying Cloud.*

on board. He also sent a messenger to the Viceroy at Mexico to say, "that as our Queene, his Soveraigne, was the King of Spaine his loving sister and friend, he would allow him to buy victuals and refit his fleet." In the middle of these negotiations in came the Spanish fleet itself, thirteen sail of great ships to our five, with 1,800,000*l.* on board, and Martin Henriguez, the new Viceroy.

Nothing but mischief could come. Sir John Hawkins could perfectly well have kept them out, but was afraid of how the Queen would take it after all, when it came to the point, and so he let them in and they made a very pleasant treaty, the first two articles of which were about victualling and being excessively fond of one another; the third regarding some ordnance on an island which Sir John Hawkins had taken possession of;* and the fourth was that twelve *gentlemen* should be delivered as hostages on either side.

The Spaniards, after their manner, dressed up twelve utterly worthless persons in the finest clothes, and sent them on board our ship. The English kept faith, and sent twelve real gentlemen, whom we shall see once more. And by degrees other symptoms of the Spaniards' treachery began to show themselves but too surely.

It was evident that they were setting guns so as

* This little island was but a few feet above water, and *made* the port, no ship being able to anchor at all unless her anchors were on shore here. Sir John Hawkins dreaded what would happen from the very first; for the harbour is so small that the ships were actually aboard of one another (see Hawkins's third voyage), which, as far as it goes with them, confirms Philips and Hartop entirely.

to command the men who were landed on the little island; and they also brought a large hulk of six hundred tons and laid her close to the *Minion*. It grew more suspicious still when they began to cut ports in her; and suspicion was raised to certainty when the Spaniards were seen swarming into their ships and batteries. Still negotiations were tried. Robert Barret, Sir John Hawkins's sailing-master, was sent on board the Spanish admiral, but was at once put in irons.

The catastrophe came suddenly upon all. One Augustine de Villanova, who was actually the guest of our admiral, was in the plot; and his share of it was no other than the assassination of Sir John Hawkins. They were actually at dinner together, and the false Spaniard had the dagger in his sleeve, when the signal was given by a small cornet. Some movement on the part of Villanova attracted the attention of one John Chamberlayne, and he seized and disarmed him. Sir John Hawkins rose hurriedly from table, and ordered him into confinement; and at that very minute the signal for onset was given by the Spanish trumpets, and the peaceful harbour was suddenly converted into a raging volcano, for a time as dangerous and as horrible as the neighbouring Popocatapetl.

Three hundred of the Spaniards in the great hulk were on board the *Minion* with a sudden dash; and Sir John Hawkins, shouting in "a loud, fierce voyce," "God and St. George upon these traitourous villains!" headed his men into the *mêlée*, while the men of the *Jesus* leaped into the *Minion* to the assistance of their brother sailors, and very rapidly beat the Spaniards back into their own ship.

Meanwhile the Spaniards on the mainland had dashed over to the little island where the English artillery was placed, and had beaten the English off it, a few of whom swam to their ships, but the rest were killed, and the ordnance directed against the ships. In the dreadful hurly-burly the enemy's admiral's ship blew up, hurling three hundred Spaniards to destruction.

The odds were bitterly cruel against the English; but there were two among those English at the sound of whose names the ears of old sailors tingle even now—Sir Francis Drake and Sir John Hawkins. We have here an anecdote of the latter. In the middle of the fight he, probably hoarse with shouting orders, called his page Samuel for a cup of beer; and, setting down the silver flagon, a demi-culverin shot struck it away. "God," said he, "who has preserved me from this shot, will preserve us from these traitors and villains."

The fight went fiercely on from ten in the morning till dark, doubtless watched by Indians from the shore, wondering if the strange Lutherans would win, and if their tyranny was overpast. But it was not so. As the swift night came down, Drake and Hawkins managed to draw away with their only remaining ships,—the *Minion* and the *Judith*,—carrying as many of the crews of the other ships as they could, in their dire necessity, cram on board—Drake, one may be allowed to fancy, thinking of vengeance. "Acapulco, beware!"

They got to sea on the morning of the 25th of September, and were at once caught by a gale of wind from the north, in which the over burdened *Minion* got separated from the *Judith*. Affairs began to look more and more serious, so that many were inclined to give themselves up as prisoners to the Spaniards to avoid perishing of hunger. The ship had nearly three crews in her (250 men), and had been driven to sea suddenly and without preparation; food failed, and in their agony they ate hides, cats, dogs, mice, rats, parrots, and monkeys.

This went on for ten days, till on the 10th of October, finding themselves near Panuco, at the bottom of the bay, and cut off from all hope, cannibalism staring them in the face, a large number begged Sir John Hawkins to put them ashore, preferring the tender mercies of Spaniard or Indian to certain starvation.

One half of the company were landed, not without disaster, for the surf was heavy, and some were drowned, having been inhumanly forced to leap into the sea by Captain Hampton a mile from shore. And so, bidding farewell to the ship,* they turned their weary faces to the desolate bush, and started on one

---

* The voyage of Sir John Hawkins home was one of the most disastrous on record. Scarcely any of them ever reached England. As Sir John himself says: "If all the miseries and troublesome affaires of this sorowful voyage should be perfectly and toroughly written, there should neede a paineful man with his pen, and as great a time as he had that wrote the lives and deathes of the Martyrs." The few miserable shadows who just managed to bring their ship to the coast of Spain were threatened by the Spaniards, and only saved by some English ships at Vigo.

of those miserable shore-walks which are among the most melancholy things in the history of adventure.

They found fresh water, of which some drank to such excess that they were got along with great difficulty. The rain was cruel and the jungle difficult; and next day they were suddenly set on by the Chichimichi Indians, who on their first onslaught, without parley or resistance, killed eight of them. Finding, however, that they were quite submissive and unarmed save for one caliver, they merely stripped those who had coloured clothes on quite naked, and directed the company to Tampico.

The unfortunate men now divided. Part, among whom was Miles Philips, went westward under one Antony Goddard (quoted to be still living at Plymouth fourteen years after); part went northward, under one John Hooper. These divided again; and it is singular that, although only two or three were killed, no less than twenty-three remained to be accounted for. They had probably become quietly naturalized.

Meanwhile poor Philips and his mates, under command of Goddard, went westward towards Panuco. They were perfectly naked, and the weather was burning, the thorns tore their flesh, and the musquitoes stung them until they were frantic. They had to beat their way through the thorny jungles with cudgels, and the happiest seemed to be those who were laid at rest suddenly and for ever by the unerring Indian arrow. For twelve days they toiled on thus, until, as one would have conceived, life was scarcely worth having on any terms. Yet life was precious, too, even with certain slavery, and possible ill-treatment. Bare, torn, and bleeding as they were, the sound of a gun on the twelfth day was pleasant to them, and the crowing of a cock immediately after "was no small ioy vnto vs." They had arrived at the river Panuco.

Sitting down and drinking greedily of this river (a bow-shot in breadth), they saw that the other side was crowded with Spaniards riding up and down. At first the Spaniards took them for their Indian enemies, the Chichimichi; but at last one of them came across in a canoe rowed by two Indians, and surveyed them. Crossing again and giving his report of them, twenty Spanish horsemen (armed) at once crossed in canoes, towing their horses behind them. Arrived at the side of the river where the poor English stood, they set their lances in rest and charged them.

Submission being made to the Spaniards, they were brought up to the town guarded by tame Indians, the boys and the more feeble being carried on their conquerors' horses. The governor was very furious with them, and demanded their money; but the Indians and Spaniards had been pretty well before him here. Still Antony Goddard had a gold chain, which he gave him, and some of the others, who had some clothes left, made up a very small sum. This got, however, did little to soften his anger. He put the whole of them into a black-hole, calling them Lutherans and English dogs; fed them with sodden maize like hogs; and when they asked for a surgeon for their wounded, offered them the hangman. And so for three days they "waited to be bereaved of their lives."

And, indeed, when on the fourth day there came a large number of Spaniards and Indians armed, bringing halters, they gave themselves up for gone, and began calling to God for mercy and forgiveness of sins. But the Spaniards' instructions were not so bad. They merely bound them two and two, and marched them away towards Mexico, distant about 270 miles, guarded by two Spaniards and many Indians.

The friars on their road were very kind to them On the second evening, coming to Santa Maria, some white friars gave them hot meat, broth, and fruit, and clothed them with white baize: and here, too, one Thomas Baker, poor fellow, wounded before by the Indians, marched no further in this weary world, but lay down and died, to see England no more. The black friars at Meititlan also were exceedingly kind to them, giving them shirts, and acting like Christians in every way. The Inquisition had not yet been established in Mexico.

The treatment they received from their two Spanish guards was singularly unequal. One, a very good old man, was most gentle and kind to them, going before to provide everything he could for them; but their other guide, a young man, was "a very cruell cative," who carried a javelin in his hand, and when our men could scarcely crawl had a horrible trick of smiting them violently on the back of the neck and knocking them down, crying, "March, English dog, Lutheran, enemy of God." All the way to Mexico this continued, the old man making them halt and rest, the young one urging them on. It was with joy, after their dreadful march, that they heard that they were within fifteen miles of Mexico, for they had little pleasure of life left, and would prefer liberty to the present state of things, even though it came through death.

He describes the shrine of one lady of Guadaloupe as being life-size, of silver and gilt ; and while the wonder of it was still on their mind they were met by a great number of horsemen who had ridden out from Mexico to meet them and stare at them, and by whom they were escorted into the Mexico of 1568 through the gate of St. Catharine, and were thence marched on to the Placa del Marquese, close by the market-place.

The Spaniards of the city loaded them with kindness. Provisions, five times more than they could eat, hats, and money were given to them ; and after a little time they were taken along the lake in two canoes to a hospital, where were many other English ; indeed that and another hospital, that of Our Lady, were full of English. No sooner did they come into hospital than the men began to die ; and in the next fortnight there were so many gone, that there was plenty of room in the ladies' hospital, whither Miles Philips was removed.

Here six months passed away with courteous treatment, and every sort of kindness. Virtuous gentlemen and ladies from the city visited them continually, bringing every kind of present, including succats and marmalade. But with restored health came fresh troubles ; orders came from the Viceroy that they were to be sent south to the prisons of Tescuco, the entrepôt of all the rascals in Mexico, of all colours, from whence they were generally sold into slavery. Evil times began again. Although set to no work, they were kept straitly in prison, and so nearly starved, in spite of one Robert Sweeting, a renegade, whose father had married a Spaniard, and who helped them, that in desperation they determined to break out, and by that means incur death or gain freedom.

They were a hundred strong still, and seemed to have no difficulty at all in getting away; but the night was dark, it rained terribly, and they had no guide, and wandered they knew not whither—but, unluckily, quite in the wrong direction, for at daybreak they found themselves close to Mexico, and were at once recaptured.

They were threatened with death, but it was not inflicted; they were ordered to the garden of the Viceroy, and great must have been their surprise when they met there the gentlemen who had been given as hostages by Sir John Hawkins and Captain Barret, the master of the *Jesus*. Here they worked for four months, with only two sheep among the hundred of them, and two halfpenny loaves for each man. At the end of this time the gentlemen hostages and Captain Barret were removed into prison; and it was announced that any Spanish gentleman who desired to have an Englishman might do so on the mere condition of having him forthcoming at one month's notice. The Spanish gentlemen flocked into the garden, and carried them off with the greatest rapidity.

The fate of the unfortunate gentlemen hostages was very miserable. Long kept in prison, they were sent to Spain in the fleet, and many of them died from the cruel handling of the Inquisition. Of Captain Barret we hear that he was kept another year in Mexico, and that, going into Spain, he was seized by the Inquisition, and after some persecution was condemned to be burnt with another Englishman, John Gilbert.

The common sailors fared much better however. They were taken as footmen and valets to the Spaniards, and were ordained to follow them when they walked abroad, at which their Spanish masters were very proud, as no Spaniard in this country would serve another, and the only available followers were Indians. By degrees too, as their worth was found, they became employed as factors in the silver mines at good wages, sixty pounds a year; and moreover, without cheating their masters, by getting the Indians by kindness to work a little for them on Saturday afternoon, they were able to make four or five pounds a week, which will give one some idea of what the masters' profits must have been. Many of our Englishmen became in this way, after three or four years, worth their six or seven hundred pounds.

But now came the detested Inquisition, for the first time established in Mexico. Six years after their first captivity, in the year 1574, came Don Pedro Moya de Contreres, as chief inquisitor, John de Bouilla, his assistant, and Pedro de los Rios for secretary, and established themselves in a fair house near the white friars, and then began looking round for a job in their line. One was ready to their hands, with which to make an "entrance and beginning." These Englishmen, who seemed thriving, must be inquired into for their souls' health and comfort. The preliminaries were soon arranged. Their goods were confiscated, and they were cast into dark dungeons in the city of Mexico.

They were never more than two together, and so did not know what had become of each other: thus in the darkness they remained one year and a half. During this time they were frequently called before the inquisitors alone, and there severely examined of their faith, commanded to say the Creed, Ave Maria, and Pater noster in Latin, which a great many were unable to do otherwise than in English. But here the half-breed Robert Sweeting, nobly and at the risk of his life, assisted them; for, being interpreter, he told the inquisitors that they could say them perfectly in English. The next demand made upon them was this; On their oaths did they believe that any bread or wine remained on the paten or in the chalice after consecration? and whether or not the host of bread which the priest held up, and the wine in the chalice, were not actually the very perfect body and blood of our Lord? To answer no to this was to die.

Next they were asked to reveal how they had been taught and what they had believed when they were in England; to which they, for the mere safety of their lives, would answer that they had never believed or been taught otherwise than as they had said before. The inquisitors would now warn them that they must give a more satisfactory answer than that on the pain of the rack, and would dismiss them to consider. When they were next brought up, it was demanded again what they had been taught and what they believed, and they were also tempted by promises of pardon to betray any of their fellows, being told that they should be set at liberty if they would tell the truth. They however, although separately examined, stuck pretty nearly to the same answer,—that as for their sins and offences in England against God and our Lady, or any of His blessed saints, they were heartily sorry for the same, and did cry God mercy; and besought the inquisitors, for God's sake, considering that they had come into that country by force of weather and against their wills, and had never in all their lives done or spoken anything against their laws, to have mercy upon them.

But they had none; and about three months before the final judgment given against them they were all racked, and some tortured into uttering things against themselves which afterwards cost them their lives. And now having got enough out of their own mouths to condemn them, they erected a great scaffold against the large church in the main square, and from it proclaimed with sound of trumpet and drum, that whoever would come there in a fortnight should hear the judgments of the Holy Inquisition against the English heretics, Lutherans, and also see the same put in execution.

There was no rest for them on the dreadful night before the judgments; for officers of the Inquisition came to them, bringing their San Benitos, which garments were of yellow cotton with red crosses upon them, and kept them up all night, drilling them in a yard, and showing them in what order they were to go to the scaffold. When the miserable morning dawned, they had for breakfast a cup of wine and a piece of bread fried in honey, and afterwards started in single file, in their yellow garments, with halters round their necks, and a green candle unlighted in their hands, each one guarded by two Spaniards. There was a vast crowd, so dense that room had to be made to pass. And, having come through it, our poor Englishmen mounted a flight of stairs, and then were seated in chairs to receive judgment. Soon after their arrival the Viceroy and the inquisitors ascended the scaffold by another flight of steps. Next 300 friars, white, black, and grey, were placed in the places appointed for them, and the judgment began.

Roger was chief armourer of the *Jesus*. He was condemned to 300 lashes on horseback, and to serve in the galleys for ten years.

John Gray, John Brown, John Rider, John Moon, James Collier, and Thomas Brown, 200 lashes and eight years in the galleys.

John Keyes, 100 lashes and six years in the galleys.

Fifty-three more men, names forgotten, probably in the agony of sitting there hour after hour awaiting one's own, were condemned to various numbers of lashes and terms of years in the galleys. At last our fate was read, and one may imagine the gust of relief when it was all over.

"And then was I, Miles Philips, called, and was adjudged to serve in a monastery five years, wearing a San Benito all the time."

So *that* was over, and he could look around now, and remember names. He had been nearly the last, and his agony had endured long; for after six more had been sentenced to servitude in monasteries, without stripes, it was nearly night—time for the great closing entertainment of the wicked day's work.

George Rively, Peter Momfrie, and Cornelius, the Irishman, were had up for judgment. Sentenced to be burned to ashes. It was done at once in the market-place, near the scaffold, and was soon over. After this good day's work the inquisitors and the others retired, and the English were taken back to prison.

The next day was Good Friday, and on this day, of all days in the year, these unutterable scoundrels put their iniquitous sentence into practice. A horse was provided for each of the sixty Englishmen, and they were mounted on them, naked from the waist upwards. They were then led through the principal streets, and before them went a couple of criers, crying, "Behold these English dogs, Lutherans, enemies to God." And as they went there were some of the inquisitors themselves, and some of the "familiars of that rake-hell order," encouraging the executioners to strike and lay on to those English heretics. The instruments of torture were whips, and the spectacle most horrible; and at last, when it was over, our poor, gory fellow-countrymen were led back to the inquisitor's house, where they were dismounted and carried to prison, to abide their passage to Spain to the galleys, to undergo the rest of their martyrdom.

Miles Philips speaks in terms of great kindness for

his treatment by the good friars, to whom he, and one William Lowe, were appointed; they were well lodged, fed, and clothed. Philips was appointed to oversee Indians in building a church, Lowe was sent into the kitchen. They had agreeable chambers, clean bedding, and plenty of hearty sympathy for their misfortunes; for these honest friars (though by their dress they seem to have been Dominicans*) hated the Inquisition with a deep hatred, which they confided to the Englishmen as far as they might, being for the most part so watched that they were afraid to let their right hand know what their left did.

The four years having expired, they were once more brought before the chief inquisitor, their fools' coats pulled off and hung up in the great church, and underneath written, "A Lutheran heretic reconciled." Likewise here were hung the coats of those who had gone to Spain to the galleys with the same inscription; but under the coats of the three who had suffered by fire was written, "A Lutheran heretic burnt." They were now free to go up and down the country and do as they liked, but continually watched both in word and deed—escape being nearly impossible.

* Here, as elsewhere, it is almost impossible to distinguish between the innumerable orders of monks, infinitely multiplied as they were in this century. "Franciscans," by the mere adoption of a stricter régime and a hood, become "Capuchins." Again they branch into "Recollects" in France, "Reformed Franciscans" in Italy, and "Barefooted Franciscans" in Spain. Vows of poverty are alternately adopted and abandoned. Even the diligent Mosheim says that it would be an endless and unprofitable labour to enumerate them. It is worthy of note, however, that all these fresh divisions were made with the object of returning to original purity of manners, one of the strongest proofs of the necessity of the Reformation.

Most of them having given up their religion, and being hopeless of escape, gave up everything, and taking wives, in some cases rich ones, settled down comfortably as citizens of Spain. These were but little watched or annoyed, their wives and their wealth being considered as sufficient hostages for their not running away. Miles Philips, however, who could not make up his mind to marry and settle, but still looked forward, however distantly, to escape from the idolatry and hypocrisy to which he was condemned, was treated very differently. He might have gone to the mines and got rich again; but he knew that the moment he was well-to-do, that "diuelish" Inquisition would be on him again, and strip him of every farthing. He therefore made it his choice to learn to weave gograms and taffeties; and so apprenticed himself to a weaver for three years, paying him 150 dollars, hoping to live quietly and without suspicion.

However, the familiars would not let him alone. They constantly charged him with intentions to run away to England, and become once more a Lutheran heretic. He pointed out to them how impossible it was that he should do so; but that was useless. They had him once more before the inquisitor, who demanded of him why he did not marry? He answered that he had bound himself to an occupation. The inquisitor answered that he knew he meant to run away, and therefore ordered him, under pain of being burnt as a relapsed heretic, not to leave the city or to go near St. John de Ulloa (Vera Cruz), or any other port.

The night was very long and dark; but at this time

there came a flash of lightning which illuminated it for one instant, and made the old blood tingle again. Drake had dashed at Acapulco.

The panic and hurly-burly were awful. The Viceroy made a levy *en masse* of the Spaniards in Mexico; and of unmarried men there were three thousand full-blooded Spaniards, and twenty thousand half-breeds. They expected an advance of the English, and the sack of the city of Mexico; the richer Spaniards began to get out of the way and secure themselves; and the Viceroy sent for Miles Philips and Paul Hersewell to see what they could tell him about this terrible fiery Drake.

Question:—Did they know one Francis Drake, brother to Captain Hawkins? *Answer:*—(very blandly, no doubt) That Captain Hawkins had only one brother; that he was sixty years old, and at this time Governor of Plymouth. *Question:*—Did they know Francis Drake at all? *Answer:*—No. (Oh, Miles Philips! Miles Philips!)

Before anything could be done, news had come that Drake was gone; nevertheless troops were despatched in all directions, and to Acapulco itself Captain Rovas de Corte, with two hundred men, was sent, accompanied by Miles Philips as an interpreter, licence being given by the inquisitors. Coming to Acapulco, Captain Rovas found that Drake had been gone a month, and plucked heart to embark in three small barks, the largest sixty tons, with 200 men, and go after him, taking Philips as interpreter, to his great joy, for he was sure enough that if the terrible Drake once got hold of them, he would account for them with the greatest ease. For twenty days did they creep down the land towards Panama without finding Drake, or anything like him; but hearing he was clean gone again, they went back to Acapulco; and it was with a bitterly sick heart that poor Miles came ashore again at Acapulco, and recommenced his journey towards the miserable priest-watched Mexico.

The Viceroy was so certain that Drake would be driven on shore somewhere on the coast by hunger, that he kept everything in readiness; and above all things kept Miles Philips under more strict surveillance night and day, lest at any moment he should be wanted for an interpreter. Things thus became utterly unendurable to him, and he determined to attempt an escape, which nearly succeeded, bold and open as it was. The fleet was to sail in three days for Spain; he was now as good a Spaniard by tongue as any of them; he determined to ride coolly down to the port and enlist on some ship for a soldier.

He had not been half an hour in Vera Cruz before he was arrested on a false suspicion. He was mistaken for a gentleman's son, of Mexico, who had bolted from his father, and intended for Spain. Denial was useless, and there happened to be no friends of the runaway youth at hand who could tell them that this was not their man, while, unfortunately, there happened to be one who recognised him; and as he was being taken to prison, out of mere kindness came forward and told them that this was one of Captain Hawkins' men, and that he had known him in a San Benito for three or four years. His kindness was ill-timed. Poor Miles was instantly put in prison with bolts on his legs. Surely nothing would save him this time.

The criminals, with whom he lay for three weeks, had some of them known him, and would pinch themselves of their victuals to give some out of kindness and compassion to him. One of them was more than friendly, for, having a friend who came often to the grate, he caused him to get Miles wine, and to buy him a knife for two dollars, with a file in the back of it; "And a happy man was I," says he, "when I slipped it into my boot." However, in four days he was taken out from the prison, and being fitted with a set of new leg-irons, made "with a bar between the shackles," and his hands also being manacled together, was cast into a waggon, one of a train of sixty, for transportation to Mexico.

He found, to his great surprise and delight, that he could slip his handcuffs on and off as he chose. So whenever the men were most busy, and the waggon made most noise, he had his hands free, and was working away with his file at the irons, which by degrees he worked through, and lay free in his waggon waiting his opportunity.

It came in this way: his waggon, which was the first of all, broke a wheel at the bottom of a very steep hill, where it was the custom to (as they would call it in California) double-bank the waggons; that is to say, put the animals of three or four waggons on to one, and having dragged that up, return for the others. While night was falling, and his driver entertaining himself in a public-house, and most of the waggoners gone away, he slipped away into the bush, carrying

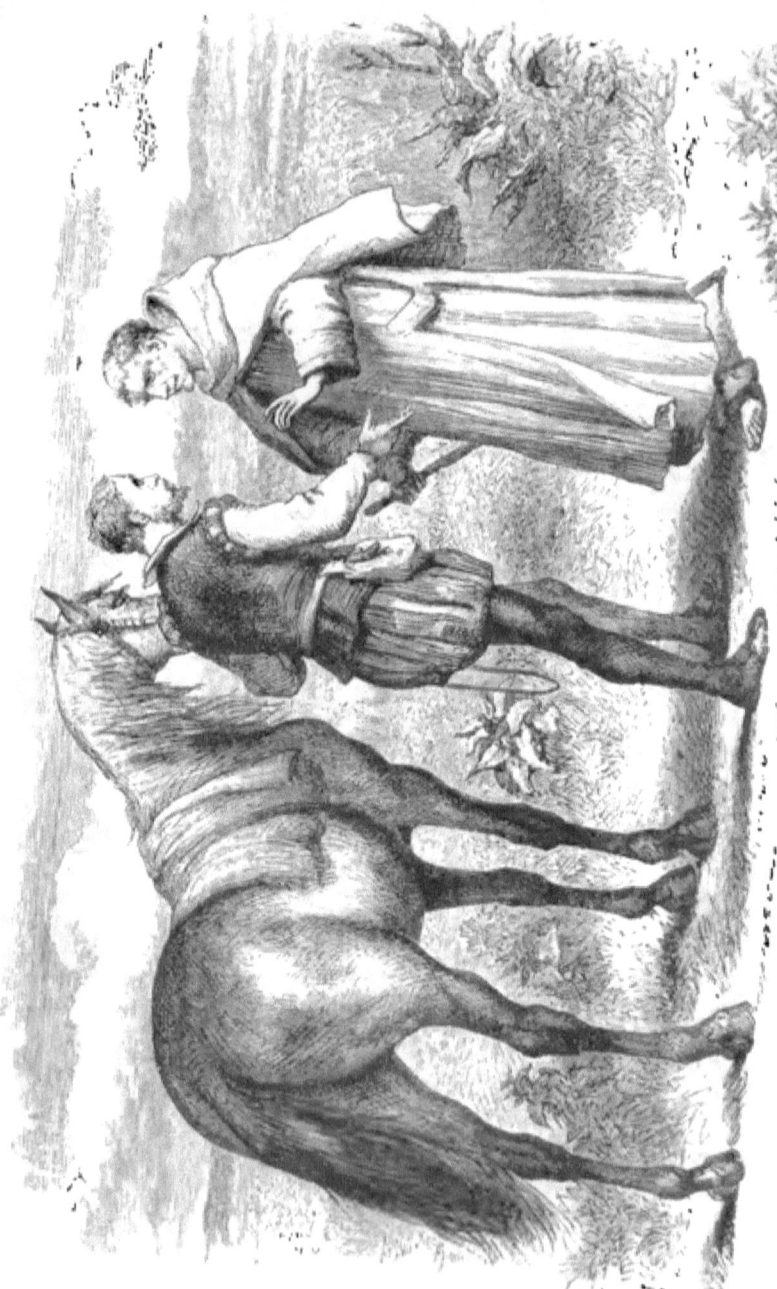

The meeting of Miles Philips and the Grey Friar.

his fetters in his hand, and found himself free, but for a great collar around his neck. His broken irons he put into a bush and covered with moss, and fled away south through the dark forest.

When morning arose, and he could see where he was, he saw high mountains to the north, with great fires on them, and very soon came upon some Indians, who were hunting deer. Having told them the tale of his escape, they sympathised profoundly with him, assisted him to file off the ring round his neck, and willingly guided him to Jalapa, at that time an Indian town, and safe : here he stayed three days, in consequence of sickness.

With some of the gold which was quilted in his doublet he bought a horse for six dollars, and still held south as he was directed. He had not gone six miles before he overtook a grey friar, a man whom he knew very well as a thorough hater of the Inquisition, to whom he told his tale, and of whom he begged direction. The worthy friar not only gave him that, but his company for three days, during which he took him to Indian houses only. As he went on among these Indians, he collected from among them in three days no less than *twenty dollars* in alms, or for masses, one would suppose, which would seem to bring us to the astounding result that a travelling friar could make his pound a day in those times. All this money he freely gave to Miles Philips, who, bidding him farewell, turned his horse's head southward towards Guatemala, on the Pacific.

He gives us no details of this very long journey,

and leaves us to find for ourselves the object of it, which, however, is not difficult. He followed an unfrequented route, leading him chiefly, if not entirely, among Indians, to a point where Central America narrows suddenly to a width of only two hundred miles, and where, by one bold push, you might cross the isthmus from Pacific to Atlantic in a few days, through an utterly desert country. He is in error about his distance; it is barely two hundred miles. Accordingly, having provided himself with provisions and guides, he started, and in twelve days reached Porto Caballos, in the Gulf of Mexico, and dismissing his Indian guides, went down to the haven, where there were ships discharging Canary wine.

Going on board one of them, he had some difficulty in getting the captain to take him, because he had no passport, in spite of his representing himself a Granada man, a countryman of the captain's. The captain was afraid that he might have killed some one, or be indebted, and flying; but in the end Miles' word was taken, and the bargain was struck for sixty dollars to Spain. Our old friend joyfully laid in his provisions, the usual "hennes and bread" of those times, and in two days was skimming over the glad blue waters of the Gulf, and Mexico, with all its hideous apparatus of priest and idol, prison and Inquisition, its weary forests and its darksome dungeons, only a faint blue cloud upon the summer sea; a thing past and gone, only to return in fearful dreams in moonless midnight.

Fortune had not done threatening him yet however. Coming to Havana, he was hired at once as a soldier in the King of Spain's fleet: here he saw those great armaments for strengthening that and other ports, and some of our own cannon out of the *Jesus*. The fleet was of thirty-seven sail, and of enormous value, but not one fit to fight except the admiral's, being all very deeply laden and badly appointed. They kept away very far north-east, to avoid the French fleet at the Azores; and, after a very bad passage, made St. Lucaz, at the mouth of the Guadalquivir.

It was by the merest accident, or, to speak more correctly, by the merciful goodness of God, that he did not end his miserable days in the Inquisition after all. His being an Englishman had been discovered, though he knew it not; and he heard one of the crew tell the master so. He pretended not to hear it, but continued jocund and merry, until the time came for leave to go ashore. When he pressed to be gone, he was answered by the master, "No, you must come to Seville with me *by water;*" *i.e.* up the river. He knew what that meant well enough, and, in spite of the sickness at his heart, he put a bold face on it, continuing to be merry, and making the master fancy that he had a safe victim wherewith to please the God of mercy, and stand well with the Inquisition. However, he had a desperate man to deal with; Miles watched till he was asleep, and then, slipping down by the chains into a little boat, hauled himself ashore by the cable, and casting the boat adrift, set off for Seville by land.

Right in the very heart of Seville, under the very bars of the Inquisition cage itself, perched this very wary old bird, knowing that it would be the very last place in which he would be looked for. He took instant service with a weaver, and plied his old trade in the most diligent fashion, never stirring abroad. Part of the gossip of the shop was about a certain Englishman who had come home in the fleet, and had escaped, and the search there was for him. "Ha!" cried Miles Philips, casting his shuttle the while, one may fancy, with a vicious and emphatic orthodoxy, "the Lutheran dog! I would I might know him; surely I would present him to the Holy House." So for three months he wove, and having now got his wages, he bought an entire suit of new clothes, and went to St. Lucaz, where he had heard of an English ship.

He asked the captain for a passage, confiding to him that he was one of Sir John Hawkins' men, but the captain dared not take him. He begged him to go back again. And so poor Philips, having heard his mother-tongue again after so long, went weeping over the side, back into captivity; and, in hopes of some change apparently, enlisted in the king's galleys.

It was a happy thing to have done, for it brought deliverance after all. Being at Minorca the very next Christmas, he found an English ship; and warned by previous experience, deceived the captain by telling him that he had been in Spain two years to learn the language. The captain gave him a passage, and after sixteen years' absence he saw the cliffs of Swanage and the brown rolling hills of Hampshire and Dorset, entering Poole Harbour February 1582.

THE SUFFERINGS OF ROBERT EVERARD.

ROBERT EVERARD, when a youth, was bound by his father, Mr. William Everard, as apprentice to Captain Crib, of the ship *Baudin*, ostensibly for a slave-hunting expedition, but in reality for almost anything which might turn up in any way of business, clean or dirty. He sailed from London in August 1686.

Passing Madeira, they made the islands of St. Jago and May, two of the Cape de Verds lying close together (visited and described by Phillips seven years after). Here they were chased by a pirate larger than themselves into St. Jago (probably the harbour of Praya*), and saved for the time by the land breeze coming off suddenly and strongly and baffling the enemy. At last, however, they were forced to go out and fight, which they did with

---

* There is also a very beautiful description of this harbour in the " Naturalist's Voyage round the World" of Darwin. Those of my readers who have not read this book have a very great pleasure still untasted before them. Some parents might be inclined to hesitate before putting the book into the hands of their household, in consequence of some of the later and bolder speculations of its author. They need not be at all afraid. It is as orthodox as Bishop Colenso's Algebra.

some success, beating off their enemy, though considerably shattered themselves.

They now went on to the east coast of Africa, apparently without adventure by the way, arriving ultimately at Delagoa Bay, where they began their ivory trade. The trade was slack, the merchant or supercargo only being able to collect about two tons. The usual remedy was applied; six or seven chiefs were seduced on board by fair words and immediately "clapped into the bilboes," or, in other words, put in irons, until more ivory should be produced. This treatment having been successful they sailed on to Talleer; where they bought sixteen or seventeen blacks, a great many cattle to salt up, four or five tons of rice, besides tamarinds, oranges, and other things. In these days a slaver of the same tonnage would have carried between two and three hundred negroes.

Hence they went to the island of Johanna, of which we have heard a great deal lately, and so held boldly across the Arabian Sea to Bombay.

A circumstance occurred at Bombay which is worth writing down, as illustrating old ship life. The first mate, Mr. Baker, went ashore with the merchant at Vosvar, about eighteen miles from Bombay, and got slightly drunk. On coming on board again some words passed between the mate and the merchant, whereupon the merchant not only put the mate into irons, but the carpenter also, *for consorting with him.* He had them carried to Bombay, put in prison, and tried by a court-martial on board the *Ruby* ship. They were flogged through the fleet, receiving ten lashes at each ship, and twenty at their own, and under the walls of the fort. A man could scarcely speak and live in those days at sea.

No wonder then, with this example before his eyes, Robert Everard, finding the master to whom he was bound dead, made but very feeble applications for the freedom which was undoubtedly his. The ship was ordered to Madagascar, and he must go with her. So she sailed south to Goa, and to Carwas, and so across through the Laccadive Islands towards Madagascar, which they sighted in ten days; "it being the Lord's Day, when we were at prayers."

After a few unsuccessful efforts to meet the inhabitants, they succeeded in getting a message from the king, who told them that if they would move their ship to another place which he indicated he would trade with them. They did so, and were met by a native who spoke both Portuguese and Arabic, as did also their coxswain: trading relations were now established on an apparently friendly footing. The king promised negroes and rice; the supercargo went on shore with beads, looking-glasses, and the usual trumpery, and received in exchange plantains, chickens, and bananas. The king drank toke, a sort of native beer, which Robert Everard tells us naively made the natives drunk, but not our people. The supercargo introduced the king to rack, and the king took to it so kindly that Robert Everard was sent on board for another bottle. Some of their negroes had run away, and the king promised to catch them for them, and indeed did get one, which however he would not give up, under the somewhat lame excuse that it would be better to wait until they were all caught. All seemed to be going smooth, save that the promised negro trade seemed unconscionably deferred.

This pleasant state of things was not, however, to last. One day the captain landed an armed boat's crew and surrounded the king's palace, terrifying the town. There was no rupture, but the captain went in to the king, asking of him when the negro trade should begin. The king said that in a month's time he should have plenty; and this satisfying the captain he departed.

On the Sunday following the captain went ashore to haul the seine, taking all the ship's company, leaving only little Everard, two men, and two black boys on board—a dangerously small complement. Some natives came out bringing a kid as a present to the captain, and no doubt saw the defenceless state of the ship. Quickly after the captain and crew returned on board, possibly much to the natives' disappointment.

Very soon, however, a canoe came alongside, with the object of tempting the captain on shore; they told him that they had some negroes for sale. Whether because the captain had conscientious scruples about buying negroes on the Sabbath, or whether he was idle, one cannot say, but even this tempting bait was ineffectual, and he refused to go on shore, sending, notwithstanding, a boat's crew, consisting of the supercargo, the coxswain, five men, and Robert Everard, on shore, with, in addition to the usual trading trumpery, guns, pistols, powder, shot, and knives, to exchange for the negroes.

They landed and carried up their goods to a house for trade, and the natives brought them food, and they sat for some little time, unsuspicious of their terrible fate. Suddenly, on hearing a noise, they thought it was the king coming, but in another moment were surrounded by an infuriated mob of natives, armed with lances. Five of the crew were instantaneously murdered, one of whom in his fall fortunately knocked down Robert Everard. The supercargo made a desperate dash at the door to get to the king, but was at once thrust through the belly and killed. The man left in charge of the boat was also killed, and Everard was alone amongst them.

Meanwhile a fearful tragedy was being played out on board the ship. The men in the canoe, which had come to tempt the captain on shore, were, as it turned out, secretly armed with short lances under their clothes: they had remained on board, and gone up on to the quarter-deck, where were the captain, the mate, the doctor, the purser, the carpenter, and several forecastle men. The captain was dining, and asked them to eat, but they refused, and he began his last meal. The natives suddenly dashed on the unarmed whites, cut the captain's throat from ear to ear, and murdered the mate and the purser.

The doctor was more dexterous, or more fortunate; he leaped off the quarter-deck, ran into the gun-room, and barred the door behind him—a piece of presence of mind which saved the rest. Some of the men ran into the shrouds, while others ran into the steerage, from whence they got to the doctor in the gun-room, through the scuttles, and to their arms, while one man leaped overboard and swam to the gun-room port, at which he was taken in. By degrees, after a loss of nine or ten men, and the partial plunder of the ship, they regained her.

We return to the poor boy on shore. They did not, when they saw he was alive, kill the lad in cold blood, but carried him to the king's house, which was next door to the house in which his shipmates had been massacred. The king treated him kindly, and bade his women give him food; "but his condition filled his stomach so, that he could not eat." It is to the credit of this savage chief that he treated this sailor lad kindly, under great injuries. It appeared, when Robert Everard had time to inquire, that an English ship had been there before them, who had "played the rogue" with the king, killing several of his men; and he had avenged himself in this way. I fear that our forefathers were but a rough-handed set of fellows, in spite of their piety.

The ship had been recovered, as we have seen, by the doctor, but had got on the rocks, the natives having cleverly cut her cables. The doctor and the ship's company spent the night in bombarding the town, making apparently tolerable practice, for one shot went clean through the palace, without however hurting any one; while the king kept his army on the alert, making them drunk with toke. In the morning she was off again and sailed away;

The Desertion of Robert Everard.

Everard being taken down by some of the king's men to see her sail. He saw that a disaster had happened, by meeting some of the natives carrying part of the bulkhead of the great cabin; four gallon bottles of Madeira wine, which he, in his capacity of cabin boy, had filled with his own hands the morning before; the captain's sword; the compasses from the binnacle; and great pieces of the ensign, which they had tied about their middles. From the negroes which had run from the ship he learnt the tale of the disaster. And then the ship sailed away, and he was left all alone.

The king now started on a tour, partly of inspection and partly of triumph, carrying the sailor boy with him as an exhibition of the power of his arms, but treating him very kindly. He travelled by boat from town to town along the coast, his men blowing a large shell whenever they neared a town, to give notice of his coming. Upon hearing this, the women turned out, dancing and waving cows'-tails tied on sticks; after which he landed, ate and drank, and then reviewed the contingent of his troops in those parts. Robert Everard had but little to complain of; the women, when they saw him, "would squeak, and run away as if affrighted;" but he seems to have had plenty to eat and drink at this time, and it must have been a pleasant change for him after being kicked into the lee-scuppers by the exceedingly energetic and godly captain, lately deceased. "The king bade his wife give me some, and she gave me some upon a plantain leaf." Fine times for a ship's apprentice! The king finished his grand tour of triumph and inspection, and returned to his capital, with Robert Everard figuratively at his chariot wheels.

Although this ungrateful youth had nothing particularly to complain of, yet, with the restlessness of a sailor, he desired his freedom.

In one of the very best sailor books ever written ("Typee") one notices that the sailor, though living in the sailor's paradise, with everything to eat, nothing to do, and with a beautiful mistress, still risks his life to get back to his old hardships; risks his life to get out of a South Sea island Eden, back to brutalities, the knuckle-dustings, the salt pork, of an American whale-ship. What looks so beautiful from amidst the tar and limejuice of a forecastle, becomes, when realized for a short time, absolutely intolerable to a restless British or American sailor. They must have change at all costs. "Rio is the finest port for a sailor in the world," says Jack; but after a fortnight at Rio he begins to ask if you were ever at Sydney. After three weeks in and about Pitt Street he begins to be pathetic over the old times at Singapore, which place he probably cursed heartily on leaving. Then it is Manilla with him; then Calcutta, which he tells you is the finest city in the world, as Sir Rummagee Bumaggee (which is his pronunciation of the late Parsee nobleman's name) is the first gentleman in the world. Then there is no place like New York, or, for a change, London. In short, your true English or American sailor always wants to be somewhere else. It has had its results: for one, among many, the language of Shakespeare bids fair to become the language of the world in time, and for a time.

This boy Everard was fully possessed with the restlessness of a sailor. He was sick of being fed by queens and petted by kings. There came, soon after the king's return to the capital, an Arabian ship to trade. He got speech with them, and prayed them to take him away, whither, he could have neither known or cared. They refused, alleging that it would involve a quarrel with the king, and that they would lose their trade with him. Robert offered to swim out to their ship in the dark to save them from responsibility, but they still refused; and having bought eight or ten negroes, sailed away and left him alone again.

I had forgotten to mention that, of those who landed on that disastrous Sabbath, there was one left alive besides Everard the cabin boy. The other member of the ship's company who survived the massacre was, in actual rating and rank, below the apprentice; in personal consideration and esteem, far higher. I allude to the ship's dog. Young Everard was not all alone then after all.

About six weeks after the ship had sailed, there arose a war, and the king crossed to fight his enemies, "carrying with him me and the dog." The march lasted six weeks, and the king picked up a large number of recruits at every town; but the dog was a very important personage apparently, at all events in Everard's eyes. "When he saw any hogs he would run and bark at them, till the negroes came and killed them with their lances; *and sometimes he would fetch a young pig and bring it to me.*"

It is a strange picture, the one which I see here.

A vast mob of tawny warriors armed with spears, restless, active. Among them all an English sailor lad, almost unclothed, barefooted, bareheaded, save for his tangled curling hair falling over his bronzed face; curiously puzzled and stupid with the whole business; and with him the only connecting link between the world he seemed to have left for ever and the hideous savagery always present—the ship's dog. To me this picture is something; to others it may be nothing at all.

The king's war lasted about two months, after which he returned home in triumph, with about one hundred slaves. Everard now had sunstroke on the march, and got his bare back burnt raw by the sun: this was only the beginning of his troubles.

The king now demanded of him if he could make powder, and he was forced to answer no, but said that he could make shot, and was accordingly set to work. He made his moulds of clay, and cast them of lead with tolerable success, making about four hundred. This pleased the king, and he treated him well; and then asked if he knew flint stones when he saw them. Everard answering yes, he was sent on an expedition to find some; but unfortunately for him, after a long search, he was unable to find any at all. The king now got tired of him, and turned him out of the house to live or die.

He was now absolutely naked, and continued in this state for two years and nine months, living the life of a hunted pariah dog, without one human being to show him pity or mercy. As he lay bare under a tree, the natives would come and throw dirt upon him in contemptuous sport, but no man offered to help him. In the rainy seasons, when it hardly held up for three months together, he would lie with a fire on each side of him to warm him; but at times, when the rain had fairly beaten through the leaves of his sheltering tree and was pouring on his body, the unhappy boy would creep under the eaves of their cottages for shelter in the dark, slinking back to his own misery before daydawn, lest they should find him and do him harm.

Few English youths have ever found themselves in worse circumstances than did Robert Everard for this weary two years and nine months. His case seems to have been worse than either that of Alexander Selkirk, or of the Musquito Indian who preceded him in his solitary occupation of Juan Fernandez. One almost wonders that he did not die; yet it is difficult to die at fifteen, when all the faculties of nature are waxing instead of waning, when life is so new and so devoid of experience, that hope, and the almost certain expectation of better things in a larger future, overbear any amount of present misery. A man would have died under this; the boy lived. Let us see as a matter of curiosity how he *did* live out this time, hunted about, naked, and alone among savages.

Apparently nature in Madagascar is in her kindest mood, or he would certainly have died. I could scarcely lay my hand on any other spot on the map where a naked lad could have suffered so much and have lived; but then he was an English lad, and lads of that race are hard to kill. "Too stupid to die," says Arminius. Very likely; still, India was not conquered by the Prussians.

His first requisite was fire. This he got by the old savage trick of working a hard piece of wood against a rotten piece; a trick which I have seen often tried without the slightest result except anger. Sir Samuel Baker confirms this matter. The getting of fire from two sticks seems to be a faculty possessed only by the most barbarous tribes; I have never seen a white man who could do it. However, Robert Everard could, and kept his fires burning, he lying, without any clothes whatever, between them.

For food: he had not so much as a knife; yet he did not fare badly. He got a piece of sharp stone, with which he dug out of the earth yams and potatoes (Mr. Ellis could tell us what these roots were, most probably); and these he roasted in the fire. Then he got plantains, bananas, oranges, and pine-apples, which wanted no roasting. Still his principal larder was the sea-shore.

He made himself a spear out of a stick, between five and six feet long, sharpened it as well as he could, and hardening it in the fire, with this he went down to the shore, and almost lived in the sea.

Sometimes he had the luck to spear a fish with his stick among the rocks. At other times, at high water, he made a dam (probably with sea-weed) among the channels of the rocks, strong enough to detain the fish when the tide went down. At another time he would wade into the water and watch for the large crabs which are common on that coast. When he saw one he would put down an elastic stick which he had between the claws, and bending it over, would hold the crab tight; then he would put his arm in the water and break off the claws, and so secure the crab without fear of being bitten. In the rainy weather he would go down to the shore to watch for turtle. Sometimes he would see one, and sometimes two, coming ashore. If they were small, he would kill them; if big, let them go, as being too large for removal: he also got many of their eggs, "which were very good meat."

"When I killed my turtles," he says, "I took a sharp rock stone, for want of a knife, and with it punched it round the belly, and so broke it open, and by such hard shifts I got out the meat; then I took as much as I could eat and laid it upon coals, which I kindled for that purpose, and the rest I hung up in some tree for another time. The callowpatch and callowpea* were my dishes to eat out of; and I used to keep yams and potatoes by me to serve me five or six days, and when they were all gone, then I went again to get more yams and potatoes; and I was to dig as deep as my arm's length for the yams, and about ten inches deep for the potatoes; and when my fish and turtle were gone, then I was to look out for some more, and I always kept good store by me."

Water, however, was almost his worst difficulty. "I had nothing to bring me a little water to set by

---

* I am so grossly ignorant that I thought these two words referred to the green and the yellow fat of the turtle, so much in request among our podagrophilists. Here they evidently refer to the upper and under shell of the turtle.

me when I was a-dry, but was always obliged to go so far (a mile) for more as I wanted it. It was also necessary for me to see that there were no blacks near the water, lest they should do me a mischief; and when I did drink at the well, I was forced to lie down upon my belly to drink." One would think that even an educated Englishman or German, the most unkillable of modern mortals, would have succumbed under such a stress of misfortune; but this sailor lad bore up and weathered worse things than these.

He was now, after two years, in addition to his other troubles, attacked by very serious illness. His body got all over sores, and he had no remedies except bathing in the salt water, which stung him to madness, and caused the fleas to torment him in a manner it is difficult to imagine. At last, however, he was so lucky as to find a wild bees' nest in a rock, and getting possession of the shard of a castaway earthen pot, he melted it down, wax, honey, and all, to use it for ointment.

This brought on delirium, but it lasted only a short space at a time, so that he was able to get about at intervals and get food. His deliverance was now, after three years of absolute nakedness and solitude, very near.

There came to the island a small Arabian vessel to buy negroes: to the captain of this vessel Robert Everard addressed himself, praying him to smuggle him away. But this the captain declined to do, as if he should in any way offend the king it would injure his negro trade. He however promised to do what he could for him, and while he stayed there told the boy to come to his house every day, and so fed him with the same victuals as he ate himself, sometimes adding a handful of candied dates; he also gave him a blue stone (probably sulphate of copper) to cure his sores.

So things went on for six weeks, until one day the Arab sent for Everard. When he arrived he was made to sit down, and a new palampere was given him to wrap himself in. The kind Arab now informed him of the good news that he had bought him of the king for twenty dollars, and that the king would never have let him go had he not believed that he would have died by the way.

He was now delivered and most kindly treated, being furnished with goods to trade with the blacks, his former persecutors, for anything he liked. Boy-like he spent it all in plantains, bananas, pine-apples, and sugar-canes: boy-like, also, he exasperated his old enemies. They, seeing him made a kind of gentleman of, were always pestering him for beads, which he, seeing that their hearts were set on them, had great pleasure in refusing them. They then used mutually to abuse one another, Everard telling them that he cared nothing for them now.

Everard must have been pretty safe under the Arab's protection, for the king seems to have had a wholesome dread of him. On one occasion some natives got drunk, and accidentally sent a bullet through the Arabian quarters. Immediately the whole crew were landed and armed, and marching to the palace they demanded instant explanations. The king was glad to give this handful of men two slaves to make it up with them for what was a mere accident.

His long captivity was drawing towards an end, although he was still a slave. The vessel in which he sailed away was an open one with only one mast, containing, besides the crew, 120 negroes, placed in rows on open spars, among which Robert Everard had his place. It was impossible to move for the whole voyage (which lasted a month); where they sat all day, there they slept all night, so that when landed at Commoro (an island in the mouth of the Mozambique Channel) they were quite unable to stand. It is impossible to go into the horrible details of the arrangements of a slaver; but dreadful as those arrangements were, they were nevertheless, as described by Everard, far superior to those which are made in a modern slaver. The consequences of fresh air alone seem to have been to reduce the death-rate to a minimum, for he does not mention a single death.

Here the slaves were landed, while they mended their ship and bought about a dozen more. Everard was well supplied with everything, and kindly treated; indeed the Arabs seem to have been in general good to their slaves. Here they stayed twelve days, and then set sail for Patta ("Bad in Ajan"?), an Arab settlement, which they reached after a stormy voyage, in this clumsy, slow-sailing slave craft, of six weeks. Here they were all, bond and free, hospitably entertained by the governor's wife with boiled rice and mutton; while the governor himself gave him a fine red turban to wear and a pair of shoes; also caused to be made for him a coat and breeches. He had the toothache also; and so the Arabs got a piece of paper, wrote on it, and put it into his tooth, which, says the boy in all simplicity, stopped it aching for two years.

While here a Portuguese slaver accidentally ran ashore. The Arabs at once attacked her, and after a fight of two hours succeeded in taking her, with 300 slaves. They were now afraid lest they should not be able to keep power over such a very large body of prisoners, so that every man in the settlement was armed to the teeth. The country people came down with bows and arrows to their assistance and to trade with them. Everard describes them as tawny men with long black hair.

He was now put on board a small open vessel, containing 100 slaves, and ivory, bound for Muscat, where he was told there were Englishmen. They had a terrible passage of above a month, the sea breaking over their deckless craft, and rendering it impossible for them to light their fires and boil their rice, which they ate raw; one of their water tanks leaked out, and they were put on half-a-pint a day.

At length they landed at Muscat. Among the Arabs and Banians looking on, there was a Banian boy, who ran up to the house where the Englishmen lived to tell them that there was a little English boy come ashore with the blacks. Three Englishmen came down at once and got hold of him. The overseer of the slaves allowed him to go home with them, and they carried him off in triumph.

He had forgotten his native tongue, and could only talk in Madagascar, but made shift to let them know that he had belonged to the *Baudin*. They boiled mutton and porridge full of onions for their precious young prize; then they took him into the market and bought him a fine cap; then they, I regret to say, took him upon the housetop and made him tipsy with punch; and at last Robert Everard found himself once more, to his great astonishment, in a real bed, "with a very good coat, sheets, and quilt."

The governor having given his sanction to his remaining with these Englishmen, he took up his abode with them, although still a slave. After about seven days living with them, his English began to come to him sufficiently well to understand who they were. One of them (Mr. King), his chief entertainer, was a ship's surgeon, and the other two apparently able seamen. Singularly enough these three had belonged to the *Baudin* themselves, and only deserted her three weeks before, and now sailed with the Arabs—the able seamen with rank of gunner, and the doctor apparently as surgeon-general to the Port of Muscat. With these generous roving sailors he stayed a fortnight, getting himself petted and spoilt like a ship's monkey; they bought him silk and chintz for his neckties, and alligar (?) for his shirts, and at length went to the man who had imported him, and after a little bargaining offered twenty dollars for him, his prime cost as will be remembered, and which strikes one as being a generous and kindly action on their part.

This, however, was refused by the governor, for reasons which I am unable to understand. He insisted on sending the boy to the English at Surat, very possibly considering that he would be held in some sort answerable for him if he gave him over to three such very loose fish as the three Englishmen who had been so kind to him: this, however, is merely conjecture on my part. Another Englishman now arrived, and was kind to the boy; but the answer was the same to him as to the others, that the boy must be handed over to the English at Surat. This Englishman however, wherefore I do not understand, wrote to our Persian agent, who immediately sent a Dutch Banian with his purchase-money, and twenty dollars more for the English sailors and doctor who had been so kind to him. He bidding them farewell went on board the little open ship in which he was to coast up the Persian Gulf. The reasons of the boy's going to Persia, and his hearsay geography, are both a little obscure, but to my judgment there is an air of simple truth about all he says, which in a narrative of mere personal adventure like this is all we want. We do not want so much startling situations, as to see life in every one of its ramifications in the long past; and to me I confess it is more interesting to know what one, dead so long, thought, ate, and clothed himself withal, than any mere fact such as his having been nearly eaten by a tiger or a crocodile. Every one acquainted with sailors knows, that they will sometimes "yarn," or invent, with regard to mere adventures to a great extent.

Robert Everard was started on his, to me, somewhat incomprehensible voyage by his kind countrymen, with store of bread, cheese, rice, salt beef, and two gallons of liquor almost as strong as brandy (which one hopes he did not drink himself). Besides this they bought him a good rug and pillow, and two earthen pots to boil his victuals in. They likewise gave him some sugar, and a dollar and a half in money to spend at the places where they should touch, like the old tip one used to get when one went to school; and so splendidly provided for the boy, not we hope without thankfulness at his extraordinary good fortune, went aboard and stayed aboard till she sailed—coming ashore however every day to spend a part of his dollar and a half, "to buy me some fresh victuals, and cucumbers, and other green trade;" from which last expression I make a guess that he hailed from the counties of Devon or Cornwall.

To such of my readers as are not used to sailors and the sea I may be allowed to point out, that at every point in this singular narrative one comes across little points, small in themselves, which force one to believe the whole. This last is one among a hundred others. If you say that this story was invented, you invest at once this sailor Robert Everard with the genius of a Shakespeare for details. It is to me absolutely incredible that it is not true; in reading it carefully you come across little personal matters, which no man, save Shakespeare, could have invented. If Robert Everard invented this story, he had sufficient genius to have written the little-cared-for dialogue of mad Tom in Lear—in some respects Shakespeare's highest effort: as for Defoe, he could have beaten him on his own ground. I have said more than once elsewhere that I believed that Defoe got the first idea of his wondrous "Bob Singleton" from Robert Everard, and I see no reason to alter my opinion, save from the reflection, "How could Defoe ever have heard of Everard's adventures?" Then again one asks, "How could Defoe have ever heard of the Victoria Nyanza and the Albert Nyanza?" yet he was familiar with them. Not to be too discursive however, and to return to Robert Everard. In the whole of his narrative there is not one single fact mentioned which is out of the most ordinary human experience; and there are internal evidences innumerable, principally of eating and drinking, which make it certain to me that it is absolutely true.

I make these remarks because I find that even now there are two sorts of travellers: the one your Palgraves, Spekes, Burtons, Bakers, Livingstones, who tell plainly what they saw, representing the Jesuits* and sailors of old times; and another more imaginative class, who tell you what they think they ought to have seen, representing the Minorites and Franciscans. In result, I merely claim that Robert Everard's narrative will hold water, in fact is one of the most reliable narratives across which I have come.

He vaguely states that he came to Persia, to what town there he does not mention. Whether he merely followed Mr. Palgrave's homeward route from Ormuz to Muscat, or whether he passed Ormuz and came on to Linga, is not very clear. He mentions passing between an island and the mainland; and this may be the

---

* Singularly enough I find, since this was written, that Mr. Darwin confirms me about the credibility of the old Jesuit travellers more than once. It is very pleasing to an unscientific person to find himself confirmed by one of the greatest scientific writers of the day. The reason is not difficult to find. The Jesuits of those times were probably the most devoted, and certainly the most highly educated, body of men in Christendom.

larger island of Dgism, or the smaller one of Ormuz. However, here was an English agent who treated him most kindly, and promised at his request to send him home in the first ship.

Soon after there came in an English ship called the *Diana*, bound up the Persian Gulf, and the master of which was very sick; and coming to stay at the agent's, in an open boat in a heavy surf, got wetted and died. The mate, who succeeded him, persuaded the boy to come with him to Bassorah, at the head of the Gulf. The *Diana*, with some goods out of a king's ship, the *Kemthorn*, which had put in leaky, and was besides too large to go up the Euphrates, went up the Gulf, apparently feeling her way very carefully, and disliking very much the sight of any strange sail; extremely anxious when they were near her in a calm, and devoutly thankful when there was breeze enough for her to give them the go-by. She got a pilot to take her into the Euphrates, which Captain Hamilton, who followed Robert Everard in a very few years, describes as being about a mile broad, and keeping the same breadth for the whole of the ninety miles up to Bassorah, or, as Mr. Palgrave, who should know if any man does, writes it, Basrah.*

He gives a ship-boy's account of some fighting which was going on here while he stayed, between the Turks and the wild Arabs. He only slightly alludes to it in mentioning that the Armenian merchants were begged by the Pasha not to bring their goods ashore, as the town was not safe; and again,

* "Botzra, on the river Tigris."—Rabbi Benjamin, anno 1160.

the captain of the *Diana* was asked by the Pasha to draw his ship up the river a little way and bombard these Arabs, which he immediately did, giving his men five dollars apiece all round immediately after the engagement. This is about all Everard says concerning this struggle, and is about as much as a sailor-boy would be likely to know or care, but it singularly confirms his veracity.

Considering him to have started from home in 1686, and to have returned in 1693, it must now have been in or about the year 1692. What was happening at Bassorah that year? A rather remarkable thing. Captain Alexander Hamilton, who came trading to these parts but a very few years after Robert Everard had left, and who may possibly have been there *before* Robert Everard, points out these facts while lamenting the extraordinary difference between the warlike, jealous Turks, the then possessors of Bassorah, and their more cosmopolitan and mercantile predecessors, the Persians. He was evidently *au fait* with the trade of Bassorah, and he tells us this story. In 1691 the plague got into the town, 80,000 Persians died and the rest fled the city, which was first of all taken possession of by the innumerable beasts of prey, which, according to every writer, abound in the neighbouring deserts, and secondly by the Arabs, who held it for nearly twelve months. The Arabs in their turn were turned out by the Turks. It was the last flying bands of the beaten Arabs, making their last furious attempt, on which the *Diana*, with Robert Everard on board, fired at the request of the Pasha. I am pleased to find in the course of reading such an undeniable proof of the veracity of my little friend. He had happened to arrive at Bassorah at the very time when that town was passing out of the Persian hands for ever.

Not for ever out of *Arab* hands nevertheless: one finds in reading Franklin's voyage from Bengal to Persia (1787) that ninety-six years afterwards a certain sheik, Twing, having been on a raid against a brother sheik, was met rather dangerously near to the desert by the Governor of Bassorah, who came out, as a kind of picnic, to congratulate the sheik, his friend, on his successful plundering expedition. Instigated by the devil no doubt, the sheik took it into his head to take the governor prisoner, to send him to the rear, and to claim the town of Bassorah as his own in right of his ancestor (doubtless the sheik who had held it for twelve months in 1691, and in whose bombardment little Robert Everard had assisted). This very clever sheik made a splendid *coup d'état* of it. He sent in fifteen hundred Arabs to take possession of the palace; they seem to have been unopposed, the inhabitants probably thinking that they could not be worse off, and might be better. After finding that they did not make their *experimentum* on the vile bodies of his fifteen hundred, Sheik Twing trusted his own sacred person in, seized the shipping, inhabited the palace, and gave the most polite assurances to the inhabitants. The next thing he did was to send a note, in a tone of injured innocence, to Constantinople, lamenting that he should have been kept out of his just rights (which he had just invented) so long; promising his allegiance to the Porte on condition of having given him the Pashalic of Bassorah and *Bagdad!* (quite a new idea, developed as rapidly as the original one). After this glorious piece of coolness, he had collected all the Jew and Armenian merchants, and had got a loan of six thousand tomauns from them. A forced loan? Oh, dear, no; only you would find it on the whole best to make it. The security? Why, the carefully worded bond of the sheik himself; who, however, as soon as he had got it, thought it just as well to get out of the mud-walled fortifications of Bassorah, and have the safe desert clear behind him.

As the news from Constantinople might be rather unfavourable, as the Grand Seigneur might not exactly like such a degree of coolness as he had exhibited, he marched up the Euphrates towards Bagdad, just to anticipate the messenger with the firman. If it was favourable, good: if unfavourable, none could be the worse except the messenger.

Now a big brother of his, who had been set aside in the succession to the sheikdom by their father, had been waiting all his life to give his younger brother what is called in low life "a hoist." When this wicked younger brother of his had so shamelessly invaded the territories of the head of the holy Mahommedan religion, had captured his governor, had marched into Bassorah, the righteous soul of the dispossessed elder brother burned with ire. His own flesh and blood was one thing, but this insult to the Sublime Porte was another. He fled into the arms of the Pasha of Bagdad, and raised such a wasp's-nest about his dear younger brother's ears, that I should fancy more than once that Sheik Twing wished that their father had left his elder brother in quiet possession of the sheikdom.

The Porte never answered his letter; they merely wrote to the Pasha of Bagdad ordering his head. The pasha made friends with a neighbouring tribe of Arabs, the Bandi, whom Twing had scorned in his prosperity, and together they attacked the audacious sheik. He very nearly won, but the allies were too strong for him. His army was as much beaten as an Arab army ever is, and he went home (with the six thousand tomauns), and up to the latest intelligence (Dec. 1787) remained there on his native desert in peace. It may be considered as highly probable that his elder brother did *not* follow him to the paternal tents.

As for the Jew and Armenian merchants who had most audaciously presumed to save their throats from being cut from one ear to another, by giving this sheik the money he demanded, you may be sure that they met with the deserts of their crime as soon as the Turks got back into Bassorah. They had to pay through the nose. Sheik Twing had plagued them with whips; the new Governor of Bassorah (one does not read what Sheik Twing did with the old one) plagued them with scorpions.

The Grand Seigneur appointed Ahmed, the traitorous elder brother, as sheik in room of his brother Twing. One cannot help wondering if he ever went and took possession.

With this Eastern episode, which seemed to me so thoroughly Eastern as to be worth disinterring, and so exceedingly amusing that I was forced to tell it in my own language (for which I hope the reader will forgive me), I take leave of my little friend Robert Everard. His adventures, after Bassorah, are scarcely worth mentioning; he went to Bombay, round the Cape to the West Indies, and so home, meeting his father at Blackwall after seven years' absence, "to the great joy of us both."

JOHN FOX.

THE escape of John Fox, an English gunner, from the captivity of the Turks in the Port of Alexandria, in the year 1577, after fourteen years, is certainly one of the most magnificent pieces of audacity known; it was evidently thought so at the time, for he received compliments, not only from the Queen's Council, but also from the Pope of Rome and the King of Spain.

During the twenty years from 1560 to 1580 the trade to the Levant and to all parts of the Turkish empire fell completely into abeyance, although there was peace between the two countries—nay, more or less of a good understanding. Bodenham* made a successful voyage in 1550; in 1553 the Grand Turk gave ample privileges to Mr. Antony Jenkinson; yet until the correspondence between Queen Elizabeth

---

* Bodenham's voyage to the Levant is very interesting; the more so, as we find that one of his shipmates was no other than Richard Chancellor, who went with Sir Hugh Willoughby on the Northern Expedition in 1553. In that expedition Chancellor got on in his ship, the *Bonadventure*, saw the Emperor of Muscovy, and earned the title of "Discoverer of Russia." Sir Hugh Willoughby, in the *Bona Esperanza*, was, as is well known, frozen to death with all his crew on the coast of Lapland.

and Sultan Murad Khan, two years after the date of the following adventure, there was actually no Levant trade whatever.

The reason for this is not difficult to seek. There were certainly commercial treaties between the Venetians, the French, and the Poles on the one hand, and the Turks on the other; but none with the English. In special cases, as in the case of Jenkinson, special free passes were given, but these were only a special, and the Turks treated every English vessel without one as fair spoil, and carried off their crews into hopeless captivity as a matter of course. In her Majesty's letter of 1579, we only find the proudest woman in Europe " entreating and using mediation" to the Sultan, in a way which would make Lord Stratford de Redcliffe open his eyes, for such of her subjects as were detained in his galleys, and praying that the safe-conduct granted to Sir Edward Osborne and Mr. Staper might be extended to all her subjects. Again, later, in 1581, one Peter Baker, of Ratcliffe, having misconducted himself inconceivably in the Levant, robbed certain Grecians among other matters, the Queen writes most deferentially to the Sultan, apologizing and promising restitution, giving him also to understand that if she should have the luck to catch this same Peter Baker she would make a most remarkable example of him; so it is to be hoped, for his own sake, that Peter Baker did not show on the stones of Ratcliffe Highway till her Grace's wrath had cooled.

These little matters seem to prove that the right of the Turks to attack English ships was acknowledged, and that to do so was no *casus belli;* moreover, the right was by no means conceded to English ships, who had the great privilege only of taking care of themselves as well as they could. No wonder that with lifelong hopeless slavery before them they fought like fiends against the Turks, preferring death to surrender.

In the year 1563, a ship called the *Three Half Moons*, Grove master, with thirty-eight men on board, sailed from Portsmouth for Seville. All went well until they were near the Straits, when they found themselves surrounded by eight Turkish galleys, who showed their intentions towards them very plainly.

The owner of the ship now made them a speech, exhorting them to bravery and to trust in God; after which they engaged in prayer for a time, and then prepared for battle.

Then up stood Grove the master, a comely man, with his sword and target, holding them in defiance against his enemies; up then stood the owner, the master's mate, the boatswain, and the purser, and gave defiance likewise; then with the sound of rattling drums, blaring trumpets, and screaming fifes Grove took his gallant little ship into action against these hopeless overwhelming odds.

John Fox had charge of the guns, and plied them wonderfully fast; but it very soon came to close quarters, as the Turks found to their cost, for our fellows sent arrows hailing in on them with such rapidity that the havoc among them was very great; but the ship, receiving the concentrated fire of so many, soon began to show signs of damage, which the Turks perceiving, ran into her and dashed aboard.

Their reception was terrible; the desperate and

furious Englishmen had now taken to their halberts and brown bills, which did fearful execution upon the lighter-armed Easterns. Chief among them all, however, was the boatswain, who astonished friend and foe alike by his splendid valour, raging among the Turks "like a wood (mad) lion," so that none dare face him; but at last a random shot from the Turks smote him on the breast where his whistle hung, and he sank down on the deck a dying man, and bidding them all farewell used his latest breath to fight on to the last.

They meant to do as their dead leader had urged them, but men cannot perform impossibilities. The Turks were so numerous that they actually crowded on them until their long weapons were useless, and they were taken in detail; and at last it was all over and the brave old flag was down.

The Turks treated them with the greatest cruelty and brutality, taking no heed of their gallant defence except to use them the worse for it. Their clothes were stripped off, and they were set at once to the oar, under their masters' whips, some of them never to leave it again.

It was not very long before the owner and the master were ransomed by friends in England, and went home; but the rest, all those whose friends were too poor, were left in their misery. Ill-usage, overwork, and starvation soon told their tale upon them; one by one these gallant sailors died off, till at the end of fourteen years only one was left, John Fox, the gunner. He was a man of great constitution, and of vast courage and resource. He was a good barber, and by exercising this trade had been able to improve his rations a little, and keep body and soul together when the others died. He also, after many years, by a small fee to the jailor, was allowed to walk in and out of the prison with irons on his legs, as were six others.

After fourteen years he devised a scheme for escape. It was the winter season. The galleys were all drawn up, their masts, sails, and oars put in store, and the captains and crews were away on furlough, and there remained 268 Christian captives in the prison, consisting of sixteen different nations, of whom but three were Englishmen, John Fox, of Woodbridge, in Suffolk, William Wickney, of Portsmouth, and Robert Moore, of Harwich.

Not far from the prison there was a little kind of public-house, kept by a prisoner who earned enough to pay the jailor's fees for the indulgence. This man's name was Unticaro; he was a Spaniard who had been thirty years a prisoner, and had kept himself so quiet that he was not in the least suspected. John Fox, coming frequently to his house, opened at last what lay on his mind, and found a willing abettor in Unticaro.

By degrees all the other six prisoners who had their partial liberty were taken into the plot, and at last, at the end of December 1576, everything was ready. Fox distributed to them files, which had been procured by Peter Unticaro, and they were ordered to be rid of their irons by eight o'clock the next night.

The next night the conspirators assembled at Unticaro's, and to all appearance made very merry to distract suspicion; and after a little Unticaro rose and went to the governor of the prison, and begged him to step round to his house, as a friend awaited him there. (He named one of the masters of the city.) The unsuspecting Turk came with him at once, telling his people not to lock up, for he should soon be home.

In the meantime the others had armed. John Fox had a rusty swordblade, the others had such spits and glaives as they could find in the house; and having put out the lights they awaited the coming of their oppressor.

When the wretched man approached the little bothy and saw it all dark, he suspected at once, and turned, but only to find John Fox in his way with his rusty sword. He pleaded to him: "Fox," he said, "what have I deserved of thee that thou shouldst seek my death?" They were his last words. "Bloodsucker of Christians!" cried John Fox; and then with the suppressed fury of fourteen miserable years concentrated into one blow he struck him down dead at his feet.

They now marched towards the prison, which had been left unlocked by the orders of the dead man, and entered it softly. The warders, of whom there were six, cried out to know who they were, but answering "All friends" Fox and his fellow-conspirators fell upon them and killed them, after which they shut the bygate and put a cannon against it.

They now entered the dead governor's lodge, where they found the keys of the fortress at his bed's head, and also a very large treasure in ducats, which Fox did not touch, but with which Unticaro and two others loaded themselves, stuffing the gold inside their shirts. Here also were plenty of arms, with which they furnished themselves.

The next thing to be done was to open the prison doors with the keys: this was soon done, and the prisoners set busily, some to barricade the gate, others to fit out, as rapidly as was possible, a splendid galley, the best in Alexandria, which happened to be handy, with oars, sails, and cordage. With the experience of this kind of work gained in many a year, and with the certainty that rapidity was their only hope, the liberated Christians worked with a will which may be imagined. Fox and the head conspirators meanwhile had rougher work in hand.

Eight Turks had retreated before them, from floor to floor, until they stood at bay on the roof in their desperation. The lives of these men were necessary to the success of the enterprise, and the Christians, by getting up a ladder, came face to face with them, when a most fell and bloody fight ensued. The Christians were victorious; but Fox himself was shot twice through his clothes, and old Peter Unticaro, with the other two who had overburdened themselves with the gold, fought so clumsily, that they were killed.

One of the Turks, driven over the side of the roof, fell to the ground still alive, and by his moans and cries roused a few of the inhabitants of the scattered suburb, who in their turn aroused all Alexandria at midnight with the news that the Christian prisoners had risen and were murdering their jailors.

Alexandria was up like a swarm of bees at the news, and the two castles which crossed fire at the mouth of the harbour were manned and on the alert.

The desperate Christians, maddened with some feeling between terror and hope, worked as men have seldom worked; some carrying on a furious battle with the Turks, who were by this time attacking the prison on the land side; others putting in oars, masts, and provisions. It was a terrible fight with time, and the Christians won.

At last they were all on board. They hoisted sail before a fair wind, and stood straight towards the two grim silent castles which stood between them and freedom. No man blenched as they swiftly approached them; and until the fortresses opened on their defenceless galley like a furious volcano

> "There was silence, deep as death,
> And the boldest held his breath
> For a time."

There was nothing to be done. The full-sailed galley sped on before the south wind, with the shots whistling and hurtling around her, the furious population swarming on the shore like bees. With the forty-eight shots which she received in her few minutes' purgatory not one of them harmed anybody. The forts passed they were on the free blue Mediterranean.

Their first act, when called together by John Fox, was to offer up thanksgiving for their wonderful delivery. They then set to work at the oars, and laboured with a will, for it was very certain that the Turks would soon be in pursuit of them.

But the wind was foul, and provisions ran out. For twenty-eight weary days they toiled on, and began to lose heart, and eight died of starvation; but when hope was nearly dead they sighted Crete.

The monks received them most kindly and joyfully. They begged of Fox his rusty sword, and hung it up as a precious relic. From hence they went to Tarento, where they sold their galley, and having divided the proceeds among one another, started on foot for Naples. The Turks scoured the seas for them in every direction but the right one. On one occasion, however, they had a narrow escape; a ship which followed them told them six Turkish galleys were only one day after them.

When they separated, John Fox went to Rome, where he was kindly received by the Pope, Gregory XIV., who rewarded him for his valour, and wrote a very kind and complimentary letter for him, in which he says: "We in his behalf do, in the bowels of Christ, desire you that, taking compassion of his former captivity and present penury, you doe not only suffer him to pass freely through all your cities and towns, but also succore him with your charitable alms; whom with tender affection of pitie we commend unto you. Rome, April, 1577."

It is very pleasant to contemplate the hearty kindness of the Pope towards the native of a country he tried so hard to ruin. Our other great foe also, the King of Spain, was almost equally kind to him; gave him a place as gunner at Valentia, with eight ducats a month (2*l.* 10*s.*). In two years he returned to England, where he was pensioned by the Court for his services. He came from Woodbridge in Suffolk. That is on the tideway of the river Deben, between Ipswich and Saxmundham.

ALVARO NUNEZ.

ALVARO NUNEZ, called also Capo de Vava,* was treasurer to the expedition sent under Navaez, the would-be superseder of Cortez, to conquer and take possession of all the country between the River of Palms and the Cape Sable. It sailed in the year 1527, consisting of five ships and 600 men, and it reached Dominica in safety, where it left 140 men; after which it proceeded to St. Iago de Cuba.

Here Navaez, looking about for men, victuals, and horses, met with one Parcalle, who promised him a good adventure if he would come with him as far as Trinidad, about 300 miles along the coast. Navaez sailed at once, but staying behind with four ships at Vera Cruz (the cape at the end of the Cobra mountain) he sent on one Captain Pantoxa with one ship to get the goods, and sent our hero, Alvaro Nunez, as treasurer, to see after him: which was the cause of Alvaro Nunez being close to the centre of the greatest cyclone which had been met with since the discovery of America, as is proved by the certificates got from

* Or Cabeza de Vaca.

T

him by the inhabitants, and shown to the King of Spain.

Alvaro Nunez happened to be on shore when it came on to blow, and was unable to get on board his ship. The wind grew worse and worse all Sunday, and on Sunday night attained its greatest horror. There was no shelter, for both houses and churches had fallen before the blast, and the fragments were flying into the forest; seven or eight men would go staggering about aimlessly in the darkness, dreading instant death, and holding on by one another to steady themselves against the wind. In the darkness of that wild Sunday night they heard noises, as of devils in the storm—bells, flutes, drums, and other instruments; but the longest night has its day, and on the Monday morning they went down to the harbour.

Nullum in conspectu navem! Only some of their furniture in the water, whereby they knew that they were cast away. They walked along the coast, but there was nothing to be found; and so they turned from the ruined shore to the ruined forest, and about three-quarters of a mile from the surf found a boat on some trees, which gave them a hint of what had happened. But walking some thirty miles along the shore Alvaro found two men of his ship, under the debris of some houses, but so changed by bruising that he could not identify them; also he found a friar's habit, and a torn coverlid. For the rest nothing whatever. Sixty men had been on board the two ships, and for them mother, sweetheart, and wife must wait until the judgment day.

A Storm in the Forest. P. 274.

The thirty men who had come on shore with Nunez and Pantoxa were all saved, but they had to live in the miserable and wasted country, as best they might, until the Admiral arrived with four other ships. After some time he came, and they were relieved.

The hurricane, however, had such an effect on the minds of the crews of the four surviving ships, that they earnestly prayed the Admiral Henrignez not to put to sea during that winter. He attended to their prejudices, and sent Alvaro Nunez to winter at Sagna (Bahia de Xagna), twelve leagues further. Here they stayed from the 5th of November to the 20th of February.

They were now joined by the Admiral Henrignez, and set sail, 400 men and eighty horses, in four ships and a brigantine. Their pilot Mirvelo ran the fleet on the sandbar in coming out, and only got off after five days, at spring tide. There is nothing to notice about them until they crossed to the south point of Florida and came into an open roadstead, which I am inclined to consider to be the sound between Great Island and the main of Florida.

Here Henrignez landed on an island and made advances to the Indians, who brought him fish and venison. He took possession of the country in the name of the Emperor, and landed his men and forty horses, all the rest being dead. Such was another conquest of Florida.

Landing at night they found the huts of the Indians empty, they being all out fishing. One house or congeries of huts was sufficiently large to contain three hundred people, and in it they found nets, and, alas! to one of the nets they found hung a golden beli.

The pilot Mirvelo now declared himself to be entirely out of reckonings, not knowing where he was: the brigantine was therefore despatched on a roving commission to find a harbour, which he said he knew, or to return to Cuba. Meanwhile those that were left began to see more of the Indians, who were not without the knowledge of white men, for they had many Spanish merchants' chests, in each of which was a corpse, embalmed in painted deer-skins. "The commissary thought it was a kind of idolatry, and so he burned the chests with the bodies."

This was in the year 1527. Bartholomew de las Casas, the Dominican monk, who sent his furious protest against the cruelties of the Spaniards towards the Indians, wrote in 1542. It is doubtful whether that magnificent book can be epitomized in a book of adventure. Still let us glance at it, for it will light our path in some degree in this adventure which we have in hand. No intelligent reader will blame me for pausing here, and giving a slight sketch of what Las Casas did, and of what he said. He is familiar to every educated man through Prescott. Let us see him and hear him speak for himself. In reading Prescott's glorious prose, you see his name often; let me humbly introduce him to you in a more familiar way than a great historian could do. One's object is to be familiar without being vulgar.

I for my part rank Bart. de las Casas,* the Dominican friar, afterwards Bishop of Chiapa, among the most noble and most fearless men who ever walked the earth. He is one of those men who takes your soul to his, and warms it by his honest warmth. Listen to him in what, I dare say, is a sufficiently clumsy English translation; listen and say if you do not love. This is his plea for the slaughtered Indians, written to Don Philip of Spain, the man whom our people know, the cruel king whom we shall hate till time be dead. Mind it is no well-backed Radical or well-backed Tory speaking in a free country; only a solitary Dominican friar, speaking to the man who was practically lord of the earth. Who dares speak so now? Is not this the purest constitutional radicalism?

"Most High and Mighty Lord, as God by His providence hath, for the guiding and commoditie of mankind in this world, in realmes and provinces, appointed Kings to be fathers, and so consequently the most noble and principall members of common-weales: so can we not justly doubt, by reason of the good wills that Kings and Princes have to minister justice, but if there be anythings amisse, either by violence or injuries committed, the only cause that they are not redressed is, that Princes have no notice of the same. For certainely if they knew them, they would employ all diligence and endeavour in the remedie thereof. For it is sufficient to be

* Since writing what follows, I perceive that Mr. Helps has written his life. The life of such a man, by such a hand, should be a very beautiful one.

presupposed, even of the kindly and natural vertue of a King, that the only notice that he taketh of any mischief tormenting his kingdom, is sufficient to procure him, if it be possible to root out the same as being a thing which he cannot tolerate even one only moment of time."

The Indians, as Las Casas goes on to tell us, were very gentle, very tender, of an easy complexion, which can sustain no travel, and die easily of any disease. He gives them the best character which any man could give to a nation, and then he says how they were treated by the Spaniards.

After forty-nine years, he gives this as the result of Spanish rule. In St. Domingo, out of the three million souls there remained two hundred. Cuba and Jamaica, with sixty other islands once as fertile as "the King's garden at Seville," were now all waste. As the inhabitants of the island of St. Domingo were used up in working in the mines, the Indians of the smaller islands were captured and set to labour also, so that these islands were left without one single inhabitant, after having sustained a population of 500,000.

What Mr. Helps has written about this glorious man, Bart. de las Casas, I have not yet read. I only hope that his estimate of him is the same as mine, that he is worthy of a place in a triptich with Savonarola and Wycliffe, as one of the three great Catholic protesters. Whether he agrees with me or not, his books are always beautiful and good, so I would recommend my younger readers to make Mr. Helps one of their "friends in council" about

Bart. de las Casas, and every other matter on which he speaks, in preference to me, as a man more able, but I hope not more diligent.

We must go on a little further with this Bart. de las Casas, before we get to Alvaro Nunez once more. We are on possibly the strangest journey ever taken by mortal man; we must illustrate it as we can.

Las Casas tells us that between 1510 and 1542 there were no less than four attacks on this country of Florida, all of which were utterly disastrous: that of Juan Ponce de Leon, with 80 men; that of Vasco D'Aylon with 220; that of Pamphilo de Navaez, with 400 (the present expedition); and lastly, the one of which every one has heard, that of Ferdinand de Soto. Of the first three, including the one we have in hand, Las Casas says, "They are dead of an evil death; and as for the houses they built in times past with the blood of mankind, their memory is abolished off the face of the earth, as if they had never been in the world."

His testimony about De Soto is still more quaint and strange. "The fourth tyrant, that came last in the yeere 1538, cunningly advized, and being fully furnished, there is, three years since (he writes in 1542), no tidings concerning him. Surely he is one of the notoriousest and best experimented in those that have done the most hurts, mischieves, and destructions in any realmes with their consorts. Wherefore I believe that God has given him like end with the others."

Strangely enough, God, who often makes vain the prophecies of men, made this friar's furiously indignant words come true, almost at the very moment they were being uttered, little as he knew it. Turn to the account of the expedition of De Soto, written by a Portuguese of the company.

Broken-hearted and fever-sticken, on the 20th of May, 1542 (just when Las Casas was writing), the Claverhouse of the Indians lay a-dying by the banks of the swift Mississippi.

"On the next day departed out of this life the valourous, virtuous, and valiant captain, Don Fernando de Soto, Governor of Cuba, and Adelantado of Florida, whom fortune advanced, as it useth to do others, that he might have the greater fall."

Strange prophecy and strange fulfilment. His followers kept his death secret from the Indians, as his personal prestige was so great among them that they dreaded being attacked if the Indians discovered De Soto's death. They buried him, first on shore, but afterwards secretly, in the dead of night, took him out in a canoe and sank him in the middle of the stream. The old legend about him, which we used to sing when we were much younger, is not correct.

> "Oh wrap me up in a banner proud,
> In the banner of old Castile,
> And let the war-drum round me roll,
> The trumpets o'er me peal.
> And bury me at the noon of night,
> When gone is the sultry beam,
> At noon of night, by torches light,
> In Mississippi's stream."

The red-handed captain had no such gaudy funeral. A solitary canoe held still on the hissing eddies of the Mississippi at midnight by two steadfast Indians; four faithful friends, who loved him, as one may read; a scared priest hurrying through his offices in the trembling boat; the solemn forests around walling the headlong river rushing on to the eternity, of ocean; above the calm stars, which had looked down upon so many of the dead man's deeds. A splash in the water, and the last was seen on earth of Ferdinand de Soto, whose name will be remembered for ever, were it only for the cry which was sent up to heaven against him from the mouth of one solitary monk.

Forgive the digression—we are speaking of a time six years previously; we will now follow Alvaro Nunez, the real discoverer of the Mississippi.

Attracted by the gold they found in the hands of the Indians, they asked them where they had got it, and the Indians replied, From Appalachen, to the north. One can only go into probabilities here, and the probability is, that the natives round the present town of Appalachicola got gold from the natives of the southern spurs of the Apalachian mountains. A local antiquarian of Milledgeville might write us a pleasant paper on the subject. It is certain that the expedition began crawling up the swampy peninsula of Florida after the metal for which they lusted.

No one who has not done a little of the "*ex-fodiuntur opes*" can understand exactly what the gold fever is like. We know estimable and wise men who will creep and crawl through a summer's day after a stag, regardless alike of scenery, dinner, and rheumatism; who will not only do this, but will talk about nothing else for weeks after, to the intolerable boredom of their friends. Dine again with a party of fox-hunters, and see how their hearts have been in it; with a party of shooters, and see how one man sits moody over a good dinner because he has missed one rocketting pheasant. Dark tongues whisper to us that Mr. Bright loves the wild swirl of a salmon dearly. All these sports are as nothing to gold hunting; especially where it runs nuggety.

To see IT—it itself, Mammon's own bait, which rules the world as at present constituted; the sweet, heavy, delicious lump of yellow metal, which marries your palm so lovingly: to see *it* itself—the thing for which parliaments legislate first, and men, otherwise good citizens, lie, forge, and cheat widow and orphan: to see this peep with its indescribable golden gleam out of dirty gravel is a thing which maddens men. See the wondrous sight for yourself before you utterly condemn the men who are driven mad by the lust of it.

The compiler, speaking in his own person from considerable experience, has seen strange things from this gold fever, which this expedition had strong on them, and which made them, like some other people, forget God and morality. I have stood, wishing to plead between two angry brothers, but have desisted in fear of the "redding straik" (this is the most absolute truth). I have seen wives deserted with promises of return; I have seen wives dragged many hundred miles on mere newspaper reports, and have seen them come back —broken people. I have helped to take out beautiful young men dead, who have gone, in spite of remonstrance, into dangerously undermined ground after this same gold. I have sat myself eight hours together by candlelight, at the end of a long dark drive, singing Lycidas and the Christmas hymn, contented and perfectly happy at seeing the metal gleam now and then among the gravel. And more, I have sat on Christmas eve waiting for those who never came, and who will come no more for ever. Dim, fever-stricken ghosts came in from the Buckland, and brought with them still dimmer ghosts from the Omeo; but some who were waited for came not. They had thrown all at the feet of Mammon, and he had devoured them.

Of all the so-called "sports" by which men have chosen to plague themselves, gold hunting is the most maddening, and in most respects the most degrading and selfish. The guiding god on the expedition we have in hand was gold. The Spaniards devastated the earth for it; we have helped to civilize the earth by it. How much less selfish we have been than the Spaniards, casuists, if they knew how, might determine. Yet we, the greatest of Teutonic pirates, have never been so cruel as the great Latin pirates.

Three hundred men started up the long point of Florida on this strange expedition; forty were on horseback, the rest on foot. For fifteen days they saw no Indians, and met with no food except dates, and at this point came to the first noticeable river.

I have reasons, which it would be wearisome to give, for thinking that the expedition headed towards the east or Atlantic coast of Florida, and that this river was the Suwanee. He talks of the large lakes and high mountains of this country, meaning, I believe, the "Sandy Ridge" and the Lakes Mayaco, and other expansions of these rivers. They crossed this river by swimming and by rafts, and having met 200 Indians without a fight, once more inquired for Appalachen, the province where the gold came from, ready to believe anything, or to do anything for their gold. What they would believe we can learn from the account of, and skirmish with, the Indians. "Some of them" (the Spanish soldiers) "swore that they had seen two okes (oaks), each of them as great as a man's legge, shot throw from side to side with the arrowes of the Indians." Nunez himself claims to have seen an arrow in the foot of an elm "a handful in," which is not incredible.

They now arrived at Appalache Bay, the time and probable distance coming quite right, and after a fight in which one was killed, came in nine days to Aute, where, resting two days, Alvaro Nunez was despatched by the governor to look for the sea, which the Indians said was near. He went, discovered no sea, but a great river, which I venture to conceive, taking times and distances, and remembering that his story was dictated from memory, was no less a river than the Alabama. He says that it was the Magdalena.

The expedition here suddenly collapsed. We can now see how our great enemies, the Spaniards, could shift for themselves in those times. I think that we must allow, nearly as well as we could.

If they were on the Alabama, they were at least, as they had come, 700 miles from their point of debarkation; if they were on the Chatahouchy, they were certainly 500 (these figures, according to the compiler's usual custom, are greatly understated). The bubble had burst, the horses were dying before their eyes; the third conquest of Florida, to live in the minds of men at all, must turn itself into a great and honourable disaster, and a glorious retreat. Next to a Jena campaign, a really fine Anabasis is the most glorious thing. A most decisive Anabasis was positively necessary, and they set about it.

They must get away by boat: but where was the timber to build them in a country of monocotyledonous trees, without iron? Why, here were bamboos, and here were stirrup-irons, and here were wild beast skins, and, more than all, the divine spark which could bring cosmos out of such queer organic and inorganic things. One of their men, a man whose name is lost for ever, a man never noticed, comes to us in this black midnight of disaster, and says to us, " Excellentissimo Adelantado Pamphilo Navaez, most noble and excellent Alvaro Nunez, Capo de Vava, our Secretary; I am Sancho Panza, a blacksmith and bellows-maker, and my brother is a carpenter, and lives on the quay of the ever-blessed St. Christopher, at St. Lucar. Now, most excellent and right admirable gentlemen, you have made a rather worse mess of this business than any of your predecessors, but if you will listen to me I will get you out of it. I will make you (by my bellows-making knowledge) rafts of inflated skins; I will float them with canes (by my brother's carpentering knowledge); and I will take your very knightly spurs off your heels, and make out of them iron bolts sufficient for the purpose."

Don Quixote did not like this last proposition very much, but he remembered that, against Sancho's recollections about the helmet of Mambrino, and the Cave of Montesinos, he had no case against Sancho, save Sancho's solitary indiscretion about the Pleiades. And when Don Quixote remembered that he also was riding cock-horse on Clavileno at the same time, he gave up his spurs, and Sancho made files of them. Our dear old Don does not seem to have remembered on this occasion the promissory note for the ass foals. Well! well! a book one loves is hard to part with.

These boats were made of cane and inflated skins, caulked with palmetto fibre and pine amber.*

Between the fourth of August and the twentieth of September five boats were finished, each thirty-three feet in length; the oars were of "savine" (most likely *Juniperus Barbadensis* or *Virginiana*), the ropes and tackle of the tails and manes of the horses on which they had been living while building their boats. Flaying these horses' legs whole, they made bottles

* Called in our great southern provinces "kawri," not from the same species of tree of course, but similar. In the old English translation from Ramusio it is called "a certain gumme, which a Grecian called Don Theodoro," which seemed difficult to class in any way, until one saw that Don Theodoro was the name of the man who fetched it, and not of the gum.

to carry their water. In "the country whereinto our sinnes conducted us" there were no stones, and so they were badly off for ballast. But at last they got afloat.

Fifty men were now dead, the rest were divided among the boats; and putting off into the river, were, after all kinds of almost incredible hardships from hunger and thirst (the water in the horseskin bottles having, of course, turned putrid), carried along the shore, among islands and reefs which it is impossible to recognise. The record of their voyage, until the eighth of November, it would be utterly useless and painful to go through.

On the eighth of November we find the boat of Alvaro Nunez in very strange case. Hunger, thirst, the wild beating of the cruel sea, the cold of the winter, had all done their work, and the crew of Alvaro's boat lay heaped on one another as they had cast themselves down in their despair. Alone erect among them stood Alvaro and the master, the latter of whom soon told Alvaro that he must take the helm, for that his time was come, and so went and cast himself down among the others.

What a night-watch for Alvaro upon the wild, wandering sea, alone, waiting for his turn to die as he thought! This is surely stranger and wilder than anything we have heard of yet. He steered the boat until after midnight, and then leaving her to herself crept forward to see if the master, the last man who had spoken, was dead. What an errand!

"The merry men so beautiful,
And they all dead did lie."

But that was not for them as yet. The apparently dead men were not dead; their end was not come, but was to come all the same. The master also was not dead. I honestly confess that my pen fails me here. The reader must trust to an older one than mine.

"Midnight being past, I went to see if the master was dead, who said vnto me, that he was suddenly better, and that he would guide the boat vntil day. Then surely I found myself in such state, that much more willingly would I haue received death than see so many men before me, in that state in which they were.

"And after the master took charge of the boat, I rested myself a little, but very vnquietly, because nothing was further from me than sleepe."

Stars, which look down on our wandering, restless brothers in bush and in jungle, listen to this awful dead voice out of the dim past, and shine kindly on them!

"And about the morning me thought that I heard the noise and roaring of the sea; because being a very lowe coast it raged much. Whereupon I called the master, who answered me, that he supposed we were now neere to the land, and, sounding, we found ourselves in seuen fathom. He thought it fit that we should remain at see until daylight appeared.

"And so I took an oare and rowed to the land's side, and put the stearne to the sea. And being neare to the land, a wave took us, which cast the boat back into the sea, as farre as a man might sling a stone. And with the great blowe which it gaue, *almost* all the men who remained there as dead recovered their senses again, and began to goe on their hands and feet."

> It had been strange, e'en in a dream,
> To see these dead men rise."

Had Coleridge read Alvaro Nunez? I think not. Candlish and Pigafetta would have given him all his materials for the "Ancient Mariner."

The men of Alvaro Nunez got on shore and managed to make fires. They were staying at one more resting-place on the road to dusky death.

Lopez d'Oviedo, the strongest among them, was sent to climb into a tree; and he reported that they were on an island, and could see an Indian town. To this they went, found it empty, and took a small pot, some thornback, and a "young whelpe." An hour or two afterwards, six hundred Indians were upon them (while only six Spaniards could rise from the ground), with bent bows. These Indians, about whom the Spanish captains will have to plead against Las Casas before the throne of God, loved them, pitied them, and brought them such store of food as enabled them to make an attempt to proceed on their voyage.

The Spaniards dug their boat out of the sand, and stripping themselves naked, got her across the surf. A heavier sea than they had calculated on capsized her near the shore, and they being naked, and the cold intense (November), let go the oars, and all was ruin and disaster once more. The controller and two others tried a swim for it, but the boat struck them and drowned them; the others, clinging to the boat were cast ashore stark naked, with the loss of everything they had in the world, and finding the brands of their fire still burning, they crowded round it.

"We stood crauing mercy from our Lord God, and pardon of our sinnes with many teares; every one of us not grieving only for himselfe, but for all the rest that hee saw in the same state. At the setting of the sunne, the *Indians*, supposing that we had not been gone, came to find vs, and brought vs somewhat to eate."

Poor, wild, forest children! But they were terrified and puzzled at seeing the Spaniards naked, and they did not know them again. The gaunt, grim, terrible Spanish soldier in his mail was one thing, the utterly naked, cowering men, whose very natural majesty was gone by starvation, were another. They knew them no more than did the wary porter know Jovinian when he came before him in such guise:

> "'We list not buy to-day or flesh or fell;
> Go home and get thyself a shirt at least,
> If thou would'st aught; for saith our vicar well,
> That God hath given clothes e'en to the beast.
> Therewith he turned to go, but as he ceased,
> The king cried out, 'Open, O foolish man!
> I am thy lord and king Jovinian.'"*

And as they cried out, the Indians knew their Jovinian at once. It seems a pretty story to tell about the way they received the poor naked Spaniards. While telling it, let us contrast the English of the verse I have quoted above—which I humbly venture to think almost the most exquisite

* Morris's "Proud King."

English we have ever had, the highest development of our great language—with the English, roughly speaking, of Shakespeare.

"The *Indians* seeing the misfortune which had befallen us, and the lamentable case wherein we were, with so great calamitie and miserie, came amongst vs, and through great griefe and compassion which they had of vs, beganne mightily to weepe and lament, and that from the heart, insomuch that they might be heard farre from thence; and they thus lamented more than halfe an houre."

To go back again from the language of Purchas to that of Chaucer, two hundred odd years before, may interest our younger readers. Let us take a fragment which Chaucer has put into the mouth of a Cambridge student, leaving the Early English Text Society to dispose of the question whether Chaucer's English was the vernacular of the day; and leaving also Tyrwhitt, who thinks it was, to fight his own battle. The two undergraduates are catching horses:

> " These sely clerkes rennen up and down,
> With Kepe, kepe; Stand, stand; Jossa, wanderere.
> Ga whistle thou, and I shall kepe him here.
> * * * *
> They coulde not, though they did all hir might,
> Hir capel catch, he ran alway so fast,
> Till in a diche they caught him at the last."

Now that I have tried by a few, I hope well-chosen, words, to take your mind for a little time from this continued history of disaster, we will follow Alvaro Nunez in his unparalleled adventure.

Strangely enough, the Indians among whom these wrecked Spaniards were, were a tribe familiar to all English mouths as household words. I find that they must have been the *Seminoles.*

Here are the historical old Seminoles for you, if you care to hear of them from the first educated man who ever saw them and lived.

They fought most stoutly and well. Their bows were terribly strong, but of no use against Spanish armour; yet they managed to kill the controller's horse under him. They lived in little huts made of straw and reeds, placed carefully out of the way of lightning, in small gullies, with a good elevation nearly round them, so that the spark was little likely to strike them, by no means a brick villa on an elevation, with metal cowls on high chimneys, like the Sydenham man's house, who lives in expectation of having that house about his ears during the next thunderstorm. They lived mainly on maize, ground in their hand-mills, and on fish. Their bows were as thick as a man's arm, and their range was two hundred paces (one Avellameda was stricken like Ahab "between the joints of his harness," and killed dead). They were gentle, brave, good-humoured, and very affectionate in their domestic relations. In stature very tall and handsome. They were apparently a very innocent set of people, but they had to go, and they went. I forget where they were shoved round to last.

Seeing in the hands of the Indians two Spanish nets, Alvaro asked the Indians, by signs, where they had got them: they replied, in the same manner, that they were got from two countrymen of theirs who were living not far off. He, sending two Spaniards and two Indians after them, found that they were two Spanish gentlemen of the expedition, in an ill case, Andrea Dorante and Alonzo di Castiglio. These poor Spanish gentlemen had kept their clothes, and were deeply distressed at finding their comrades naked, but they could do nothing at all for them.

Their only chance now was to get at what they believed to be the nearest Spanish settlement to them, Panuco, of which place we have heard before in this book. The first attempt was to launch the remaining boat, but she was at once swamped.

One more chance remained. The main body might possibly winter at Appalache Bay, but four of the lustiest and strongest swimmers might desperately go round the head of the gully, swimming the rivers and creeks, and bring assistance. The names of the four valiant naked Spaniards who were, in an entire absence of all geography, set to swim the Alabama, the Mississippi, the Sabine, the Trinity, the Colorado, and the Bravo del Norte, at the place where Brownsville now stands; these men's names, I say, shall not be lost, "carent quia vate sacro." They were: Alonzo Ferrante, a Portuguese, carpenter and mariner; Mendoz, of whom nothing more is said; Figueroa, a native of Toledo; and a fourth, who had, apparently, like Hans Andersen's magician, no name at all—so I cannot assist him further.

They passed away, and the others were left without

clothes, and the winter settled down. The head party under Alvaro Nunez seem to have known how to die like Spanish gentlemen; but five isolated men, leaderless, along the coast, in their hunger, their despair, and their fury at being brought by their leaders to die in such a place, grew devilish, and ate one another, until only one solitary man remained.

The horror that this catastrophe caused among the Seminoles was very great. The eighty Spaniards were now reduced to fifteen.

Their fury against the Spaniards was increased by the belief that an epidemic dysentery, from which the Seminoles were suffering, was caused by witchcraft of the Spaniards. Alvaro Nunez pointed out to them that if they had ever had this power, they would never have allowed their own men to die. The argument prevailed with the kindly Seminoles. But there is very little doubt, from his account, that if the Seminoles had dreamed of the ghastly horror of cannibalism being enacted in their territory, they would have murdered every Spaniard at once. The savages spared them as men smitten of God, and therefore sacred from the stroke of man.

A singular and strange custom, of which I have never read before, prevailed among these Seminoles, so fantastic and almost frantic, that it seems to put them in a rather high class of civilization, and makes one wonder that they did not use hair powder and chignons, like the Latookas of Baker. When anybody died, these Seminoles "initiated a function" (I believe that is correct American)

When any one died in a house, they instantly left off providing supplies for that house, and the house left off providing supplies for itself. There is surely more midsummer madness in this piece of religion than in any other one has heard of, not excepting suttee or witch-swimming. Until April he stayed with them, and then the tribe migrated to get mulberries (whether Morus rubra or scabra I cannot say, but he says they grew by the sea).

These Seminoles now got it into their poor heads that these Spaniards, so different from them, who prayed to gods other than theirs, and had been honoured by being smitten and afflicted by those gods, must have miraculous powers of healing. Cooper the novelist, who knew much about the Indians, was the first who ever called my attention to this strange respect for the dignity of sorrow existing among these forest children. One is glad to find it cropping out here again, were it only that one is glad to find that a man who has given us so much pleasure was right. The Spaniards laughed at the Indian nonsense, but the Seminoles deprived them of food until they undertook cures. And of course, having little more to deal with than flatulent dyspepsia, accompanied with nervous symptoms, succeeded. Homœopathy and spirit-rapping were alive among ourselves till very lately; brain waves are the last thing; Greatrakes may write to the papers to-morrow, for aught one knows, and give us the details of his stroking cure.

However, Alvaro Nunez undertook cures, and

expresses to us his unutterable astonishment at finding them quite successful.

Having done a little doctoring, he now took to merchandise, travelling about, as I believe, into the country of Indians scarcely less historical than the Seminoles, that of the Choctaws. They were as different from the Seminoles as the Mandans are from the Arrapahoes, the Comanches, or the Sioux. Had this expedition landed west of the Alabama, they would have had short shrift, and we should have heard no more of them for ever. It is to the gentle kindness of the Seminoles that we are indebted for this story; clumsily told enough in the first instance, and possibly not less so now. The story is the wildest and strangest I have ever read, "like a fire seen far off in waste places," as Swinburne says of Blake.

Now, wandering among these Choctaws in the lonely, swampy forests which maddened Dred, he took for five solitary years to trading. The world was *past* the man. Everything was entirely gone from him, as he believed; the broad sweeping reaches of the Guadalquivir, crowded by the fantastic and beautiful στεφάνωμα πυργάτων which men call Seville, gone utterly, and in their place the swamps of Florida, and the brutal Choctaws, with their indescribable vices and cruelties.

Now for five years this Spanish gentleman, preserving his form of faith in Christ, lacking the ordinances of his form of religion, without clothes, without companions, save for occasional interviews with the other three who were left now, Andrea Dorante,

Estenamico, and Figueroa, lived, if it may be called living.

He describes the buffalo* as being met within fifty leagues of the mouth of the Alabama (which river he never named, I am merely guessing) : for the rest he tells us little about either Choctaw or Seminole, which we cannot learn from Catlin.

He now traded, a matter his nation has always been famous for, but has very often only performed one half of the task—in buying they are apt not to pay. This poor Spanish gentleman went into trade, and sold reeds for arrows, and strung shells and nuts to be used for festival dances, which I take to be wampum. About this time I think that he passed a little westward into the country of the Moscagas (he says Marianes), in the direction of Mobile.

So time went on, and he lived and did not die. One attempt he and a few others made to escape westward round the head of the gulf, but it was detected by the Indians and prevented. It caused them to treat the Christians with great jealousy and harshness, and separate them one from another. But the next time that the Indians went away into the woods to drink what he calls June, Alvaro Nunez, Dorante, Castiglio, and a negro started for their lives.

It was late autumn, and there was no time to spare. Two days' quick walking, however, got them to a fresh tribe of Indians, whom he calls Ananares, whom we

---

* "These came from the north, further through the land unto the coast of Florida; little horns, like the Moresche cattle" (the bull of the arena?). "They have very long hair, and extend themselves into the country more than four hundred leagues." Evidently the bison.

may guess were between Appalachicola and Mobile, and were so far safe.

They had been heard of here for their great healing powers, and Alvaro Nunez tells us this story in perfect good faith. I make no comments on it, disliking such stories. Indians came to them afflicted with pains in their heads, requiring to be healed. Castiglio blessed them, and commended them to God, whereupon they were instantly well. The Indians believed in the miracle, and it was a splendid thing for the Spaniards; venison and "Tune" they might have now as much as they would. They were now certainly west of St. George's Sound. Their new friends seem to have been Moscagas, for the Creeks lay up country, about the lower slopes of the Appallachian mountains. Here they determined to winter.

The Indians, however, were migrating in search of food, and almost at first Alvaro got lost and left behind. Five days he wandered alone, carrying firebrands to make four great fires to lie between every night, utterly without food and without clothes.*

For some time Castiglio seems to have done almost all the healing. His prayers seemed to have worked wonders, though he deeply distrusted the effect of them himself in consequence of his numerous sins. They were intensely believed in. Nunez, a polished Spanish gentleman, was evidently puzzled by the cures wrought, and gave God thanks always for His mercies, hoping that He would soon remove him to a place where he could serve Him better. The only theory I can advance is, that the Indians had over-

* " *As naked as ever I was born* " in trans.

fed themselves with the "Tune" and venison, and were suffering from nervous dyspepsia, a disease always instantly cured by pulling the patient's nose, or being rude to his wife. Few students over thirty have not known those singular reflected actions of stomach on to brain, which are instantly removed and forgotten by action or pleasure. Certain sermons bring those symptoms on, but while Maurice is preaching they disappear. A street organ may make an over-worked man feel ill, but I never heard that Madam Schuman and Joachim interpreting Beethoven ever did.

Besides, I know from personal experience that savages, starved at one time, over-eaten at another, are singularly subject to nervous dyspepsia. They are *always* seeing the devil. The grasshopper is a burden unto them. Their remedy, when they have found it out, is brandy or whisky. "Plenty mine, tumble down die to-morrow, Mr. Overseer. See um debbil debbil along a creek in a tea scub. Give it nobler brandy, Mr. Overseer." Give him a couple or so of charges of powder and shot, and tell him that when he brings you half a dozen ducks he shall have tea and bread, and he is well in an instant. His debbil debbil disappears, as the rackshass or shietan of Brahmins or Mussulman East Indian disappears before the vigorous bullying of Captain Jones, Bengal Artillery.

I want to believe in my troublesome friend Alvaro Nunez, and so I have defended him at some length. He did not believe in these apparent cures himself, but wondered at them.

The Indians among whom he passed now are utterly undistinguishable by me from any atlas (and I have been favoured in that respect) which I can get hold of. The antiquarians of New Orleans must settle the matter between these tribes, amongst which the discoverer of the Mississippi passed: Cucalenches, Maticoles, Coaios, Sofalas, and Ataios. It appears to me that, whatever they were, they were not Choctaws. There appears an internal evidence in this quaintest of quaint stories that the Seminoles were gentle and the Choctaws violent. Perhaps some American gentleman will come across, write the history of Berkshire, and survive. However, one man turned up at the end of his journey, and saw the Mississippi first of Europeans; enough for a book of adventure.

The Sofala Indians came to Castiglio and begged him to come and heal some of their sick. But Castiglio was a "very fearful physician," and distrusted the whole business from beginning to end. And so that great Spanish gentleman Alvaro Nunez was sent on the errand.

Among the Sofala Indians Alvaro found a man apparently dead; he actually believed that he was: though the symptoms, as described by him, are certainly those of a man in a state of coma after a singularly violent epileptic fit. After Alvaro had roused him, and blown on his face a little, he came to himself, to the wonder and delight of the Indians. They entertained him with the greatest hospitality, such as they had, but it was little enough. These Indians of Florida were wretchedly poor for three-quarters of the year, the strength they got at the

Tune harvest being obliged to carry them on for a long time. With these people he abode no less than eight months, before he and his three companions resumed their walk round the gulf.

Among the next Indians with whom he sojourned he had to sell a net, and, what was worse, a skin he had to cover him, to buy provisions; so he now had to go naked again in the broiling sun, "which caused them," he says, "to change their skins twice a year." The packages they had to carry cut their flesh, and the thorns tore them. "Once," poor Alvaro says, that "being terribly torn, and losing much blood in seeking wood, he could comfort himself no other way than by thinking of the Passion of our Lord, and the blood which had been shed for him." The poor treasurer had need of some comfort now, for he was in evil case. He contracted with these Indians to make combs, bows, arrows, and nets. What he liked best was to get a job of scraping a hide thin, for then he could eat the scrapings.

I put him now in and about the Alabama and the Chickasawshay, in the country of the people known familiarly to us as the Choctaws, or (?) flat-heads. This nation was evidently divided into nearly innumerable tribes, each one of which could hardly have consisted of many families, yet which all had right of war. Seventeen tribes are named in the Choctaw country alone, between the Alabama and Lake Pontchartrain. It would be utterly ridiculous for me to plague my reader and exhibit my own ignorance in trying to localize these little tribes of those three great groups which we now popularly know as Seminoles, Choctaws, and Creeks, none of which three names are mentioned by Nunez at all. Some American antiquary should epitomize it for us; it would be very interesting. No name of a tribe is mentioned by Nunez in any way familiar to European ears, except one which bears a slight similitude to "Arrapahoe;" no geographical name known to me, or to modern atlases (from 1808 to Keith Johnston), except Appallache.

Nunez, however, was the first educated European who saw the red man of Florida and Louisiana, and lived to write about him.* A few facts about these great historical tribes may not be uninteresting.

It seems that they were singularly (when first seen) like the Australian savage in more than one point. They showed most unmistakably the signs of an older civilization decaying among outlying tribes, by dispersion in quest of the necessaries of life. In a case of dispersion, in consequence of utter poverty, when ἀνάγκη becomes God, the first traditions which go are the old forms of culture; the last, the traditions necessary for the preservation of human existence. None of these men had art to *invent* their terrible bows and arrows, any more than an Australian could invent that marvellous thing, the boomerang. But their necessity was so great, that they had kept hold of the traditions necessary for their dog-like existence, and had abandoned all those which were not necessary for it.

That they were not so far fallen away as the Australians, it is unnecessary to say; for, instead of

* But compare the narrative of De Soto.

dying out like the Australians, they had sufficient vitality left in them to become partially civilized, to become very dangerous and troublesome. They were soon splendid riders of the horses which, as Nunez tells us, so terrified them at first. They took to the gun, and by all accounts used it with a superior dexterity to our own. In fine, the strongest of them were driven westward, and I believe that, getting more into the real buffalo track, they got turned into Comanches, and Arrapahoes, and such people. This however is more the business of the Pacific Railway Company than ours. Aboriginal tribes will certainly coalesce if there is a sufficient amount of vitality left in them. For example, the Sioux. One would like to know the pedigree of some of the Sioux chiefs. You may consult the "Almanach de Gotha" and get no information. Are there none of the gentler Pawnee, and the still gentler Mandan, among them, not to say Chickasaws, Choctaws, Kickapoos, and Cherokees? Are they an Adullamite coalition? I do not know, whatever I may think, and so will say not one word.

Another fact about these noble red men is noticeable in comparison with the Australian savage, the very last one which has been brought face to face with civilization. Their languages seem to have been absolutely *infinite*. To claim precedence for the Tower of Babel would be to speak slightingly of the Capitol at Washington in this case. We wish to give no further national offence, and so will pay the United States the compliment of saying that the country they took possession of beat (whipped?)

Babel in the matter of the confusion of tongues hollow.

It would be incredible that two petty tribes, consisting of about a dozen families each, divided by a brook, should speak a different language. But one finds it exactly the case in Australia to the present day. Let us give a ghost of a guess at this very strange fact.

Necessity. You must live, you can't starve, "at least *I* can't," as that jolly convict says in "Great Expectations." And even though you have fallen so low in the dim dark night of savagery that you do not care for your own children, yet you will still care for your wife, as long as she is a patient drudge for you. And you must feed her when she cannot feed herself. You naturally being a brute, do so with as little trouble as possible; consequently you take possession of the best bit of country you can get hold of, and hold it if you can. Dynastic traditions step in to assist family necessities, and it becomes entirely impossible that you can give up your patrimony to your dearly beloved and anointed brother at Berlin.

It is however among savage tribes not like any little difference between Nassau and Prussia. If you give way, you get your throat cut. Consequently you fight for it, your sons fight for it, your grandsons fight for it (in the barbarous manner). If you fall, there is an hegemony of Cherokees or Kickapoos, as the case may be. But no interchange of articulate speech; no Talleyrand or Londonderry; only arrows which will go half through a small tree.

Then you cannot read or write, not even novels or newspapers. So there is no interchange of literature, which has done so much to cause the present existing good feeling between the United Kingdom and the United States.

So in fifty or sixty years, if you can hold your own for so long, you will find that, never having held articulate speech with any one but your own tribe, you will have developed a new language.

Seriously, however, I do believe that this wonderful variety of languages among savage tribes arises from isolation, continuous necessitous war, and utter absence of written speech.* from languages whose words had entirely lost their first intention, and had become mere arbitrary sounds, utterly without any form of inflexion.

The people who seem to me to be the Choctaws, of various septs, entertained them very well. Their character for miraculous cures had gone before them, and the further they went the greater was their prestige. Alvaro Nunez himself says that human memory cannot recall the innumerable tribes through which he passed. They were received everywhere as great "Medicine Men," few natives daring to eat anything unless they had blown upon it. The first sign of Mexican civilization which they met was a copper bell with a face engraved on it.

When and where he crossed the Mississippi it is extremely difficult to decide; in fact, I think impossible. While he dawdled one has a hope of tracking him, but when he got among more civilized

* One need only go to Eyre's Australian vocabularies to prove it.

tribes, with his prestige as a great physician, he is nearly impossible to trace.

But he was the first European who saw the Mississippi; of that I think there is little doubt. If not he, who? I believe, after a certain amount of careful thought, that in his zeal he kept north of Lake Pontchartrain and crossed the Mississippi just below Baton Rouge. By this route he would get to Requiza, and so by Rio Bravo del Norte, and by the towns of Loredo and Revilla to Panuco.

But he confuses counsel by saying that he came to the South Sea. Now if it can be only granted that the South Sea only means the Gulf of Mexico, my theory would hold water beautifully. But he gives us so many facts to prove that he actually crossed to the Pacific that one must give up this theory. About his crossing the Mississippi there is, of course, no doubt.

He arrived at the desert which the advanced Spaniards had made and called it Peace. His fellow-countrymen entreated him most grossly at first, but much better afterwards. The discoverer of the Mississippi was sent home with all honour, and arrived in Lisbon in 1537.

He had been ten years in this unutterable misery and confusion; ten years of hopelessness, anxiety, and starvation. There was nothing left for him but to go home to Spain and die comfortably. To go home to Spain? Certainly. But to die? No. There was no "die" in the man. On his arrival home he demanded the Governorship of Florida, but Hernando de Soto, the man of whose death I have spoken above, had been beforehand with him there. His vast wealth overpowered the petty claims of our Alvaro Nunez. But in 1540 we find the naked Nunez, maker of nets, scraper of hides, afloat once more, as Governor of Buenos Ayres. Losing two ships on the coast of the Brazils, this unkillable man landed his men and marched them overland to the heads of the Parana, whence in canoes he took them to his capital—an adventure greater than his first. If the Latin nations could hold as well as they can conquer, where should *we* be?

Poor Alvaro! His end is very problematical. Everybody seems to contradict every one else about it, as is generally the case in what is called history. Perhaps somebody may find something at Simancas or Fetter Lane about him. That he was sent as prisoner to Spain by the colonists in 1544 (like our Governor Bligh) there is little doubt. Some say that, like Bart. de las Casas, he took the side of the Indians too strongly; some, on the other hand, say that it was nothing of the kind. Sent home prisoner he was however, and had to wait eight years for trial. Some say he was honourably acquitted; some say, on the other hand, that he was banished to Africa. Two things about him are certain however: that he was a man made of stuff rarely found in these days, and that he discovered the Mississippi.

THE FOUNDATION OF AN EMPIRE.

It may be, as some say, that we British are the greatest pirates on the earth; or, on the other hand, it may be said that we have been civilizing the earth and subduing it, in the way God has shown us, with many mistakes, many errors, many cruelties, many sins, many sad ferocities. But if piracy means the United States, Canada, Australia, New Zealand, this magnificent regenerated India (our great future work, leaving Western civilization to the United States), the suppression of the slave trade, and last, not perhaps (who can tell yet?) least, the civilization of the Nile Basin, all I can say is, "Piracy go on and prosper!"

We have seen in this little volume the beginning of several things which have collapsed. Notably, the Mogul invasion of China; the attempt of the Papacy on the Mogul emperor; the works of the brave monks in West Africa; the slave trade; the attempts against Mother Carey in Spitzbergen. Let me close my little book with an account of a matter which does not seem inclined to collapse in any way at all.

There lies among the pleasant Southern Seas an island as large as Europe—an island lone, melancholy, until lately desolate. The traveller approaching that island even now is struck with the awful melancholy of its high-piled forest capes ; for, like Ireland, its mountains are near its coast, and it has a great central basin, in trying to cross which our poor brothers have fallen down and died, leaving their bones to whiten in the scorching sun.

The largest, and possibly the grandest, island in the world—not so much because its flora and fauna have not one solitary plant, animal, or bird in common with the nearest point of Asia, Malacca ; but because there, among its strange, wandering savages, you find the traces of a civilization, never, in all probability, high, but which has left at least one puzzling trace behind it. The natives of Australia acknowledge no God, and are loth to hear of any, as the brave Moravians will tell you ; yet who can still make a boomerang and throw it ?

The land of lonely rivers and level grey plains ; the land of wool and of corn incalculable to the human mind ; the land of gold and of jewels— 11,000,000*l.* sterling of gold passed out of Port Philip heads in one year, beating by 3,000,000*l.* the largest export ever made from the Minas Geraes in Brazil. The present writer used at one time to cast away from the surface of his gold blue stones of great specific gravity. It occurred to him in an idle moment to ask a jeweller in Melbourne what they were : he said, " Sapphires !"

Who were to have this wondrous land, which lay for countless thousands of years in a summer sea, waiting for its owners ? Whom had God selected out of those who had done their best to serve Him to be owners of this wondrous land? Was it to be a Latin colony, priest-plagued, and torn to pieces with ever-recurring petulant revolutions? Was it to fall to the Dutch? Was it to go to the Dutch, those glorious rovers, to be tied hand and foot with over-government, like Java, farmed only for the benefit of the mother country? No, readers! God designed that country for *us*.

I want shortly to show you, before we part, by what silent and wise ways He gave it to us. I think that we have done our duty by it.

I for myself (as an erring brother may confess and ask mercy) can find no mention of the country at all before 1616, not believing that Saris (1606) got to the country at all. I believe that Theodoric Hertog (better known to English readers as Dirk Hartog) was the first educated European who ever set eyes on the land some of us love so well. But when a man begins saying that he believes such and such a thing, you cannot argue with him. Some believe that St. Bridget nursed St. Patrick. It is no use telling them that she was only one year old when he died, as seems undoubtedly the case; and then in comes your cranking man who denies the existence of St. Bridget altogether. I only say that I believe in Dirk Hartog, as did also President De Broisey—no small authority.

1619, 1622, 1628, Edels, Flamming, De Witte, coasted down the west coast of Australia, but made nothing of it. In 1628 also (*most decidedly*) Carpenter discovered Carpentaria. Prevost says 1662.

In 1642 Tasman discovered Van Dieman's Land

and New Zealand. Of Van Dieman one knows mainly that he returned to Europe with vast riches in 1631. Good Tasman—probably put on his legs by the wealth of Anthony Van Dieman—called the country Van Dieman's Land. But the name got to smell so very unsavoury in the nose of every decent mainland colonist, that our good Queen, on humble petition, whitewashed it (as far as she could) by calling it Tasmania. So Abel Tasman has got his due from the Queen of England and Empress of India.

Before us everywhere (with the Spaniards), behind us everywhere now, the Dutch seemed to have had, and to have, every facility which one could possibly wish for; but I fancy that they had too small a population from which to select. Comparing our population and resources against the Dutch, it would be like a united Trinity against such a College as Christ's or Jesus for a boat race. I can draw no illustration from Oxford, for all the Colleges are small.

So much did the Dutch do, and the land was left in peace. They seemed to be wanting in dash here— the dash which we have got partly from Celt, partly from Norseman. They slept over it, and the sun rose and set on the beloved old land. And the world wagged on there, as it did here; and, to avoid being wearisome, I will pass over Dampier, and come right on to Captain Cook at once, in his first voyage in 1770.

Leaving New Zealand, he held twenty days northwest, and, on the 19th of April, Lieutenant Hicks saw Australia, and left his name for ever on Point Hicks.

He now entered Botany Bay, from the swamp at the head of which Sydney is now supplied with water. It was Sir Joseph Banks—a man of a high-renowned old family, and of very great fortune, who had given up luxury, ease, marriage, everything, to come with Cook—who had it named Botany Bay, from the innumerable flowers he found there—a certain sign in Australia of barren and worthless land. Surely stranger mates were never found than Cook and Banks: Banks, one of the high old noblesse; Cook, the son of a common agricultural labourer, who had run away to sea and turned collier's boy, and who, in the Wolf-Montcalm war in Canada, had sounded and buoyed a channel in the St. Lawrence under fire. These men sailed together, in all hearty love, with Solander, a Swedish naturalist, pupil of Linnæus; and they all three died, but not, as they were willing to do, together. Wolf and Montcalm have one monument, these three true friends have none.

They had been but a short time in Botany Bay when La Perouse sailed in, and, having met Cook, sailed away again, to be seen by civilized eye no more. Our brothers, the Australians, have had the good taste to erect a pillar to him on the shores of Botany Bay. A noble man in every respect he seems, but gone into utter dim, dark night. It was forty years before a trace was recovered of him, and after that one only finds that some of his company had built a schooner out of the wreck of his two ships, and had sailed away, and in their turn had been lost utterly to human knowledge.

At about this time the British Government were

beginning to find out that hanging some ten or a dozen persons per month for petty theft was by no means decreasing crime, but *increasing* it. I cannot explain this phenomenon in any way. One would fancy that if you wanted anything, you would sooner steal it under the penalty of imprisonment than under that of hanging ; but it was not so. For myself, I simply confess that I have not sufficient personal courage to commit a burglary; I believe that I should half die of fright if I met the housemaid. What must the terror of hanging be ? Possibly the case was that prison was then worse than death. Anyhow, hanging did no good ; transportation was tried, and the great dominion of Australia founded.

They knew nothing of the wealth of the land. I think that they thought it was a hopeless, God-forgotten place. How can one go into details here ? I have read nearly every account of the settlement, and really I am getting to the state of mind in which Mr. Matthew Arnold was when he said that history was a Mississippi of lies.

Before, however, I begin to give the words of another, I will give the legend (for it is really nothing more) of the discovery of Port Jackson. " The story goes," said Mr. Willet to Mr. Solomon Daisy, " that you saw a ghost last March, but nobody believes it." The story goes that one Jackson, a sailor, was on the maintop on the look-out as Cook was sailing by Sydney heads. Jackson reported that there was a large harbour inland. Captain Cook told him that he (from the deck) could see nothing but a small boat harbour, and that were there such a harbour, it should be called after him. It is a good story, but I do not find confirmation of it. They believed it, however, for Sydney harbour is Port Jackson to this day; and on that then desolate shore, beside the green sea-water, with flying violet shadows, stands a white-walled city of 60,000 inhabitants—as some say, the most beautiful city in her Majesty's dominions.

Governor Phillip, mentioned below, John Hunter the great physiologist, and my grandfather Doctor Lucas were great intimates. There is now in the family a tea-caddy made of the first wood sent from Australia. My grandfather, again, was the intimate friend of Lord Rodney, and knew Gibbon. The foundation of this empire seems so old, and is yet so new, that I mention these facts.

The reason of this seems to me to be, that the French Revolution, and the wars which followed it, made a terrible gap, which nothing seems able to fill up. As to Australia, it was left alone to sink or swim, we having command of the seas. It was a case of

"Crescit occulto velut arbor ævo."

Now I will leave my own words, and give you those of an eye-witness. This is dated the 5th of March, 1787—a day which will be memorable for ever to (potentially) 25,000,000 souls. What follows is an extract from Mr. White's journal, surgeon-general under Captain Phillip, my grandfather's friend.

"I this day left London, charged with dispatches from the Secretary of State's office, and from the Admiralty, relative to the embarkation of that part of the marines and convicts intended for Botany Bay; and on the evening of the seventh, after travelling two days of the most incessant rain I ever remember, arrived at Plymouth, where the *Charlotte* and *Friendship* transports were in readiness to receive them.

"General Collins, commander-in-chief at that port, lost no time in carrying the orders I had brought into execution; so that, on the morning of the ninth, the detachment of marines were on board, with all the baggage. But the next day being ushered in with a very heavy gale of wind, made it impracticable to remove the convicts from on board the *Dunkirk* prison-ship, where they were confined. So violent was the gale, that his Majesty's ship the *Druid*, of thirty-two guns, was forced to cut away her mainmast to prevent her driving on shore.

"The weather being moderate the following day, the convicts were put on board the transports, and placed in the different apartments allotted for them—all secured in irons, except the women. In the evening, as there was but little wind, we were towed by the boats belonging to the guardships out of the Hamoaze, where the *Dunkirk* lay, into Plymouth Sound. When this duty was completed, the boats returned; and the wind now freshening so as to enable us to clear the land, we proceeded to Spithead, where we arrived on the 17th, and anchored on the Mother Bank, among the rest of the transports and victuallers intended for the same expedition, under the conduct of his Majesty's ship the *Sirius*. As soon as the ship came to anchor, I visited all the other transports, and was really surprised to find the convicts on board them so very healthy. When I got on board the *Alexander*, I found there a medical gentleman from Portsmouth, among whose acquaintance I had not the honour to be numbered. He scarcely gave me time to get upon the quarter-deck before he thus addressed me: 'I am very glad you are arrived, sir; for your people have got a *malignant* disease among them of a most dangerous kind, and it will be necessary for their preservation to get them immediately relanded.' Surprised at such a salutation, and alarmed at the purport of it, I requested of my assistant, Mr. Balmain, an intelligent young man, whom I had appointed to this ship for the voyage, to let me see the people who were ill. 'Sir,' returned Mr. Balmain, taking me aside, 'you will not find things by any means so bad as this gentleman represents them to be; they are made much worse by him than they really are. Unlike a person wishing to administer comfort to those who are afflicted, either in body or in mind, he has publicly declared before the poor creatures who are ill, that they must inevitably fall a sacrifice to the malignant disorder with which they are afflicted—the malignity of which appears to me to exist only in his own imagination. I did not, however,' continued Mr. Balmain, 'think proper to contradict the gentleman, supposing, from the consequence he assumed, and the ease with which he had given his opinion, or more properly his *directions*, that he was some person appointed by the Secretary of State to officiate for you till your arrival. When you go among the people, you will be better able to judge of the propriety of what I have said.' Mr. Balmain had no sooner concluded than I went between decks, and found everything just as he had represented it to be. There were several in bed with slight inflammatory complaints; some there were who kept their bed to avoid the inconvenience of the cold, which was at this time very piercing, and whose wretched clothing was but a poor defence against the rigour of it; others were confined to their bed through the effects of long imprisonment, a weakened habit, and lowness of spirits, which was not a little added to by the declaration of the medical gentleman abovementioned, whom they concluded to be the principal surgeon to the expedition. However, on my undeceiving them in that point, and at the same time confirming what Mr. Balmain had from the first told them, viz. *that their complaints were neither malignant nor dangerous*, their fears abated. To this I added, that I would immediately give orders for such as were in want of clothing to be supplied with what was needful—a power delegated to me by Captain Phillip, together with the liberty of giving such other directions as I thought would tend to the recovery or preservation of their health. And further, as they had been *nearly four months on board, and during that time had been kept upon salt provisions*, I would endeavour to get fresh for them while in port. This short conversation had so sudden an effect on those I addressed, and was of so opposite a tendency to that of the gentleman alluded to, that before we got from between decks I had the pleasure to see several of them put on such clothes as they had, and look a little cheerful. I then pointed out to Lieutenant Johnson, commanding officer of the marines on board and to the master of the ship, the necessity there was of admitting the convicts upon the deck, one half at a time, during the course of the day, in order that they might breathe a purer air, as nothing would conduce more to the preservation of their health, To this these gentlemen readily assented, adding that they had no objection to the whole number coming upon deck at once, if I thought it necessary, as they were not apprehensive of any danger from the indulgence. On returning to the quarter-deck, I found my new medical acquaintance still there; and before I could give some directions to Mr. Balmain, as I was about to do, he thus once more addressed me: 'I suppose you are now convinced of the dangerous disease that prevails among these people, and of the necessity of having them landed in order to get rid of it.' Not a little hurt at the absurd part the gentleman had acted, and at his repeated importunity, I replied, with some warmth, 'that I was very sorry to differ so essentially in opinion from him as to be obliged to tell him that there was not *the least appearance* of malignity in the disease under which the convicts laboured, but that it wholly proceeded from the cold, and was nearly similar to a complaint then prevalent, even among the better sort of people, in and about Portsmouth.' Notwithstanding this, he still persisted so much in the propriety of their being landed, and the necessity there was for an application to the Secretary of State upon the occasion, that I could no longer keep my temper, and I freely told him 'that the idea of landing them was as improper as it was absurd.' And, in order to make him perfectly easy on that head, I assured him that when any disease rendered it necessary to call in medical aid, he might rest satisfied I would not trouble *him;* but would apply to Doctor Lind, Physician to the Royal Hospital at Hasler, a gentleman as eminently distinguished for his professional abilities as his other amiable qualities; or else to some of the surgeons of his Majesty's ships in Portsmouth harbour, or at Spithead, most of whom I had the pleasure of knowing, and on whose medical knowledge I was certain I could depend. This peremptory declaration had the desired effect. The gentleman took his leave, to my great satisfaction, and thereby gave me an opportunity of writing by that evening's post to inform the Secretary of State and Captain Phillip of the real state of the sick, and at the same time to urge the necessity of having fresh provisions served to the whole of the convicts while in port, as well as a little wine for those who were ill. Fresh provisions I dwelt most on, as being not only needful for the recovery of the sick, but otherwise essential, in order to prevent any of them commencing so long and tedious a voyage as they had before them with a scorbutic taint; a consequence that would most likely attend their living upon salt food, and which, added to their needful confinement and great numbers, would, in all probability, prove fatal to them, and thereby defeat the intention of Government.

"The return of the post brought me an answer, and likewise an order to the contractor for supplying the marines and convicts daily with fresh beef and vegetables, while in port. A similar order I found had been given long before my arrival; but, by some strange mistake or other, had not been complied with. The salutary effect of this change of diet, with the addition of some wine and other necessaries ordered for the sick, through the humanity of Lord Sydney, manifested itself so suddenly, that in the space of a fortnight, on comparing my list of sick with that of a surgeon belonging to one of the guardships, allowing for the disproportion of numbers, mine did not exceed his. And yet, notwithstanding this, which is a well-known fact, the report of a most malignant disease still prevailed; and so industriously was the report promulgated and kept alive by some evil-minded people, who either wished to throw an odium on the humane promoters of the plan, or to give uneasiness to the friends and relations of those engaged in the expedition, that letters from all quarters were pouring in upon us, commiserating our state. The newspapers were daily filled with alarming accounts of a disease which only existed in the imagination. But with some more delays we at last sailed towards our destination, and in eight months were off the coast of Australia.

"*9th.*—Wind variable, and weather hazy, damp, and dark; with some vivid flashes of lightning, succeeded by distant peals of loud thunder. On the morning of this day died Edward Thomson, a convict, worn out with a melancholy and long confinement. Had he lived, I think he would have proved a deserving member of society, as he seemed sensible of the impropriety and imprudence of his former life, and studious to atone for it.

"10*th.*—The wind variable, and weather dark and gloomy, with a very troublesome high sea. About two o'clock P.M. we had one of the most sudden gusts of wind I ever remember to have known. In an instant it split our mainsail; and but for the activity shown by the sailors in letting fly the sheets and lowering the topsails, the masts must have gone over the side. The *Prince of Wales*, who was close to us, had her mainyard carried away in the slings. Fortunately for us the squall was of short duration; otherwise the ships must have suffered considerably from the uncommon cross sea that was running, which we had found to be the case ever since we reached this coast.

"11*th* and 12*th.*—The wind variable, inclining to the southward and westward, and still an unpleasant cross troublesome sea. We saw a whale, several seals, and many large oceanous birds, which we frequently fired at, without their betraying the smallest symptom of fear either at the report or at the balls, which frequently dropped close to them. A conclusion may be drawn from hence that they had never been harassed with fire-arms before; if they had, they would undoubtedly have shown some fear, a sensation they seemed to be totally unacquainted with. In all our firings we did not kill one of them.

"19*th.*—In the evening we saw the land over Red Point, bearing W. by N., the extremes of the land from S.S.W. to N. We were then about three leagues from the shore; and finding it unlikely to get in that night, Captain Hunter made the signal for the convoy to come within hail, when he acquainted them that the entrance into Botany Bay bore N.N.W.; adding, that for the night he intended to stand off and on, and early in the morning make sail for the bay.

"20th.—At four in the morning the *Sirius* and convoy made sail, and at eight o'clock anchored in eight fathom water; Cape Banks E.S.E., Point Solander S.S.E., and the entrance of the bay, between these two lands, W.S.W. We found here the *Supply* tender, which had arrived the 18th, and the *Alexander*, *Scarborough*, and *Friendship* transports, who had only arrived the day before. To see all the ships safe in their destined port, without ever having, by any accident, been one hour separated, and all the people in as good health as could be expected or hoped for, after so long a voyage, was a sight truly pleasing, and at which every heart must rejoice. As we sailed into the bay, some of the natives were on the shore, looking with seeming attention at such large moving bodies coming amongst them. In the evening the boats were permitted to land on the north side, in order to get water and grass for the little stock we had remaining. An officers' guard was placed there to prevent the seamen from straggling. Captain Hunter, after anchoring, waited on the governor, on board the *Supply*; who, with several other officers, landed. As they rowed along the shore, some of the natives followed the boat; but on her putting in for the shore, they ran into the woods. Some of the gentlemen, however, before they returned on board, obtained an interview with them, during which they showed some distrust, but, upon the whole, were civilly inclined. The boats sent to haul the seine returned, having had tolerable success. The fish they caught were bream, mullet, large rays, besides many other smaller species.

"21st.—The governor, Captain Hunter, and the two masters of the men of war, with a party of marines, set off this morning, in two rigged long-boats, to examine Port Jackson, a harbour lying a little to the northward, which was discovered by Captain Cook.

"23d.—The party returned this evening, full of praises on the extent and excellence of the harbour, as well as the superiority of the ground, water, and situation, to that of Botany Bay; which I own does not, in my opinion, by any means merit the commendations bestowed on it by the much-lamented Cook and others, whose names and judgments are no less admired and esteemed. During his Excellency's absence, the lieutenant-governor had issued his orders to land all the artificers that could be found among the convicts, and a party of others, to clear the ground for the intended town, to dig sawpits, and to perform everything that was essential towards the works purposed to be carried on. Although the spot fixed on for the town was the most eligible that could be chosen, yet I think it would never have answered, the ground around it being sandy, poor, and swampy, and but very indifferently supplied with water. The fine meadows talked of in Captain Cook's voyage I could never see, though I took some pains to find them out [they came at another time of year, when the grass was grey, not green, as Cook saw it]; nor have I ever heard of a person that has seen any parts resembling them. While the people were employed on shore, the natives came several times among them, and behaved with a kind of cautious friendship. One evening, while the seine was hauling, some of them were present, and expressed great surprise at what they saw, giving a shout expressive of astonishment and joy when they perceived the quantity that was caught. No sooner were the fish out of the water than they began to lay hold of them, as if they had a right to them, or that they were their own; upon which the officer of the boat, I think very properly, restrained them, giving, however, to each of them a part. They did not at first seem very well pleased with this mode of procedure, but on observing with what justice the fish was distributed they appeared content.

"While we remained at Botany Bay, as I was one morning on board the *Supply*, we saw twenty-nine of the natives on the beach, looking towards the shipping, upon which Lieutenants Ball and King, Mr. Dawes, and myself, went on shore, landing at the place where they were. They were friendly and pacific, though each of them was armed with a spear or long dart, and had a stick, with a shell at the end, used by them in throwing their weapons [the wommera, or throwing-stick, which some say is only a corruption of *boomerang*]. Besides these, some few had shields made of the bark of the cork tree, of a plain appearance, but sufficient to ward off or turn their own weapons, some of which were pointed and barbed with the bones of fish, fastened on with some kind of adhesive gum. One of the most friendly, and who appeared to be the most confident, on signs being made to him, stuck the end of his shield in the sand, but could not be prevailed upon to throw his spear at it. Finding he declined it, I fired a pistol ball through it. The explosion frightened him, as well as his companions, a little; but they soon got over it, and on my putting the pistol into my pocket, he took up the shield, and appeared to be much surprised at finding it perforated. He then by signs and gestures seemed to ask if the pistol would make a hole through him, and on being made sensible that it would, he showed not the smallest signs of fear; on the contrary, he endeavoured, as we construed his motions, to impress us with an idea of the superiority of his own arms, which he applied to his breast, and by staggering, and a show of falling, seemed to wish us to understand that the force and effect of them was mortal, and not to be resisted. However, I am well convinced that they know and dread the superiority of our arms, notwithstanding this show of indifference, as they, on all occasions, have discovered a dislike to a musket; and so very soon did they make themselves acquainted with the nature of our military dress, that, from the first, they carefully avoided a soldier or any person wearing a red coat, which they seem to have marked as a fighting vesture. Many of their warriors, or distinguished men, we observed to be painted in stripes across the breast and back, which, at some little distance, appears not unlike our soldiers' cross-belts.

"24*th*.—The boats were employed in getting water and grass for the live stock, as the governor, finding

Port Jackson more suited to his wishes, had determined to remove to that place, and form the settlement there. While these preparations were making, every person in the fleet were surprised to see, in this part of the world, two large ships [these were the ships of La Perouse] plying hard in the offing to get into the bay. It was seen, in the evening, that they had French colours flying; but the wind blowing pretty strong out of the bay, they were unable to get in, and the weather becoming thick and hazy, we soon lost sight of them.

"25*th.*—Nothing of the strange ships to be seen. The governor, with a detachment of marines, sailed in the *Supply* tender for Port Jackson, leaving instructions with Captain Hunter to follow him with all the transports and victuallers, as soon as the wind and weather would permit.

"26*th.*—We again descried the French ships standing in for the bay, with a leading wind, upon which Captain Hunter sent his first lieutenant on board the commanding officer's ship, which was distinguished by a broad pendant, to assist them in coming in. Soon after the lieutenants were returned to the *Sirius*, Captain Clonnard, the French commodore's captain (who during the late war commanded the *Artois*, taken by the *Bienfaisant*, Captain Macbride), waited on Captain Hunter, and informed him that the ships were the *Astrolabe* and the *Boussale*, which sailed from France in the year 1786, under the command of Messieurs de la Perouse and De Langle. He further acquainted him that, having touched at Navigator's Isles, they had had the misfortune to lose Captain

De Langle, the second in command, with ten other officers, and two boats' crews, all of whom were cut off by the natives of those islands, who appeared to be numerous and warlike. This accident induced them to put into this port in order to build some boats, which they had in frames. It also had afforded room for the promotion of Monsieur Clonnard, who, on their leaving France, was only the commodore's first lieutenant.

"At ten o'clock the *Sirius*, with all the ships, weighed, and in the evening anchored in Port Jackson, with a few trifling damages done to some of them who had run foul of each other in working out of Botany Bay. *Port Jackson I believe to be, without exception, the finest and most extensive harbour in the universe, and at the same time the most secure, being safe from all the winds that blow.* [True enough, were the entrance larger. When you have *got* in you are safe enough, but *getting* in without steam is not always easy.] It is divided into a great number of coves, to which his Excellency has given different names. That on which the town is to be built is called Sydney Cove. It is one of the smallest in the harbour, but the most convenient, as ships of the greatest burden can with ease go into it, and heave out close to the shore. Trincomalé, acknowledged to be one of the best harbours in the world, is by no means to be compared to it. In a word, Port Jackson would afford sufficient and safe anchorage for all the navies of Europe. The *Supply* had arrived the day before, and the governor, with every person that could be spared from the ship, were on shore clearing the ground for the encampment. In the evening, when all the ships had anchored, the English colours were displayed; and at the foot of the flag-staff his Majesty's health, and success to the settlement, was drank by the governor, many of the principal officers, and private men, who were present upon the occasion.

"27th.—A number of convicts from the different transports were landed to assist in clearing the ground for the encampment. His Excellency marked the outlines, and as much as possible to prevent irregularity, and to keep the convicts from straggling, the provost-marshal, aided by the patrole, had orders to take into custody all convicts that should be found without the lines, and to leave them in charge of the main or quarter guard. The boats sent this day to fish were successful. Some of the natives came into the little bay or cove where the seine was hauled, and behaved very friendly. Indeed they carried their civility so far, although a people that appeared to be averse to work, as to assist in dragging it ashore. For this kind office they were liberally rewarded with fish, which seemed to please them, and give general satisfaction.

"29th.—A convenient place for the cattle being found, the few that remained were landed. The frame and materials for the governor's house, constructed by Smith, in St. George's Fields, were likewise sent on shore, and some preparations made for erecting it. This day Captain Hunter and Lieutenant Bradley began to take a survey of the harbour. In the course of the last week all the marines, their wives and children, together with all the convicts, male and female, were landed. The laboratory and sick tents were erected, and, I am sorry to say, were soon filled with patients afflicted with the true camp dysentery and the scurvy. More pitiable objects were perhaps never seen. Not a comfort or convenience could be got for them, besides the very few we had with us. His Excellency, seeing the state these poor objects were in, ordered a piece of ground to be enclosed for the purpose of raising vegetables for them. The seeds that were sown upon this occasion, on first appearing above ground, looked promising and well, but soon after withered away; which was not indeed extraordinary, as they were not sown at a proper season of the year. The sick have increased since our landing to such a degree, that a spot for a general hospital has been marked out, and artificers already employed on it. A proper spot, contiguous to the hospital, has been chosen to raise such vegetables as can be produced at this season of the year, and where a permanent garden for the use of the hospital is to be established.

"*February* 1*st*.—We had the most tremendous thunder and lightning,* with heavy rain, I ever remember to have seen.

"2*d*.—This morning five sheep, belonging to the lieutenant-governor and quarter-master, were killed by the lightning under a tree, at the foot of which

---

* White was not yet accustomed to the fearful concussion of Australian electrical storms. From comparison of human experience I believe that the centre and metropolis of thunderstorms is the island of Celebes. When you get your ship struck twice a day for a week, you may be allowed to hold an opinion.

a shed had been built for them. The branches and trunk of the tree were shivered and rent in a very extraordinary manner.

"*5th.*—A storehouse has been begun for the purpose of receiving the stores and provisions of the three transports bound to China. On a muster of the convicts this morning some were found to be missing, and supposed to have gone to Botany Bay in hopes of being received on board the French ships, which are said to be short of hands, and made more so by the loss they had recently sustained, as before mentioned.

"*7th.*—The governor's commission, and that for establishing a criminal court of judicature, admiralty court, &c., were read. After this was done the troops under arms fired three volleys, when his Excellency thanked the soldiers for their steady and good conduct, which Major Ross caused to be inserted in the general order-book. The governor then addressed the convicts in a short speech extremely well adapted to the people he had to govern, and who were then before him. Among many circumstances that would tend to their future happiness and comfort he recommended marriage, assuring them that an indiscriminate and illegal intercourse would be punished with the greatest severity and rigour. Honesty, obedience, and industry, he told them, would make their situation comfortable, whereas a contrary line of conduct would subject them to ignominy, severities, and punishment. When the ceremony was concluded his Excellency, attended by all the officers of the colony, withdrew to a tent pitched for the occasion, where a cold dinner was laid out ; and after the cloth was removed many loyal and public toasts were drank.

"*8th.*—A party of the gentlemen of the garrison set out by land to pay a visit to the French at Botany Bay, from whom they met with the most hospitable, polite, and friendly reception and treatment. Many of the convicts who had been missing had been at Botany Bay. They had offered themselves to the French navigators on any terms, but not one of them had been received.* This refusal obliged them to return, and when they came back they were real objects of pity. Conscious of the punishment that awaited so imprudent and improper an experiment, they had stayed out as long as the cravings of nature would permit, and were nearly half starved. A woman, named Ann Smith, and a man have never since been heard of. They are supposed to have missed their way as they returned, and to have perished for want. As the French commodore had given his honour that he would not admit any of them on board, it cannot be thought he would take them. The convict, it is true, was a Frenchman, named Peter Paris,† and it is possible, on that account, he might have been concealed through pity by his countrymen, and carried off without the knowledge of the commanding officer. At the very time the party from hence were gone by land to Botany Bay, Captain Clonnard came round in a boat on a visit

---

* Probably the last political act of La Perouse with Europeans. He carried his great name most nobly to his unknown grave.

† I doubt he had been coining, but had been recommended to mercy by a mixed jury.

of ceremony from Monsieur de la Peyrouse to the governor. He brought with him some dispatches, which he requested might be forwarded to the French ambassador at the court of London by the first transports that sailed for England. The captain stayed all night, and returned the next morning. This day, for the first time, a kangaroo was shot and brought into camp. Some of the natives passed pretty close to the *Sirius* without seeming to express, by their countenance or actions, either fear, curiosity, or surprise. During the course of this week fourteen marriages were solemnized. The criminal court, consisting of six officers of his Majesty's forces by land or sea, with the judge-advocate, sat for the first time before whom several convicts were tried for petty larceny. Some of them were acquitted, others sentenced to receive corporal punishment, and one or two were, by the decision of the court, ordered to a barren rock or little island in the middle of the harbour, there to remain on bread and water for a stated time.

"12th.—The commissions were read a second time, at the desire of some of the officers, whose situation with the battalion prevented them from being present at the first reading; after which the lieutenant-governor and judge-advocate were sworn in justices of the peace, and Lieutenant King (second of the *Sirius*) superintendent and commanding officer of New Norfolk Island, an appointment given him by the governor.

"14th.—The *Supply* sailed for Norfolk Island, with Lieutenant King and his detachment, consisting of

Mr. Cunningham, master's mate, and Mr. Jameson, surgeon's first mate, of the *Sirius*, two marines, and twelve male and female convicts. The governor furnished him with provisions and stores of every kind for six months, and with tools for cutting down timber; which last employment was the purpose of his mission.

"27*th*.—Thomas Barrett, Henry Lovel, and Joseph Hall were brought before the criminal court, and tried for feloniously and fraudulently taking away from the public store beef and pease, the property of the Crown. They were convicted on the clearest evidence; and sentence of death being passed on them, they were, about six o'clock the same evening, taken to the fatal tree, where Barrett was launched into eternity, after having confessed to the Rev. Mr. Johnson, who attended him, that he was guilty of the crime, and had long merited the ignominious death which he was about to suffer, and to which he said he had been brought by bad company and evil example. Lovel and Hall were respited until six o'clock the next evening. When that awful hour arrived, they were led to the place of execution, and just as they were on the point of ascending the ladder, the judge-advocate arrived with the governor's pardon, on condition of their being banished to some uninhabited place.

"29*th*.—Daniel Gordon and John Williams were tried and convicted of stealing wine, the property of Mr. Zachariah Clarke. Williams being an ignorant black youth, the court recommended him to the governor as a proper object of mercy, and he was accordingly pardoned. Gordon, who was another black, had his sentence of death, while at the gallows, changed to banishment with Lovel and Hall.

"30th.—John Freeman was tried for stealing from another convict seven pounds of flour. He was convicted, and sentenced to be hanged; but while under the ladder, with the rope about his neck, he was offered his free pardon on condition of performing the duty of the common executioner as long as he remained in this country; which, after some little pause, he reluctantly accepted. William Sheerman, his accomplice, was sentenced to receive on his bare back, with a cat-o'-nine-tails, three hundred lashes, which were inflicted.

"A New Holland Cassowary* was brought into camp. This bird stands seven feet high, measuring from the ground to the upper part of the head, and in every respect is much larger than the Common Cassowary of all authors, and differs so much therefrom, in its form, as to clearly prove it a new species.

"*March* 9th.—The governor, with two long-boats manned and armed, returned from Broken Bay, situated a little to the northward, which he had been exploring for several days. It affords good shelter for shipping, and the entrance is bold; it cannot, however, be compared with Port Jackson. While he was there he saw a great many of the natives, some of whom he thinks he had observed before, either at Botany Bay or in the neighbourhood of Port Jackson. One of the females happened to fall in love with his greatcoat; and to obtain it she

* This is the Emu. A foolish bird, which I have often attempted to kill, but have never succeeded.

used a variety of means. First, she danced and played a number of antic tricks; but finding this mode ineffectual, she had recourse to tears, which she shed plentifully. This expedient not answering, she ceased from weeping, and appeared as cheerful as any of the party around her. From this little incident it may be seen that they are not a people devoid of art. At Broken Bay many of the females, young and old, had the first joint of the little finger on their left hand cut off. As this was the case with those who were married, or appeared to be so from their having young children, as well as with those who were too young for a connexion of that nature, it was not possible to account for the cause of such an amputation. Thefts and depredations on one another have become so very frequent and glaring among the convicts, that scarcely a day passes without some of these miserable delinquents being punished. So hardened in wickedness and depravity are many of them, that they seem insensible to the fear of corporal punishment, or even death itself.

"The principal business going forward at present is erecting cabbage-tree huts for the officers, soldiers, and convicts; some store-houses, &c.; and a very good hospital; all which in the completion will cost a great deal of time and trouble, as the timber of this country is very unfit for the purpose of building. Nor do I know any one purpose for which it will answer, except for firewood, and for that it is excellent; but in other respects it is the worst wood that any country or climate ever produced; although some of the trees, when standing, appear fit for any use whatever, masts for shipping not excepted. Strange as it may be imagined, no wood in this country, though sawed ever so thin, and dried ever so well, will float. Repeated trials have only served to convince me that, immediately on immersion, it sinks to the bottom like a stone.*

"The stone of this country is excellent for building, could any kind of cement be found to keep it together. There is not any limestone (I believe)† in New South Wales. The governor, notwithstanding that he had collected together all the shells which could be found, for the purpose of obtaining from them the lime necessary to the construction of a house of his own residence, did not procure even a fourth part of the quantity which was wanted. The foundation stone of a private house for him has been laid; and a plate of copper, with the following inscription engraved on it, is to be placed in the wall:

ARTHUR PHILLIP, ESQ.,
CAPTAIN-GENERAL IN AND OVER HIS MAJESTY'S TERRITORY OF
NEW SOUTH WALES, AND ITS DEPENDENCIES,
ARRIVED IN THIS COUNTRY ON THE 18TH DAY OF JANUARY, 1788, WITH THE
FIRST SETTLERS;
AND ON THE 15TH DAY OF MAY, IN THE SAME YEAR, THE FIRST OF
THESE STONES WAS LAID.

* This is perfectly true. I had once to point out this fact to a gentleman who proposed to get up a Great Lumber Company (Limited). The first basis of operations was to have been the "Yarra." Coming two hundred miles through splendid forests, I challenged him to find a solitary tree on its banks which would float.

† He may well say, like an honest man, "I believe." Now-a-days they would write it down for a fact. In reality there are no such fantastic developments of magnesian limestone (with the exception of Virginia) as those of New South Wales. The awful, unapproached caverns off the Mitta Mitta, into which our friends crept to die, are limestone.

"The *Supply* tender returned from Norfolk Island; where, with great difficulty and danger, the stores sent with Lieutenant King were landed, on account of the rockiness of its shore, and the violence of the surf that almost continually beats upon it. In her passage there she fell in with an island, in lat. 31° 36' S. long. 159° 4' E. never before discovered, to which Lieutenant Ball, who commanded the *Supply* on this occasion, gave the name of Lord Howe's Island. On her return to this port she stopped at it, and found the landing nearly, if not quite, as difficult as at Norfolk Island. The shore in many places was covered with excellent turtle, eighteen of which were brought here, and proved a seasonable supply to the convicts afflicted with the scurvy, many of whom were in a deplorable situation.

"The smallest turtle brought from Lord Howe's Island did not weigh less than 150 lbs. They also found on it, in great plenty, a kind of fowl, resembling much the Guinea fowl in shape and size, but widely different in colour; they being in general all white, with a red fleshy substance rising, like a cock's comb, from the head, and not unlike a piece of sealing-wax. These not being birds of flight, nor in the least wild, the sailors availing themselves of their gentleness and inability to take wing from their pursuits, easily struck them down with sticks. There were also many birds of the dove kind, as tame as the former, and caught with equal facility. Some of them were brought alive to this place. Besides these, the shore abounded with sea birds of several species. The island is very barren, and not more than twenty miles in circumference.

"*April* 15*th*.—His Excellency, attended by Lieutenant Ball of the navy, Lieutenant George Johnston of the marines, the judge advocate, myself, three soldiers, and two seamen, landed in Manly Cove (so called from the manly conduct of the natives when the governor first visited it), on the north side of the entrance into Port Jackson harbour, in order to trace to its source a river which had been discovered a few days before. We, however, found this impracticable, owing to a thicket and swamp which ran along the side of it. The governor, anxious to acquire all the knowledge of the country in his power, forded the river in two places, and more than up to our waists in water, in hopes of being able to avoid the thicket and swamp; but, notwithstanding all his perseverance, we were at length obliged to return, and to proceed along the sea-shore, a mile or two to the northward. At the end of this we fell in with a small salt water lagoon, on which we found nine birds, that, whilst swimming, most perfectly resembled the *rara avis* of the ancients—a *black* swan. We discharged several shot at them, but the distance was too great for execution. Our frequent firing, however, caused them to take wing, and they flew towards the sea, which was very near, in the order that wild geese generally preserve—the one before the other. Had we not raised them we should certainly have concluded that they were black swans; but their flight gave us an opportunity of seeing some white feathers which terminated the tip of each wing; in every other part they were perfectly black. Their size appeared not equal to that of an European swan, but the shape exactly corresponded, except about the wings, which seemed rather small for the body. We not long after discovered the great brown kingfisher.*

"We rounded this lagoon, and proceeded four or five miles westward, along the banks of a small fresh-water river which emptied itself into it, and had for its source only a swamp or boggy ground. After we had passed this swamp, we got into an immense wood, the trees of which were very high and large and a considerable distance apart, with little under or brushwood. The ground was not very good, although it produced a luxuriant coat of a kind of sour grass growing in tufts or bushes, which at some distance had the appearance of meadow land, and might be mistaken for it by superficial examiners. Here we pitched our tents (without which the governor never travelled) for the night, near a swamp, out of which we were supplied with water, not indeed either of the best or clearest kind. The night being cold, and a heavy dew falling, we kept up a large fire before the tents, which, though in one respect an excellent precaution, far from chasing away, seemed to allure the musquitoes, which tormented us inexpressibly during the whole

* The *Alcedo gigantea*, or "Laughing Jackass." His merry shouts and shrieks of laughter echo through the wood at sundown. He is a sacred bird now, for he lives on deadly snakes.

night. We this day discovered the Banksian cockatoo.*

"16*th*.—We pursued our route westward, proceeding many miles inland, without being able to trace, by a single vestige, that the natives had been recently in those parts. We saw, however, some proofs of their ingenuity, in various figures cut on the smooth surface of some large stones. They consisted chiefly of representations of themselves in different attitudes, of their canoes, of several sorts of fish and animals; and, considering the rudeness of the instruments with which the figures must have been executed, they seemed to exhibit tolerably strong likenesses. On the stones where the natives had been thus exercising their abilities in sculpture were several weather-beaten shells. The country all around this place was was rather high and rocky; and the soil arid, parched, and inhospitable.

"In the evening, after a long and fatiguing march, we fell in with the north-west branch of Port Jackson harbour. Here the two seamen, overcome with fatigue, and having their shoes torn from their feet through the ruggedness of the road along which we had travelled, could proceed no further. This circumstance induced the governor to consign them to the care of Lieutenant Ball and a marine, supplying them with provisions sufficient to last them till they reached the ships. His Excellency, with the rest of the party, pushed on to the westward, by the water-

* The black Cockatoo with the *ruby* tail. Not the larger and savage Wee Wah with the yellow tail, the untameable eagle among Scansores.

side, in hopes of finding better land, and a more open country. About four o'clock in the afternoon we came to a steep valley, where the flowing of the tide ceased, and a fresh-water stream commenced. Here, in the most desert, wild, and solitary seclusion that the imagination can form any idea of, we took up our abode for the night, dressed our provisions, washed our shirts and stockings, and turned our inconvenient situation to the best advantage in our power.

"The next morning we hid our tents and the remains of our provisions, and with only a little rum, and a small quantity of bread, made a forced march into the country, to the westward, of about fourteen miles, without being able to succeed in the object of our search, which was for good land well watered. Indeed the land here, although covered with an endless wood, was better than the parts which we had already explored. Finding it, however, very unlikely that we should be able to penetrate through this immense forest, and circumstanced as we were, it was thought more prudent to return. We accordingly, after an expeditious walk, reached the stream from whence we had set out in the morning, and taking up the tents and provisions which we had left, proceeded a little farther down, to the flowing of the tide, and there pitched our tents for the night; during which it rained very heavily, with thunder and lightning.

"18th.—We began our progress early in the morning, bending our course down the river. Some places along the shore, where the tide had flowed so as to obstruct our passage, we were obliged to ford; and at times we were under the necessity of climbing heights nearly inaccessible. At length, after undergoing much fatigue, we were agreeably surprised, and cheered with the sight of two boats, sent by Captain Hunter to meet us, and just then coming up with the tide. By them we learnt that Lieutenant Ball with his enfeebled party had arrived safe at the ship the day after they had quitted us. We all went on board the boats, and fell down the river till we got to a pleasant little cove, where we dined, with great satisfaction and comfort, upon the welcome provisions which were sent in the boats by the governor's steward. After having refreshed ourselves, we again embarked, and about six o'clock in the evening arrived in Sydney Cove.

"22d.—On the morning of this day the governor, accompanied by the same party, with the addition of Lieutenant Cresswell of the marines and six privates, landed at the head of the harbour, with an intention of penetrating into the country westward, as far as seven days' provisions would admit of, every individual carrying his own allowance of bread, beef, rum, and water. The soldiers, beside their own provisions, carried a camp kettle, and two tents, with their poles, &c. Thus equipped, with the additional weight of spare shoes, shirts, trousers, together with a great coat or Scotch plaid, for the purpose of sleeping in, as the nights were cold, we proceeded on our destination. We likewise took with us a small hand hatchet, in order to mark the trees as we went on; those marks (called in America *blazing*) being the only guide to direct us in our return. The country was so rugged as to render it almost impossible to explore our way by the assistance of the compass.

"In this manner we proceeded for a mile or two through a part well covered with enormous trees, free from underwood. We then reached a thicket of brushwood, which we found so impervious as to oblige us to return nearly to the place from whence we had set out in the morning. Here we encamped, near some stagnant water, for the night, during which it thundered, lightened, and rained. About eleven o'clock the governor was suddenly attacked with a most violent complaint in his side and loins,* brought on by cold and fatigue, not having perfectly gotten the better of the last expedition. The next morning being fine, his Excellency, who was rather better, though still in pain, would not relinquish the object of his pursuit; and therefore we proceeded, and soon got round the wood or thicket which had harassed us so much the day before. After we had passed it, we fell in with an hitherto unperceived branch of Port Jackson harbour, along the bank of which the grass was tolerably rich and succulent, and in height nearly up to the middle, interspersed with a plant much resembling the indigo. We followed this branch westward for a few miles, until we came to a small fresh water stream that emptied itself into it. Here we took up our quarters for the night, as our halts were always regulated by fresh water, an essential point by no means to be dispensed with, and not very abundant, or frequently to be met with, in this country. We made a kettle of excellent soup out of a white cockatoo and

* Bush lumbago.

two crows which I had shot, as we came along. The land all around us was similar to that which we had passed. At night we had thunder, lightning, and rain. The governor, though not free from pain, was rather recovering.

"*24th.*—As soon as the dew, which is remarkably heavy in this country, was off the ground, we proceeded to trace the river, or small arm of the sea. The banks of it were now pleasant, the trees immensely large, and at a considerable distance from each other; and the land around us flat, and rather low, but well covered with the kind of grass just mentioned. Here the tide ceased to flow; and all further progress for boats was stopped by a flat space of large broad stones, over which a fresh water stream ran. Just above this flat, close to the water side, we discovered a quarry of slates, from which we expected to derive great advantage in respect to covering our houses, stores, &c. it being a material beyond conception difficult to be procured in this country; but on trial it was found of no use, as it proved to be of a crumbling and rotten nature. On this fresh water stream, as well as on the salt, we saw a great many ducks and teal, three of which we shot in the course of the day, besides two crows, and some loraquets.* About four in the afternoon, being near the head of the stream, and somewhat apprehensive of rain, we pitched our tents before the grass became wet, a circumstance which would have proved very uncom-

---

* Scarlet, purple, and blue; one of the most splendid of all Scansors. A long-tailed parrot as big as a small pigeon, which the colonists misname "Lories."

fortable during the night. Here we had our ducks picked, stuffed with some slices of salt beef, and roasted; and never did a repast seem more delicious; the salt beef, serving as a palatable substitute for the want of salt, gave it an agreeable relish. The evening cleared up, and the night proved dry. During the latter, we heard a noise which not a little surprised us, on account of its resemblance to the human voice. What it proceeded from we could not discover; but I am of opinion that it was made by a bird, or some animal.* The country round us was by no means so good, or the grass so abundant, as that which we had passed. The water, though neither clear, nor in any great quantity, was neither of a bad quality nor ill-tasted.

"The next day, after having sowed some seeds, we pursued our route for three or four miles west, where we met with a mean hut, belonging to some of the natives, but could not perceive the smallest trace of their having been there lately. Close to this hut we saw a kangaroo, which had come to drink at an adjacent pool of stagnated water, but we could not get within shot of it. A little farther on, we fell in with three huts, as deserted as the former, and a swamp, not unlike the American rice grounds. Near this we saw a tree in flames, without the least appearance of any natives, from which we suspected that it had been

* Almost certainly the great Caprimulgus, or goat-sucker, who spends the watches of the night by crying out in a loud voice, "More Pork! More pork!" as well as a man could say it himself. A man told me that their real name was 'Mope-hawk," because they were like hawks, and moped. For me, I believe in the onomatopœia.

set on fire by lightning. This circumstance was first suggested by Lieutenant Ball, who had remarked, as well as myself, that every part of the country, though the most inaccessible and rocky, appeared as if, at certain times of the year, it had been all on fire. Indeed in many parts we met with very large trees, the trunks of which and branches were evidently rent, and demolished by lightning. Close by the burning tree we saw three kangaroos. Though by this time very much fatigued, we proceeded about two miles farther on, in hopes of finding some good water, but without effect; and about half-past four o'clock we took up our quarters near a stagnant pool. The ground was so very dry and parched, that it was with some difficulty we could drive either our tent pegs or poles into it. The country about this spot was much clearer of underwood than that which we had passed during the day. The trees around us were immensely large, and the tops of them filled with loraquets and paroquets of exquisite beauty, which chattered to such a degree that we could scarcely hear each other speak. We fired several times at them, but the trees were so very high that we killed but few.

"26th.—We still directed our course westward, and passed another tree on fire; and others which were hollow, and perforated by a small hole at the bottom, in which the natives seemed to have snared some animal. It was certainly done by the natives, as the trees where these holes or perforations were, had in general many notches cut, for the purpose of getting to the top of them. After this we crossed a watercourse, which shows that at some seasons the rain is very heavy here notwithstanding that there was at present but little water in it. Beyond the chasm we came to a pleasant hill, the top of which was tolerably clear of trees, and perfectly free from underwood. His Excellency gave it the name of *Belle Veüe.* From the top of this hill we saw a chain of hills or mountains, which appeared to be thirty or forty miles distant, running in a north and south direction. The northernmost being conspicuously higher than any of the rest, the governor called it *Richmond Hill;* the next, or those in the centre, *Lansdown Hills;* and those to the southward, which are by much the lowest, *Carmarthen Hills.*

"In a valley below *Belle Veüe*, we saw a fire, and by it found some chewed roots of a saline taste,* which showed that the natives had recently been there. The country hereabout was pleasant to the eye, well wooded, and covered with long sour grass, growing in tufts. At the bottom of this valley or flat, we crossed another water-course, and ascended a hill, where the wood was so very thick as to obstruct our view. Here, finding our provisions to run short, our return was concluded on, though with great reluctance, as it was our wish, and had been our determination, to reach the hills before us if it had been possible. In our way back, which we easily discovered by the marks made in the trees, we saw a hollow tree on fire, the smoke issuing out of the top part as through a chimney. On coming near, and minutely examining it, we found that it had been set on fire by the natives; for there was some dry grass

* I think *Mesembrianthemum equilaterale.*

lighted and put into the hole wherein we had supposed they used to snare or take the animal before alluded to.* In the evening, where we pitched our tents, we shot two crows and some loraquets for supper. The night was fine and clear; during which we often heard, as before, a sound like the human voice, and, from its continuance on one spot, we concluded it to proceed from a bird perched on some of the trees near us.

"*27th.*—We now found ourselves obliged to make a forced march back, as our provisions were quite exhausted—a circumstance rather alarming, in case of losing our way, which, however, we met with no difficulty in discovering by the marked trees. By our calculation we had penetrated into the country, to the westward, not less than thirty-two or thirty-three miles. This day we saw the dung of an animal as large as that of a horse, but it was more like the excrement of a hog, intermixed with grass.† When we got as far back as the arm or branch of the sea which forms the upper part of Port Jackson harbour we saw many ducks, but could not get within shot of any of them. It was now growing late; and the governor being apprehensive that the boats which he had ordered to attend daily might be, for that day, returning before we could reach them, he sent Lieutenants Johnston and Cresswell, with a marine, a-head, in order to secure such provisions as might have been sent up, and to give directions for the

---

* Done to smoke out a poor opossum. There is a capital drawing of the thing being done in Sturt's Travels, fifty years later, and 1,000 miles away.

† Emu.

boats to come for us the next morning, as it then appeared very unlikely that all the party, who were, without exception, much fatigued, could be there soon enough to save the tide down. Those gentlemen accordingly went forward, and were so fortunate as to be just in time; and they returned to us with a seasonable supply of bread, beef, rum, and wine. As soon as they had joined us, we encamped for the night on a spot about the distance of a mile from the place where the boats were to take us up in the morning. His Excellency was again indisposed, occasioned by a return of his complaint, which had been brought on by a fall into a hollow place in the ground, that, being concealed by the long grass, he was unable to discern. We passed the next day in examining different inlets in the upper part of the harbour. We saw there some of the natives, who, in their canoes, came alongside of the boat to receive some trifles which the governor held out to them. In the evening we returned to Sydney Cove.

"*May 1st.*—James Bennet, a youth, was executed for robbing a tent belonging to the *Charlotte* transport, of sugar and some other articles. Before he was turned off he confessed his guilt, and acknowledged that, young as he was, he had been an old offender. Some other trifling thefts were brought before the court at the same time, and those concerned in them sentenced to receive corporal punishment.

"The *Supply* tender sailed for Lord Howe's Island to fetch turtle; as did the *Lady Penrhyn* transport for China. The *Scarborough* dropped down the harbour; she was followed the next day by the *Char-*

lotte, and they sailed in company for China. Some of the natives came alongside the *Sirius*, and made signs to have their beards taken off. One of them patiently, and without fear or distrust, underwent the operation from the ship's barber, and seemed much delighted with it.

"21*st*.—William Ayres, a convict, who was in a state of convalescence, and to whom I had given permission to go a little way into the country for the purpose of gathering a few herbs wherewith to make tea, was, after night, brought to the hospital, with one of the spears used by the natives sticking in his loins.* It had been darted at him as he was stooping, and while his back was turned to the assailant. The weapon was barbed, and stuck so very fast, that it would admit of no motion. After dilating the wound to a considerable length and depth, with some difficulty I extracted the spear, which had penetrated the flesh nearly three inches. After the operation he informed us that he received his wound from three of the natives, who came behind him at a time when he suspected no person to be near him except Peter Burn, whom he had met a little before, employed on the same business as himself. He added, that after they had wounded him they beat him in a cruel manner, and stripping the clothes from his back, carried them off, making signs to him (as he interpreted them) to return to the camp. He further related, that after they had left him, he saw Burn in the possession of another party of the natives, who were dragging him along, with his head bleeding, and

* The beginning of the end.

seemingly in great distress; while he himself was so exhausted with loss of blood, that, instead of being able to assist his companion, he was happy to escape with his life.

"The *Port Jackson thrush* inhabits the neighbourhood of Port Jackson.*

"25*th*.—The *Supply* arrived from Lord Howe's Island without a single turtle, the object for which she was sent; a dreadful disappointment to those who were languishing under the scurvy, many of whom are since dead, and there is great reason to fear that several others will soon share the same fate. This disorder has now risen to a most alarming height, without any possibility of checking it until some vegetables can be raised, which, from the season of the year, cannot take place for many months; and even then I am apprehensive that there will not be a sufficiency produced, such are the labour and difficulty which attend the clearing of the ground. It will scarcely be credited, when I declare that I have known twelve men employed for five days in grubbing up one tree; and when this has been effected, the timber (as already observed) has been only fit for firewood; so that in consequence of the great labour in clearing of the ground, and the weak state of the people, to which may be added the scarcity of tools, most of those we had being either worn out by the hardness of the timber, or lost in the woods among

---

* Now called White's Thrush, after our present good author. It is the only vertebrate creature found universally in all divisions of the earth. I have shot the poor innocent things, I am sure I do not know why.

the grass, through the carelessness of the convicts, the prospect before us is not of the most pleasing kind. All the stock that was landed, both public and private, seems, instead of thriving, to fall off exceedingly. The number at first was but inconsiderable, and even that number is at present much diminished. The sheep, in particular, decrease rapidly, very few being now alive in the colony, although there were numbers, the property of Government or individuals, when first landed.

"26th.—Two men of the *Sirius* were brought before the criminal court, and tried for assaulting and beating in a cruel manner another man belonging to the same vessel while employed on an island appropriated by the governor to the use of the ship. They were sentenced to receive five hundred lashes each, but could not undergo the whole of that punishment, as, like most of the persons in the colony, they were much afflicted with the scurvy.

"28th.—Captain Hunter, his first lieutenant, and the surgeon of the *Sirius*, went to the point of land which forms the north head of Port Jackson. In going there they discovered an old man, with a little girl about five years of age, lying close to the ground watching their motions, and at the same time endeavouring to conceal themselves. The surgeon had his gun with him, the effects of which he let the old man see, by shooting a bird which fell at his feet. The explosion at first greatly alarmed him, but perceiving that they intended him no ill, he soon got over his fears. The bird was then given to him, which (having barely plucked and not more than half broiled it) he devoured, entrails, bones, and all. The little girl was much frightened, and endeavoured to hide herself behind the old man, to escape the least observation.

"30th.—Captain Campbell of the marines, who had been up the harbour to procure some rushes for thatch, brought to the hospital the bodies of William Okey and Samuel Davis, two rush-cutters, whom he had found murdered by the natives in a shocking manner. Okey was transfixed through the breast with one of their spears, which with great difficulty and force was pulled out. He had two other spears sticking in him to a depth which must have proved mortal. His skull was divided and comminuted so much that his brains easily found a passage through. His eyes were out, but these might have been picked away by birds. Davis was a youth, and had only some trifling marks of violence about him. This lad could not have been many hours dead; for when Captain Campbell found him, which was among some mangrove-trees, and at a considerable distance from the place where the other man lay, he was not stiff, nor very cold; nor was he perfectly so when brought to the hospital. From these circumstances we have been led to think that while they were despatching Okey he had crept to the trees, among which he was found; and that fear, united with the cold and wet, in a great degree contributed to his death. What was the motive or cause of this melancholy catastrophe we have not been able to discover; but from the civility

A A

shown on all occasions to the officers by the natives, whenever any of them were met, I am strongly inclined to think that they must have been provoked and injured by the convicts.

"Early the next morning the governor, lieutenants G. Johnston and Kellow, myself, six soldiers, and two armed convicts, whom we took as guides, went to the place where the murder had been committed, in hopes, by some means or other, to be able to find out either the actual perpetrators, or those concerned. As most of their clothes, and all their working tools were carried off, we expected that these might furnish us with some clue; but in this we were disappointed. We could not observe a single trace of the natives ever having been there. We then crossed the country to Botany Bay, still flattering ourselves that we might be able to discover, among a tribe at that place, some proof that they had been concerned; as the governor was resolved, on whomsoever he found any of the tools or clothing, to show them his displeasure, and by every means in his power endeavour to convince them of his motives for such a procedure.* In our route we saw several kangaroos, and shot a very fine teal. A little before sunset, after a long and fatiguing march, we arrived at Botany Bay. When we approached the bay, we saw eleven canoes, with two persons in each, fishing; most of them had a fire in their canoe, a convenience which they seldom go without at any time or season, but particularly

---

* It is evident that the unhappy blacks began the war of extermination.

at this, as the weather was very cold. Here we pitched our tents, for (as I have before observed) we never travel without them, and kindled large fires both in front and rear; still, however, the cold was so very intense that we could scarcely close our eyes during the night. In the morning the grass was quite white with a hoar frost, so as to crackle under our feet.* After breakfast we visited the grave of the French abbé, who died whilst the Count de Peyrouse was here. It was truly humble indeed, being distinguished only by a common head-stone, stuck slightly into the loose earth which covered it. Against a tree, just above it, was nailed a board, with the following inscription on it:—

HIC JACET
LE RECEVEUR
EX F. F. MINORIBUS GALLIA SACERDOS
PHYSICUS IN CIRCUMNAVIGATIONE MUNDI
DUCE D. DE LA PEYROUSE.
OBIIT DIE 17TH FEBR. ANNO 1788.

As the painting on the board could not be permanent, Governor Phillip had the inscription engraved on a plate of copper, and nailed to the same tree; and at some future day he intends to have a handsome head-stone placed at the grave. We cut down some trees which stood between that on which the

* Our gardeners insist on putting everything which comes from any part of Australia into a tropical oven house. If they had had their clothes frozen as stiff as a board, after trying to ford a creek, as I have, it is possible that they would not do so. Also Alsophilla Australis, the verdant fern tree, will flourish where there is severe frost; but as it looks like a palm tree, it is smothered in a hot-house.

inscription is fixed and the shore, as they prevented persons passing in boats from seeing it.

"Between this and the harbour's mouth we found forty-nine canoes hauled upon the beach, but not a native to be seen. After we had passed them, we fell in with an Indian path; and, as it took a turn towards the camp, we followed it about two miles; when on a sudden, in a valley or little bay to the northward of Botany Bay, we were surprised at hearing the sound of voices, which we instantly found to proceed from a great number of the natives sitting behind a rock, who appeared to be equally astonished with ourselves, as, from the silence we observed, they had not perceived us till we were within twenty yards of them. Every one of them, as they got up, armed himself with a long spear, the short stick before described used in throwing it, a shield made of bark, and either a large club, pointed at one end, or a stone hatchet. At first they seemed rather hostilely inclined, and made signs, with apparent tokens of anger, for us to return; but when they saw the governor advance towards them, unarmed, and with his hands opened wide (a signal we had observed among them of amity and peace), they, with great confidence, came up to him, and received from him some trifles which he had in his pocket, such as fish-hooks, beads, and a looking-glass. As there appeared not to be less than three hundred of them in this bay, all armed, the soldiers were ordered to fix their bayonets, and to observe a close, well-connected order of march as they descended the hill. These people (as already mentioned) seemed to dislike red coats, and those who carry arms; but on the present occasion they showed very little fear or distrust; on the contrary, they in a few minutes mixed with us, and conducted us to a very fine stream of water, out of which some of them drank, to show that it was good. The women and children kept at some distance, one or two more forward than the rest excepted, who came to the governor for some presents. While he was distributing his gifts, the women danced (an exercise every description of people in this country seemed fond of).

"The men in general had their skins smeared all over with grease, or some stinking, oily substance; some wore a small stick, or fishbone, fixed crossways in the division of the nose, which had a very strange appearance; others were painted in a variety of ways, and had their hair ornamented with the teeth of fish, fastened on by gum, and the skin of the kangaroo. As they conducted us to the water, a toadstool* was picked up by one of our company, which some of the natives perceiving, they made signs for us to throw it away, as not being good to eat. Soon after I gathered some wood-sorrel, which grew in our way, but none of them endeavoured to prevent me from eating it; on the contrary, if a conclusion may be drawn from the signs which they made rela-

* I have no hesitation in asserting my opinion that the *Agaricus campestris* or common mushroom, now so amazingly abundant in Australia, was introduced accidentally by Europeans. The marsh mallow and the thistle seem for the first time to have found their natural habitat ; while the salmon seems to be a dead failure at present.

tive to the toadstool, they showed by their looks that there was nothing hurtful in it.

"We halted but a short time with them, as it was growing late, and we had a long way to walk. Before we parted from them, the governor gave them two small hand axes in exchange for some of their stone axes and two of their spears. As we ascended a hill, after our departure from them, eight of them followed us until we had nearly reached the top, where one of those who had been most familiar with us made signs for us to stop, which we readily complying with, he ran to the summit, and made a strange kind of hallooing, holding at the same time hands open above his head. As soon as we came up to him, we discovered another large body of them in a bay, about half a mile below us. Our new friend seemed anxious to carry us down to them, but it not being in our way we declined his offer. Seeing us take another direction he halted, and opened his hands, in order, as we supposed, to put us in mind that he had received nothing from us, upon which we presented him with a bird, the only thing we had, with which he returned, to appearance, fully content and satisfied. We now proceeded towards the camp, where we arrived about sunset.

"This was the greatest number of the natives we had ever seen together since our coming among them. What could be the cause of their assembling in such numbers gave rise to a variety of conjectures. Some thought they were going to war among themselves, as they had with them a temporary store of half-stinking fish and fern-root, the latter of which they use for bread. This we remarked, as several of them were eating it at the time we were among them. Others conjectured that some of them had been concerned in the murder of our men, notwithstanding we did not meet with the smallest trace to countenance such an opinion, and that fearing we should revenge it, they had formed this convention in order to defend themselves against us. Others imagined that the assemblage might be occasioned by a burial, a marriage, or some religious meeting.

"*The 4th of June, The King's Birthday.*—His Excellency ordered every soldier a pint of porter, besides his allowance of grog; and every convict half a pint of spirits, made into grog, that they all may drink his Majesty's health; and, as it was a day of general rejoicing and festivity, he likewise made it a day of forgiveness—remitting the remainder of the punishment to which the sailors of the *Sirius* were subject, and pardoning Lovel, Sideway, Hall, and Gordon, who had been confined on a little sterile island, or rather rock, situated in the harbour, until a place of banishment could be found. This act of lenity and mercy, added to many others which the governor had shown, it is to be hoped will work some change on the minds of these men. Indeed some good may be expected from Hall and Gordon, who, since their sentence, have appeared penitent; but from Lovel and Sideway very little change for the better can be expected, because they seem so truly abandoned and incorrigible. At night every person attended an immense bonfire that was lighted for the occasion; after which the principal officers of the settlement, and of the men-of-war, supped at the governor's, where they terminated the day in pleasantry, good humour, and cheerfulness.

"The next morning we were astonished at the number of thefts which had been committed during the general festivity by the villainous part of the convicts on one another, and on some of the officers whose servants did not keep a strict look-out after their marquees. Availing themselves thus of the particular circumstances of the day is a strong instance of their unabated depravity and want of principle. Scarcely a day passes without an example being made of some one or other of these wretches; but it seems to have no manner of effect upon them.

"10th.—John Ascott and Patrick Burn, two convicts, were brought before the criminal court, and prosecuted by Lieutenant G. William Maxwell of the *Sirius*, and Mr. Kelter the master of the same ship, for having, a few nights before, in a riotous manner, with many more of the convicts, attacked some seamen belonging to the men-of-war, and behaving in an insolent and contemptuous manner to them. After a long and judicious hearing, the prisoners were acquitted, as the charge brought against them was by no means substantiated.

"26th.—About four in the afternoon a slight shock of an earthquake was felt at Sydney Cove and its environs. This incident had so wonderful an effect on Edward Corbett, a convict, who had eloped about three weeks before, on a discovery being made of his having stolen a frock, that he returned and gave himself up to justice. A few days antecedent to his return he had been outlawed, and was supposed to have driven off with him four cows, the only animals of this kind in the colony.* This, however, he declared himself innocent of, but confessed his having committed the theft laid to his charge. The strictest search was made, but in vain, after the cows. It is probable that they have strayed so far off in this endless wild as to be irrecoverably lost. Previously to the return of Corbett, he must have suffered very severely from hunger; his eyes were sunk into his head, and his whole appearance showed that he had been half starved. While he was absent, he says, he frequently fell in with the natives, who, though they never treated him ill, did not seem to like his company. He informed us, that in a bay adjacent to that where the governor and his party had met with so many of the natives, he saw the head of one of the convicts lying near the place where the body had been burnt in a large fire. This, in all likelihood, was Burn, who was carried off at the time Ayres was wounded, as he has not been heard of since.

"The natives of this country, though their mode of subsisting seems to be so very scanty and pre-

---

* In 1788 there were four cows and a bull on the Australian continent. In 1868 there were 960,000 horned cattle in New South Wales alone, leaving out the three other splendid provinces of Victoria, South Australia, and Queensland. "Verily, the earth is the Lord's, and the fulness thereof."

carious, are, I am convinced, not cannibals.* One of their graves, which I saw opened, the only one I have met with, contained a body which had evidently been burned, as small pieces of the bones lay in the bottom of it. The grave was neatly made, and well covered with earth and boughs of trees."

So began a terrible fight, lasting for so many years, of which we now begin to see some of the results. On the one side were five or six gentlemen and 150 troops, and the desert and the savages on the other. Of the convicts one can hardly say which way they were. They were in overwhelming majority, a mass of desperate men, who had all forfeited their lives by the then existing laws, and no doubt would have risen if they could. Some showed signs of amendment, and seem to have been as well used as was possible. Others were hopelessly depraved, and extreme repressive measures were necessary. Phillip seems to have been spoken of by those who knew him as a humane and excellent man, but it fell to him to put the laws of those times in force, and he did it. He pardoned where he could. On the 4th of June, as we see, he pardoned every body, but it was little good.

How Phillip, Hunter, and King kept their wits at all, in the seething hell of abominations and massacres which followed, is a great wonder; but they did right nobly. They had to do some very severe things; it becomes most necessary among swarms of enlarged

---

* Not habitually, but occasionally. On this point consult Eyre, late Governor of Jamaica, their friend and protector. Even he does not hesitate to pronounce against them in this respect.

and desperate convicts;* but by degrees they got order out of confusion, staggering and uncertain cosmos out of utter chaos, and the thing throve. They were hard-fisted men who hit. Neither the United States or Australia were founded by kid gloves and rose water. Those who sneer at these men who bore the burden and heat of the day, had better undertake a similar job on their own account, which, happily, thanks partly to the hard hitting of the men who founded America and Australia, they will find difficult. The men who landed "at the bottom of Bridge Street, Sydney, near the colonnade," had to hit out from the shoulder, and did so.

It was a miserable struggle for a long time, but Civilization won steadily, in spite of all the terrible elements she had to contend with. She had for her assistance a young race, quite indomitable, and in the long run she won.

The first real sign of civilization was, of course, a revolution. Our old friend and hero, Bligh, of the *Bounty*, who had successfully proved that his temper was so atrocious that he could not keep a picked crew of excellent men in order, was, for some inscrutable reason, "told off" to administer this colony just at the very time when free settlers were becoming powerful, and when the most perfect tact and caution

* The Governor of Norfolk Island told me once in private conversation, that he gave 300 convicts 100 lashes a-piece one night. The island was all but gone, but he did not like to shed blood. A gentler or more humane being than this man does not walk this earth. He was a man who got a nickname for his extreme good-nature. He had to do *something*, and he did that—and won.

were required. The end was an explosion. The troops mutinied, and in January 1806 seized him, and put him on board ship, with orders to leave the colony. So ended the great Australian Revolution, without one solitary black eye to any person concerned. Major Johnson, the leader of the insurgent troops, was tried by court-martial at Chelsea Hospital, and what—hung? Shot?—no, quietly cashiered. He lived and died happily in Australia. Bligh lived until 1817.

While these little matters were happening, the roar of Trafalgar was still in our fathers' ears, the great Moravian battle had been won, and Pitt lay dead at Putney, "with the look of Austerlitz in his face." It was no time to bother about small majors of infantry who had squabbled with a not very successful captain of the navy. The hurricane of great desolation was sweeping over the earth, and in front of the swift hurrying cloud sped the War Eagle, Napoleon, who guided it. Cease your babbling, you Sydney gaol birds, lest a worse thing befall you. We are all alone, and our temper is gone. Disband your mutinous troops. Here is Macquarie and the 73d Regiment to knock you into shape.*

Australia had been getting ready for Macquarie, and Macquarie was exactly the man for Australia. In twelve years he had made a country of it. MacArthur had introduced the merino sheep in 1803. Under the wise and good rule of Macquarie, these had increased enormously, and Sydney was built. In Europe these

* The exact dates of the news arriving in England are very confused, so one has to be very vague.

twelve years of Australian prosperity are noted in men's minds by such words as Wagram, Torres Vedras, advance of Wellington through the Peninsula, Moscow, Passage of the Beresina, Leipsig, Elba, Waterloo, St. Helena. In Australia these echoes came dimly deadened by long distance,

" Like footsteps upon wool."

Macquarie all this time was civilizing, road-making, bridge building, nay, street building, for the infant colony, while the old parent land was fighting her hardest for them and theirs. When you show me a successful Latin colony, I will confess that we wasted all our money in getting command of the seas.

There is little more to chronicle: the great colony squabbled on, scolding a great deal, until it came to what it is now. The natives, of course, went on, one way or another, by drink or by sheer butchery, in spite of some splendid efforts to save them: notably by ecclesiastics of all persuasions (who have fairly earned *their* salt in *that* colony). But even the glorious Moravians could do nothing with them. By degrees the land throve so gloriously that it had to be divided, and South Australia (the country discovered by Sturt) and Tasmania (the great island to the south) had to be pared off the parent stem, even before the tremendous prize of gold was found.

It is wonderful to think of the way in which God hides things from men until His time is ready. Sir Thomas Mitchell, a meritorious and excellent man, in one of his numerous expeditions, crossed Expedition Pass, by Mount Alexander, through a long valley, leading over some 10,000,000*l.* of gold, *an immense quantity of which must have been actuallly visible after a shower of rain.* The gold about Expedition Pass (we used to call it Sawpit Gully, I do not know what they call it now), was actually so thick on the very surface, that the children used to go out "nuggetting" with knives on Sunday. The "squatters" (wool growers) had no notion that they were walking upon half the interest of the National Debt, until Lyell gave the word, and Hargreaves followed it, but not in Victoria, in New South Wales. That colony did well in gold, but the new colony, only just separated from her, did better.

Victoria, the richest of our colonies save India, was but a district of New South Wales: a small and not very important district, principally separated because it was considered hard that honourable members should be required to go 500 miles to Sydney to attend to their legislative duties. This trifling province exported in 1852, 11,000,000*l.* in gold alone.

Now just cast your mind back for a few moments for eighty-one years. Many whom we know were alive then. What did we see at that time?

A band of sailors and soldiers, landing in a hopeless swamp, on a continent as large as Europe, in charge of a band of hopeless, godless, convicts, 700 strong. Not one solitary white man was on that continent at that time. An old lady who walks about the streets at Clifton now, and is as good at a crossing as another, was then a bright child of seven years old.

Now just read the statistics which follow, and see what man can do when God will back him.

The Australian continent is divided into five nearly independent republics, the presidents of which are, at the desire of the colonists, nominated by the Imperial Government. The first which claims our attention is, of course, the oldest :—

NEW SOUTH WALES—
  Population, 440,000.
  Revenue, £3,000,000.
  Population of its chief town, Sydney, about 60,000.

VICTORIA (*its offshoot*)—
  Population, 660,000.
  Revenue, £2,991,000.
  Population of its chief town, Melbourne, 130,000.

SOUTH AUSTRALIA—
  Population, 170,000.
  Revenue, 975,000.
  Population of the chief town, Adelaide, 30,000.

QUEENSLAND (*possessing twice the acreage of the Canadas*)—
  Population, 96,000.
  Revenue, £593,000.
  Population of chief town, Brisbane, 10,000.

TASMANIA—
  Population, 98,000.
  Revenue, £270,000.
  Population of chief town, Hobart Town, 25,000.

WEST AUSTRALIA, *Convict Settlement*—
  Population, 21,000.

Summed up, then :—

AUSTRALIAN UNITED PROVINCES—
  Population, 1,670,000.
  Revenue, £10,194,000.

This is a lame conclusion to a book of spirited adventure you say. I say no. Where would the great Australian United Provinces be now, had it not been for the glorious band of adventurers who made her? The object of our race is to civilize the earth, and we have not done very badly with such figures as these before us.

THE END

LONDON: R. CLAY, SONS, AND TAYLOR, PRINTERS.

www.ingramcontent.com/pod-product-compliance
Lightning Source LLC
Chambersburg PA
CBHW032020220426
43664CB00006B/306